# The Book of
# Whippingham

By

Sarah Burdett

First published in Great Britain in 2006

British Library Cataloguing-in-Publication Data.
A CIP record for this title is available from the British Library.

ISBN 1 84114 501 7
ISBN 978 1 84114 501 3

HALSGROVE

Halsgrove House
Lower Moor Way
Tiverton, Devon EX16 6SS
Tel: 01884 243242
Fax: 01884 243325
email: sales@halsgrove.com
website: www.halsgrove.com

Title page photograph: *The Folly Regatta in 1948.*

Printed and bound in Great Britain by CPI Bath.

# Acknowledgements & Associated Reading

I would like to thank everyone who has lent photographs of Whippingham for this project, or who has talked to me about their life in the village. I dare not mention names or I might miss someone out, so thank you all! Whippingham School, and Mrs Nicci Billington in particular, have shared with me the material that they have gleaned over the years about both the school and village.

The staff at the Isle of Wight County Records Office have shown me many interesting documents over the years, knowing my interest in the village, and have always been most helpful. We also received great help from the staff at Windsor Royal Archives and Photographic Collection. One could spend months there examining Queen Victoria's original documents relating to her estate here.

East Cowes Heritage Centre was the catalyst for my initial research about the village. We wanted to put on an exhibition about Whippingham, and it grew... and grew! Having started the research, it was the Workers' Educational Association (WEA) who asked me to run a course about Whippingham, which provided the impetus for further research, and consequently a need to write this book.

My thanks go to the Whippingham Partnership who provided some expenses towards this project. I hope that the book will provide more information for a Heritage Trail around the village and other projects.

Please accept my apologies if you lent us a photograph or gave us information and it is not in the book. Eventually we had more photographs and information than we could use. However, a complete set of all the photographs will be kept at the Community Centre and at East Cowes Heritage Centre, so the information is preserved. Also accept my apologies if I did not obtain information from you. There was a limit to what could be achieved within the timescale. We would welcome any additional material about Whippingham from anyone for the files at the centres.

Finally, I wish to offer my sincere thanks to Brian Taylor who nobly undertook all the scanning of loaned material, trying to achieve the best from every photograph. I would also like to thank my husband for putting up with me over the last year – perhaps next year we will have more time to get out on the boat at The Folly, now that I have finished the book!

*Sarah Burdett*
*2006*

Brading, Rosetta, *East Cowes and Whippingham 1303–1914*. J. Arthur Dixon, 1990.
Brading, Rosetta, *East Cowes and Whippingham 1914–1939*. J. Arthur Dixon, 1990.
Brinton, Marion, *Farmhouses and Cottages on the Isle of Wight*. IWCC, 1987.
Britton, Andrew, *Once Upon a Line*, Volume 4. Oxford Publishing Company, 1983.
Daniels, S.B., *Rescue From the Skies – The Story of the Airborne Lifeboat*. HMSO, 1994.
Fox, Uffa, *Joys of Life*. George Newnes Ltd, 1966.
Fox, Uffa, *More Joys of Living*. Nautical Publishing Company, 1971.
Hockey, S.F., *Insula Vecta*. Phillimore, 1982.
Isle of Wight Women's Institutes, *Within Living Memory*. Countryside Books, 1994.
Jaffe, Deborah, *Victoria, A Celebration*. Carlton Books, 2000.
Moore, Hilda Alice, *Arreton All My Days*. Homespun Publications, 1997.
Partridge, Michael, *The Royal Naval College Osborne, 1903–1921*. Sutton Publishing, 1999.
Prothero, Rowland (Lord Ernle), *From Whippingham to Westminster*. John Murray, 1938.
Searle, Adrian, *Isle of Wight at War, 1939–1945*. Dovecote Press, 1989.
Snow, Victoria, *Wootton Bridge and Whippingham on the Isle of Wight*. Stockwell Ltd, 1986.
Snow, Victoria, *Queen Victoria's Osborne Estate, Royal and Rural*. 1987.
Tagg, A.E. and Wheeler, R.L., *From Sea to Air – The Heritage of Sam Saunders*. Crossprint, 1989.
Wheeler, R.L., *River to Sea – The Maritime Heritage of Sam Saunders*. Crossprint, 1993.
Winter, C.W.R., *The Manor House of the Isle of Wight*. Dovecote Press, 1984.
Woodhams, John, *Paddle Steamers*. Oakfield Publications, 1991.
York, Sarah, Duchess of, *Victoria and Albert*. Weidenfeld and Nicolson Ltd, 1991.

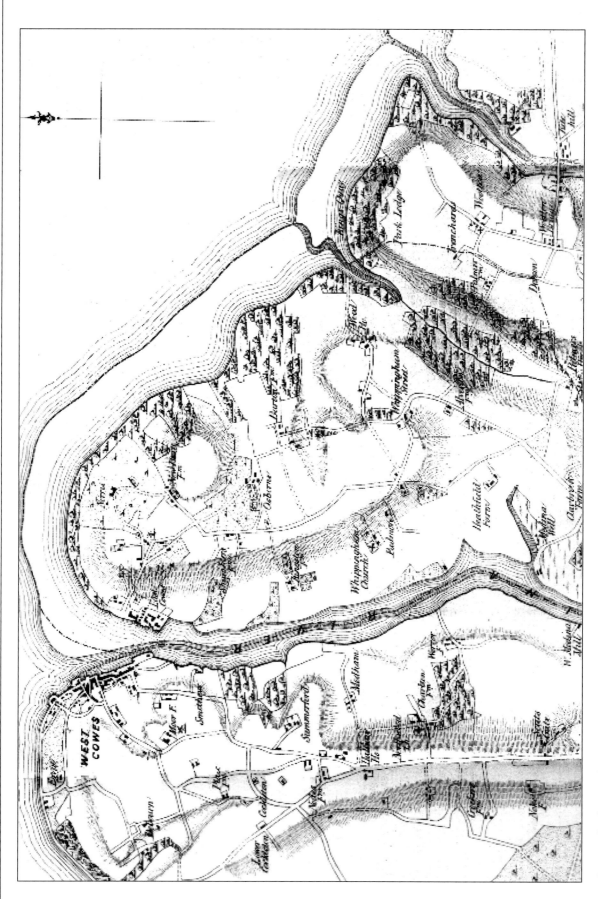

*A map of Whippingham, c.1810. This was used for implementing the Public Heath Act in 1853 in East Cowes.*

# Contents

*The Barton estate workers and their families in 1923.* The picture includes, in the back row: *Ted Street* (seventh from left), *Mr Brown the head cowman* (eighth from left), *Harry Hatcher the pigman* (nineteenth from left), *Charlie Snow whose father was copseman for Queen Victoria* (twenty-first from left); men standing on the right, fully visible, from the right: *Mr Mullet, Mr Gregory, Fred Loader*; ladies seated, left to right: *Mrs Ellen Snow of Primrose Cottage who washed handkerchiefs for the Royalty* (far left), *Mrs Nellie Snow* (second from left), *Mrs Foss* (tenth from left), *Mrs Brown a seamstress and gate opener at Alverstone* (ninth from left), *Mrs Lily Snow and baby Grace* (fourteenth from left), *Mrs Street* (sixteenth from left). Children on the ground: *Bert Loader* (fourth from left) *and Arthur Loader* (first from right).

*Visitors to Whippingham Church, c.1910. Note the lady precariously climbing a ladder to reach the top of the coach.* (REPRODUCED COURTESY OF W.J. NIGH & SONS LTD)

# Chapter 1

# Introduction

Whippingham was mentioned in the Domesday Book. Some 900 years later Whippingham is part of the Island's 'Tourist Trail'. In summer Beatrice Avenue is filled with coaches while they disgorge their occupants for the obligatory ramble around the church and churchyard, before moving off half an hour later towards Osborne House. By teatime all is quiet again. The Almshouses bask in the evening sun, the river sparkles, the jackdaws squawk in the church chimney and peace returns to the countryside.

So many people have passed through the church gates. Many parishioners have been forgotten. The aim of this book is to tell a few of their stories, to tell of their homes, and of their work in the village.

Just pick a local place name – Clavell. Clavell's Copse still stands along Mount Road on the Barton estate. Did Lord Robert de Claville worship at the old church of St Mildred's in 1220? He had two sons, Henry and Hugh. We know that Henry Claville's wife gave land to Stephen, rector of Whippingham in 1266. It was worth a few prayers for her soul after she departed from this life!

Pick a family name – Snow. Les Snow plays the organ at the church. His family lived and worked on the Osborne and Barton estates. Mrs Grace Davison (née Snow) can be seen on her mother's knee in the estate workers' photograph of 1922 *(opposite page)*. A vast number of people are shown on that one photo-graph, all working on or supported by the Barton estate. In the twenty-first century, mechanisation has changed the face of farming; the dairy herds have gone, and the workforce has dwindled to just a few.

Much of old Whippingham that we see in 2006 is a product of its royal connection. When Queen Victoria bought Osborne and Barton in 1845, she and Albert set about a massive rebuilding programme, not only of their own house and the church, but also of all the cottages on the estate. She wanted to visit 'her people', but if they lived in rough conditions it wasn't seemly. So Prince Albert drew up plans for new cottages, and all but two of the old ones were knocked down. This improvement continued even after Prince Albert died.

Queen Victoria had the new school built in 1863, visited it frequently and looked at the children's work and gave prizes. What an incentive to always produce your best work!

The Almshouses were constructed in 1875 for aged retainers from the Queen's estate. Six new farmhouses were built and the latest innovations appeared. Millions of drainage tiles and bricks were produced in the Queen's own brickyard, the bricks all with 'VR' in the frog. Progress was the word.

After Victoria died in 1901, life carried on more quietly, although there were some changes. The hospital for the Royal Naval College Osborne was

*Whippingham School in 1994. This side of the school is as it was in Queen Victoria's time, although then the grass area was the teachers' gardens.*

CORONATION OF
King Edward VII. & Queen Alexandra.

Commemoration Festival,
WHIPPINGHAM,
FRIDAY, JUNE 27th, 1902.

Service at Parish Church ... ... ... 2-0 p.m.
Children's Tea ... ... ... ... 3-30 ,,
Adult's Tea ... ... ... ... ... 4-30 ,,
Music and Sports.

*The Rectory Grounds will be open from 3 to 9 p.m.*

*Above: A service was to be held at the church and tea and games at the Rectory to celebrate the coronation of Edward VII. However, the King had appendicitis, so the coronation was postponed until 9 August 1902. At this time he was landlord to most of the village.*

*Left: The Folly Works were a hive of activity in the 1940s. Lorries are unloading wood veneers, from which the plywood will be made.*

*Many postcards were produced as sightseers flocked to view Osborne House and the Queen's church. This one of 'the late Queen's Almshouses' probably dates from 1905.*

*The church as built under Prince Albert's direction, photographed in the early 1970s. (REPRODUCED COURTESY OF W.J. NIGH & SONS LTD)*

built opposite Barton Gates. By the start of the First World War, however, Sam Saunders was producing aeroplanes just south of The Folly Inn. These took off from an airfield there, or the amphibious planes taxied away along the river.

The Folly Inn by the river continued to serve beer to the men from the sailing barges, who might have had to wait there before sailing on up to Newport with the tide to unload their cargoes. Even East Cowes residents rowed up river for an 'egg tea' at The Folly.

By the Second World War 40 per cent of the nation's plywood was being produced at the Saunders Roe (Saro) Folly Works. One night in 1942 bombing sent much of it up in smoke. An anti-aircraft battery appeared at the Heights and the noise of the guns could be heard and felt as far away as Parkhurst. Saunders Roe took over the Naval College hospital site and the Osborne works of GKN Aerospace continue there to the time of writing. Thousands of people have worked for the different companies here.

In postwar years the village relapsed into quiet backwaters off the main East Cowes Road. New houses were built on the Heights and Medina Park static caravan site grew to its 150 homes. The Post Office and shop moved along Alverstone Road, and the Community Centre reverted to its original use. The school has grown in size, providing a living heart to the village, and the Forge continues to thrive in 2006.

The traffic now pours past the village at 40mph, although local people are hoping for speed restrictions. There is not too much impact on village homes. Visitors come to enjoy the peaceful river and the church. The coastal footpath and cycle track pass through the village. The Barton estate is still almost intact and many of the Victorian houses remain.

So much can still be seen here. We hope this book will help you to understand the history behind the village and the lives of those who have lived here.

*The Folly Inn, a friendly inn beside the River Medina, c.1910.*

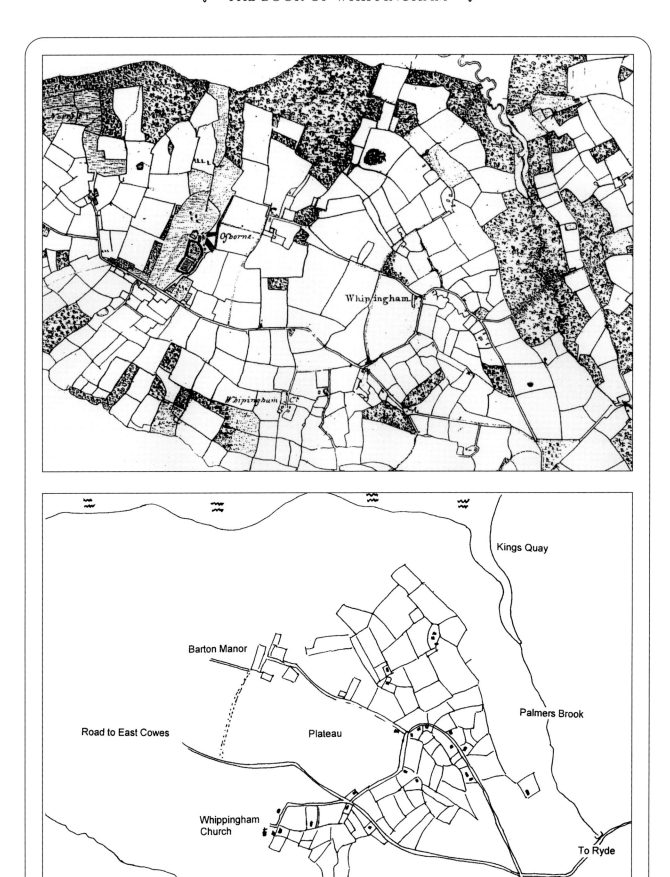

*A diagrammatic map based on the map of 1793 (top), which shows the crescent of settlement along, or just above, the 'spring line'. The smaller fields at this level show plots of cultivation around homes. Larger fields are located on the plateau top.*

# Chapter 2
# Before Domesday & Medieval Whippingham

About 8,000 years ago the sea broke through the chalk cliffs at the western end of the Needles and the Isle of Wight was separated from the mainland. The glaciers of the last Ice Age were melting and the River Solent was expanding. Boats were now the only way that people could get on or off the Island. As the sea rose the inlet of the Medina estuary gave easy sheltered access to the centre of the Island. The hunter gatherers of the Mesolithic Stone Age were the early occupants of the estuary. Evidence has been found of these people settling in sheltered spots such as Werrar, opposite the present Folly Inn, near to an easy source of food. Shellfish would have been collected, and geese and duck would have been trapped, along with fish. The landscape would have been dominated by woodland. Finds of scattered burnt flint have been found in the fields between the Alverstone and Whippingham Roads, suggesting prehistoric activity.

The Bronze Age people followed, and the first evidence of settlement lies in a ring ditch identified in a crop just to the north of Whippingham Heights. This almost certainly points to a Bronze Age bowl barrow, suitably sited on a high point. Burial mounds were intended to be seen from nearby settlements and this shows that some woodland clearance had taken place. Struck flint finds of late Neolithic/Bronze Age, half a mile to the west of the barrow, may be related to these.

Any Bronze Age settlement would have probably evolved around livestock farming. The heavy clay soils of Whippingham would have presented too much of a challenge for prehistoric cultivation. The more intensive reliance on crop farming by Iron Age peoples may account for the lack of any local evidence from this period in this area. Iron Age technology spread to the Island shortly before the arrival of the more sophisticated Roman way of life in AD43. There is no evidence of fighting on the Island at that stage as it was probably more of a diplomatic takeover.

For almost 400 years the people of Whippingham lived under the rule of the Romans. Roman settlements tended to be based around existing Iron Age farms, and so far none have been found in Whippingham. A few scattered Roman finds have arisen towards the river between The Folly and Island Harbour, but these may just suggest a travel route along the bank. Towards the end of the third century marauding tribes arrived from present-day Denmark and Germany. The Medina was one of their targets. The Romans officially left Britain in AD410. Pagan Jutes soon invaded the Island, and any vestiges of Christianity left from late-Roman times disappeared.

The Anglo Saxon Chronicle is the oldest historical record of the Dark Ages. From it we learn that in AD530 Cerdic and his son Cynric captured the Isle of Wight and slew many men. It was best not to live too near to the coast or river. In 661 the King of Mercia, Wulfhere, ravaged the Island. He gave the Island to Athelwald, King of Sussex. Eoppa, a priest, was sent to bring Christianity to the Island, but we don't know if he visited the area we now know as Whippingham. It would seem that he had little success, as in 686 Caedwalla of Wessex laid waste to the Island. His official reason was that the people were not Christian, but he was probably just trying to regain lost land. It was recorded that 'by cruel slaughter he endeavoured to destroy all the inhabitants thereof and to place in their stead people from his own province.' Around 1,200 families inhabited the Island at that time.

So any residents of Whippingham were replaced in 686 by Saxons. In this period, the name Whippingham evolved. Whippa was probably the chap put in charge of this area by Caedwalla. 'Ham' means settlement, and 'ing' means people, so the name means 'Whippa's people's settlement' – or manor in later terms. Later there was reference to the 'manors' of Whippingham. A total of 32 hides of the manors were given by Cutred, kinsman of Ethelard, King of the West Saxons, to the church of Winchester. 'Manor' meant an area of land and there is no evidence of a manor house of Whippingham.

Following the Island's conversion to Christianity, eight Island parishes were established, each with its own church. Whippingham parish ran from the Medina to the western side of Wootton, and from the Solent as far south as Shide. It is probable that the earliest church was built on the site of the present church at this stage, probably of wood, but possibly

*An old pump in one of the cottage outhouses along the spring line.*

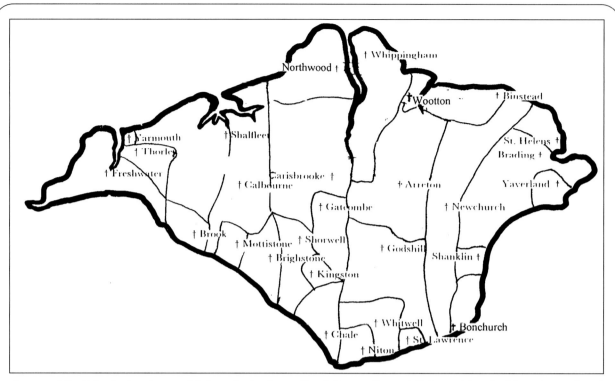

*A map of the Island, showing parish boundaries in medieval times. Several little parishes had been 'carved out' from the original eight.*

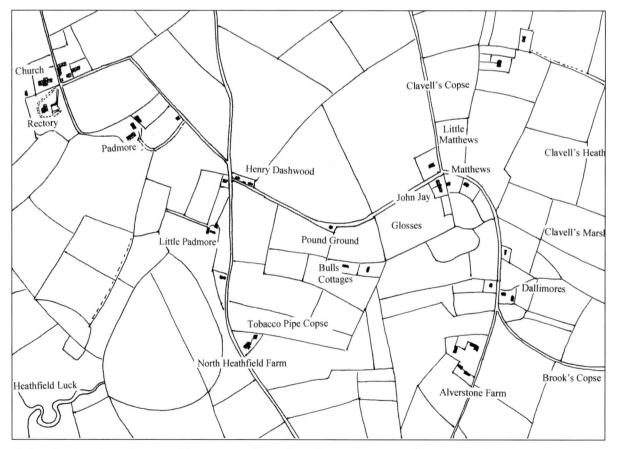

*A drawing based on the 1841 tithe map. It shows the Whippingham Street area at Matthews, which may have been the hub of the village, near the present Coburg Cottage.*

of stone, as there is a Saxon carving included in the present church. Mildred was the name of a Kentish Saxon saint, and she was made the patron saint of the parish church here.

Peaceful times ended when the Vikings started sending raiding parties to the Island in search of more land and booty. We know that they did great damage in 897, and King Alfred brought nine of his ships out to attack the Vikings. Gradually, some of the Vikings started to settle here during the winter season. There is some evidence that the settlement of Werrar, opposite The Folly, may have been used by them from 999 to 1006, so in all probability the Vikings would have visited Whippingham as well. Opposite Whippingham Church, on the plateau to the west of the river, Northwood Church was built. These two churches perhaps provided safe refuge in times of trouble, as parishioners could hide there during a Viking attack.

After the Norman Conquest of 1066, William kindly had a record made that tells us much about the use of the land 20 years later. In fact, two sets of commissioners were sent around in case one got it wrong.

At Whippingham, we read in the Domesday record that the land belonged to the King, and Wulfward rented it from him. Bolla had held it from King Edward, and it paid tax for one hide. In the lordship's land there was enough work for half a plough, and there were three villagers and two smallholders with one plough between them. The value of the land was only 10 shillings. The second surveyor said that the tax was only on half a hide of land. One hide was equivalent to 120 acres.

By comparison, Briddlesford had one hide of land being cultivated, but with four ploughs, and it was worth 40 shillings. So Whippingham was worth much less as it had poor soil and obviously did not produce very good crops in 1086.

Earl William Fitz Osbern was made lord of the Island by King William the Conqueror. In 1070 Fitz Osbern decreed that the rents from the lands belonging to the parish church of Whippingham should be given to the Abbey of St Mary of Lyre in Normandy. Whippingham was one of six Island churches he gave to Lyre.

So Whippingham entered a new stage – Saxons being ruled by Normans.

## The Early Village

Whippingham does not fit the popular stereotype of an old village. There is no village green, and no cluster of little cottages next to a pond by the old church. In those days the most necessary commodities were water and workable land. Whippingham as we know it in 2006 lies around the southern edge of a plateau. That plateau is composed of gravels washed out by rivers from the ice caps further north during the last Ice Age. Rain falling on the plateau filters through the gravelly soil until it comes to a clay layer underneath. The clay is impermeable, water cannot get through it, so springs appear at the junction of the gravels and clay. For many years the water board had difficulty diverting a spring that persistently erupted in the middle of the main road at Whippingham Shute. At the time of writing they seem to have succeeded. In cold winters the road was frequently impassable due to a sheet of ice on the hill! A second stream, that can be easily seen, emerges along Folly Lane, at various levels according to the height of the water table. Other streams collect in small valleys and make their way through the countryside either westwards to the Medina or north-east to the Solent.

The early residents of Whippingham would have used the water from these springs. As technology improved, wells were dug just above the spring line through the gravel to give access to a clean water-supply for the houses, livestock and crops. If we plot the early settlements on a map they ring the plateau. Looking at the 1863 map we see 'w' for well next to nearly every building. Ask a resident of an old house in Whippingham and they may be able to show you where their well was.

So Whippingham is categorised as a 'Spring Line' village. This gives it a scattered pattern, with no visible old nucleus. We know that there were two more cottages in the field just to the north of the church. These were empty in 1944 and used to destruction by soldiers practising for the D-Day landings.

At the eastern end of the village is an interesting area called Whippingham Street on some old maps, and Alverstone or even Elverton Street on others. This is 200 metres along the private road to Barton Farm, almost opposite Coburg Cottage. On the 1841 map several dwellings are shown, but these were demolished by order of Victoria and Albert and new improved cottages built on other sites. The field still has a few remains of old foundations, and more are visible in dry weather as parched grass outlines. This eastern end of the village would also have been convenient for access to what we now call King's Quay.

King's Quay may have been called Shoflet 1,000 years ago. Shoflet is mentioned in the Domesday Book of 1086 as being a manor held by the King. The manor would not necessarily mean that there was a house built there, but simply an area of land. It was probably adjacent to Woodhouse Farm, and could have been an important sheltered landing-place for craft crossing the Solent. As the creek silted up it became less important. It is still shown on a map of 1590 as Showflyt.

The name King's Quay is said to derive from the suggestion that it was here that King John landed when coming to the Isle of Wight shortly after signing the Magna Carta in 1215. We are not sure of the truth in this legend as the name first appeared in print in 1769.

A survey of the area was carried out in 1570. The resulting map shows an important anchorage a mile to the north-west of Showflyt where vessels sheltered from south-westerly gales. This was referred to as Meade Hole. In the early-twenty-first century it is known as Osborne Bay. Meade Hole was where the pirates exchanged their wares, either for goods or money. Much of this trade appears to have been carried out with the knowledge of Sir George Carey, the Island's Captain. That year, the Spanish Ambassador sent an agent to the Island to see what was going on. The report sent to Phillip of Spain said that there was a 'Great Fayre' of spices, wines, wool, saffron, oil, soap and a great number of other goods stolen from the Spanish King's subjects, and some from the French and Portuguese. In 1581 another witness spoke of over 30 ships, all buying, selling and bartering. He saw woollen cloth and linen, clothing, jewellery, shoes, beef, mutton, beer and bread, with the boatmen doing a good trade rowing customers from ship to ship. The people of Whippingham must have taken part in this, if they could, as it was right on their doorstep!

One can imagine smugglers using the King's Quay creek, nicely tucked away from the excise men who were stationed in East Cowes in the eighteenth century.

In 2006 the Shoflet, Showflyt or King's Quay creek has silted up and alders have started growing in the mud. The stream still flows under Palmer's Brook and Brock's Copse Bridge, and seagoing eels have been known to swim up it as far as the old railway bridge near Whippingham Station en masse, creating a seething, squirming knot in the pool there.

In late-Victorian times there was a footbridge across the mouth of King's Quay creek. Workers on the Queen's estate and children on their way to school at Whippingham would cross the bridge. Queen Victoria owned some property on the eastern side of the creek. Estate children would play on the beach. Today the creek is simply a haven for wildlife, and inaccessible to the general public.

Returning to medieval times, the settlement of Whippingham developed along the spring line around the top of the hill. From deeds in the County Record Office we can see various names appearing that give us a little insight into the people living here.

Records of the Clavell family, also spelt Clavill, Clavyle and Claville according to the whim of the scribe, begin with Henry de Clavell who was lord of the manor of Alverstone in 1222. We know then that his brother Hugh had 'land in the cultures called the Heth in the field of Whippingham in various strips.' So Heathfield was cultivated in the strip fashion, whereby different people owned strips of the same

*A sketch of King's Quay after Tomkins painting of 1809.*

field. The Clavells gave the revenue of some of their land to the Abbey of Quarr. In 1247 one acre east of Padmore, owned by Mary Clavell, widow of Henry, was being rented by Simon Othyn for 6d. a year. In 1266 this land was given by the Clavells to Stephen, rector of Whippingham, and his successors.

Ralph Lete was the son of Richard Taylor, and they farmed two acres in the field called Petenee in 1247. Where was Petenee, or perhaps Petheye, as it appeared later? Richard Taylor had land alongside.

A century later, there were arguments over landownership between Thomas le Clavell and Maud, late wife of John Othyn, in Whippingham. In 1342 the abbot of Quarr leased, for two lives, nine acres and a croft at Petheye to Thomas the elder and Thomas the younger, both sons of Thomas at Fayrelie. The land was between that held by William Othyn and John Clavell.

The medieval farmer would often work for his lord for a set number of days in lieu of paying rent. Mention is made of a 'croft', which would have been a smallholding. Houses would have been made of cheap materials which were readily available. In Whippingham this would have been wood and wattle and daub, none of which survive well, so we have no remaining examples of old wooden cottages. There was no handy stone with which to build. The manor of Woodhouse was bought by Sir Harry Worsley in 1620, Alverstone Farm being part of this. It was not until 1715 that Alverstone Old Farmhouse was built from stone and brick.

The Clavell family seem to have moved south to Pann, where they owned the manor in 1657, leaving the name Clavell's Copse behind them in Whippingham. The Othyn family continued to rent farm land. In the 1930s, a Mr Othen rented the field south of the present GKN Osborne Works and ran a successful piggery and horticultural business with his son, who died in 2003. Was he related to Simon Othyn who rented an acre east of Padmore in 1247? The Thomas family still farm in Whippingham in 2006 – perhaps descendants of the Thomas family of Fayrelie?

# Chapter 3

# Whippingham Church & Rectory

This chapter is not intended to be a guide to the present church. There is an excellent illustrated guidebook available at the church. Here we will take a look at some aspects that are not included in that guidebook.

Little is known about the earliest Whippingham Church. Saint Mildred was a Kentish Anglo-Saxon princess who became an abbess, dying in about AD700. Her remains were buried at Canterbury in 1033. Only seven other English churches are dedicated to her.

The only authenticated carved stonework from the early Saxon church has been built into the west wall of the entrance porch. There is just one engraving of the church as it was before 1800, drawn by Tomkins in the 1790s. This shows a possibly twelfth-century nave, and a thirteenth-century chancel with a fourteenth-century tower with a saddleback roof.

We do know that when an oratory was built nearby at Barton, the rights of the mother church at Whippingham were safeguarded by a special agreement, made in 1273. The people of Whippingham were not allowed to worship at Barton. Eight days after his installation, the archpriest of Barton was to go to St Mildred's and swear fidelity to the rector, promising that he would undertake no parochial functions in Whippingham. Barton would pay a tithe to Whippingham and recognise the rights of the mother church by going there as a community in procession on the day of the annual feast of St Mildred.

Like some other parish churches on the Island, Whippingham appears to have had its share of disputes with Quarr Abbey. The abbey owned Claybrook Farm, now Binfield Farm, and a dispute arose as to how the tithes should be paid. In 1266 the rector of Whippingham, Stephen, reached a compromise with Quarr whereby the abbey gave four acres of land in lieu of further receipt of tithes. This land may have been Clavell's Heath near old Alverstone Farm. In 1305 a subsequent rector renegotiated the deal to five shillings per annum in lieu of tithes. This amount was still being paid to the church in the nineteenth century.

St Mildred's was the parish church. In medieval times the parish boundary stretched from the Solent southwards to include Shide, south-east of Newport. This seems a large area, but there were only 17 households on the lay subsidy. Employees were not included in this, only those landowners liable to tax. We think of taxation as a modern phenomenon, but in 1334 an assessment of personal property was made and the same scale was used for the next 300 years. Whippingham had a lay subsidy of £1.2s., placing it at the bottom of the roll for the eastern half of the Island.

In 1377 tax inspectors considered the war damage to the Island after the French invasion. This lay subsidy revealed that there were only agricultural workers in Whippingham, no trades or craftsmen.

The Hundred Years War with France meant that there was difficulty in paying the rents owed by Whippingham to the Abbey of Lyre in France. The payment in 1189 had been fixed at ten shillings a year, but often this was not paid. In 1415, all proceeds of Isle of Wight property previously paid to Lyre were taken by King Henry V and bestowed upon the Abbey of Sheen in Surrey, which he had founded during the previous year. Sheen received the dues and also appointed the rectors of Whippingham.

Rector John Glazier was appointed by Sheen but in 1533 he was visiting London. Whippingham was then being served by, 'a layman only in reading the pistells and gospelles with the procession.' Eventually Glazier became Bishop of Hereford until he retired in 1555 with a pension of £6.13s.4d. He died in 1563, having lived through all the changes to the English religion, probably guiding the parishioners of Whippingham in the new faith.

Life must have been very hard during the sixteenth century. Whippingham Church was first Catholic, then Henry VIII introduced Protestantism. It was dangerous to disagree, but when Mary became Queen, Catholicism was reintroduced. Then followed Queen Elizabeth, and the protestant religion was again celebrated in Whippingham. Not everyone followed the changing religions. Recusancy appeared in Whippingham! (This meant that the person refused to go to church, preferring to maintain his

*An engraving of St Mildred's from 1794.*

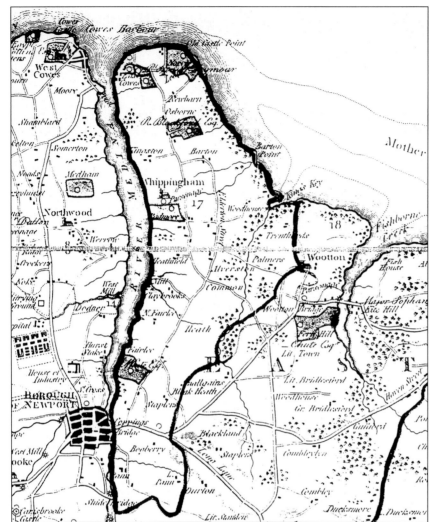

Left: *This map has the outline of the parish of Whippingham drawn on it and dates from 1810. The parish was reduced in size when 'daughter' churches were built in the 1830s and '40s in East Cowes and Barton, Newport.*

*A Brannon engraving of 1851 showing the 'Nash' church and the view up the River Medina towards Newport.*

*An engraving showing the church, spire and external galleries, rebuilt between 1804 and 1811.*

own Catholic beliefs). Richard Hobson, a gentleman of the Isle of Wight, was in prison in 1592 for recusancy, and in 1607 Edward Hobson of Whippingham was cited as not having received communion. Perhaps life was becoming more lenient, as no mention is made of prison for him, nor for Samuel Pratt of Whippingham who was also 'not receiveing communion, nor cometh he orderly to church!'

Writing in the 1600s, John Oglander dismissed Whippingham Church as being insignificant because nobody of note was buried there. Oglander probably touched on the reason for the church, and Whippingham itself, remaining something of a sleepy backwater. From medieval times the surrounding area mainly belonged to landowners who lived elsewhere, leasing to tenant farmers, some of whom may have been little more than crofters. The lack of any residential wealth, leadership and church patronage doubtless discouraged the development of a strong local community.

By 1803 the parish church of Whippingham was 'in a state of great ruin and dilapidation and in want of much repair.' It was 'too small to receive and contain its number of inhabitants.' The village of East Cowes was growing as trade and shipbuilding increased, and several influential people from there were on the Parish Council. One of these was John Nash Esq. John Nash had built himself a home on the slopes above East Cowes. He called it East Cowes Castle. He was a renowned architect, building expensive terraces in London, the Brighton Pavilion for the Prince Regent, and then Buckingham Palace when the Regent became King. The Prince Regent visited Nash in East Cowes during regatta week in 1817.

Nash also bought a farm in Whippingham – North Heathfield. This was on the left going down Whippingham Shute, opposite Heathfield Cottages. He turned his attentions to Whippingham Church, helping to draw up plans for extensions and improvements for the Parochial Church Council. A builder by

the name of James Guy was contracted to 'perform the said repairs, additions, alterations and improvements... for the sum of six hundred and fifty pounds.'

A new schoolroom was built at the west end of the church, the church was enlarged on the north side, gable-ends built and a new roof made, two new galleries constructed with external staircases, the existing gallery was taken back, and the font moved. The ceilings were repaired and painted, old decayed wood replaced, and new pews fitted up. All this work was to be carried out in just three months, but we do not know if he kept to the deadline!

Several rich parishioners, many from East Cowes, contributed to the cost of rebuilding the church and agreed to pay for their own pews. Richard Whitmaich from South Heathfield Farm and John Nash also purchased their own pews. The Nash alterations completed in 1804 do not show a spire, but later illustrations of the church do. Work continued on various parts of the church until 1813.

Other builders worked in the churchyard. One of these, Thomas Denyer, a bricklayer of Newport, was still trying to obtain his payment four years after the work was completed. His detailed invoice may throw some light on some very interesting bricks which reappeared in the southern wall of the churchyard in the year 2000. These small yellow-grey handmade clay bricks are Flemish, and pre-date 1804. They may possibly have arrived on the Island as ships' ballast, and were used in a path Denyer moved. He stated that he reused old bricks in building the

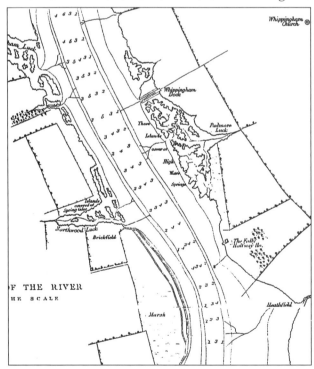

*An Admiralty Chart of 1856 showing Whippingham Dock on the River Medina, directly below Whippingham Church. (Reproduced from the 1856 Admiralty Chart courtesy of the UK Hydrographic Department. www.ukho.gov.uk)*

Above: *The remains of Whippingham dock in 2005. These stones could have originally been rubble from the medieval church.*

Above left: *An internal view in the 'Nash' church, showing the galleries, which were reached via external staircases. The Queen's pews were screened by curtains to the right.*

Left: *The Queen arrives for morning service. This picture is dated before 1875 as Truckles farmyard can be seen in the background. (*Reproduced courtesy of the County Record Office, Newport*)*

*A drawing from the Prosser sketch showing the church as it looked between 1811 and 1854.*

wall near the Rectory, and it may have been these that were found during repairs in the 1990s.

By 1804 little remained of the Norman church. Much of the stone was reused, but new stone would also have been needed. Transport at this time was by water wherever possible. On the River Medina, just below Whippingham Church, a 'dock' was constructed for the delivery of new stone to build the church. In 2005 the two arms of the dock project out into the river at right angles, each just a jumbled heap of stones covered thickly by seaweed, and marked at the western end by a warning pole. It is interesting to conjecture that some of this jumble of stones may be waste Norman or even Saxon material from the old church. Surely the builders of the pier would not have used costly new stone for building their dock. This dock was put to use once more in 1854 when Whippingham Church was again under reconstruction, this time to the form we know today.

Queen Victoria and Prince Albert bought Osborne House in 1845. Although it was their own private residence, accommodation was built for numerous household staff, visiting officials and an increasingly large family. Naturally, attendance at church was expected and if the weather was fine the royal family would walk to Whippingham, when in residence at Osborne, rather than drive.

Writing in 1854 the Bishop of Winchester commented that:

*... the parish church of Whippingham does not afford sufficient accommodation for Her Majesty, the Prince and their Royal family and suite at Divine Service, and... it is desirable that for such purposes adequate and appropriate accommodation should be provided.*

Designs for the enlargement of St Mildred's were prepared once again. The Prince Consort had considerable input into these, working with the architect, Albert Jenkins Humbert. The first stage was the enlargement of the chancel. The Bishop wrote:

*It is proposed to take down the present chancel and to rebuild in an inspired manner, and build in the churchyard two aisles – looking into such new chancel but separated therefrom by a series of six arches.*

The fact that part of the churchyard was to be incorporated into the building necessitated the removal of some of the graves and copious instructions were provided as to how this should be done.

The Queen was given her own private entrance door to the church, leading directly into the southern of the two royal chapels either side of the chancel. Chairs, not pews, were provided for the royal family and the household. After the Queen's death Edward VII ordered the present pews to be placed in the southern chapel, and most of the chairs were removed.

*A 1855 engraving showing the new chancel, which was added to the 1804 church.*

In 1860 plans were made for the rebuilding of the remainder of the church. This was to be one of Albert's last projects, as he died in 1861. The central lantern tower, 30 metres high, has at its centre a replica of the Order of the Garter. The two transepts have rose windows which are based on the designs of those at Notre Dame Cathedral in Paris. Externally, the spire and turrets have a rather Germanic feel to them, reminiscent of the Prince's homeland.

Many small touches were added to the church by the royal family. The new font was designed by Princess Louise and given by the Queen, who also donated the simple handmade wrought-iron candelabra with their glass shades. These still give the church a special touch, especially when lit at Christmas. Princess Beatrice and Princess Louise made a font carpet. The lych-gate was given by the Queen.

The newly completed church became very important to Victoria after the death of Albert. In spite of his dislike of memorials, Queen Victoria immediately had an elaborate marble one to Albert carved for the royal chapel. Other memorials followed – one to Prince Leopold who died quite young, and to various grandchildren who died in their youth. The windows were erected by the Queen in memory of her second son, Prince Alfred. Two windows were sent to an exhibition, and the Queen was asked if more could be removed for display. Her emphatic answer came back, 'No, certainly not.'

Queen Victoria took an interest in the services, to the extent of giving £10 to pay for the organist to take further instruction. Ronald Jackman was the organist in 1898, and the Queen thought that 'he seemed to distinctly benefit from the hints given to him by Sir Walter Parratt.' The East Cowes rector at the time, Revd Barnaby, wrote to Mr Jackman: 'It is indeed something for you to be jolly proud of and thankful for that the Queen wishes you to have lessons and offers to pay for them for free!'

The Queen's youngest daughter, Princess Beatrice, was married at Whippingham Church in 1885 to Henry of Battenburg. The wedding was a grand affair for Whippingham, with numerous royalty from

*Princess Beatrice and her mother enter the church.* (REPRODUCED COURTESY OF THE COUNTY RECORD OFFICE, NEWPORT)

*Beatrice and her husband Henry of Battenburg come out of the church.* (REPRODUCED COURTESY OF THE COUNTY RECORD OFFICE, NEWPORT)

various countries attending. The church was filled with beautiful flowers for the occasion. It had been intended to open the church to visitors afterwards so that they could see the flowers, and raise money for a worthy cause. However, the plans failed as the guests at the wedding helped themselves to bouquets before they left!

Sadly, Henry died 11 years later. By this time Queen Victoria had had her own chapel built at Osborne House as she was unable to attend Whippingham as frequently. It was decided to create a Battenburg memorial chapel out of the northern 'household' chapel at Whippingham, and he was laid to rest there. Henry had been made Governor of the Isle of Wight, a role that was now taken on by his widow. In 1914 Princess Beatrice moved into Carisbrooke Castle, and at the outbreak of the Second World War the Government decided she should move to the safer mainland. While there she died, but after the war her remains were returned to Whippingham to lie beside her husband.

The Battenburg (later changed to Mountbatten) link is still strong with Whippingham. The parents of Lord Louis Mountbatten are buried in the church-yard. They were living in the parish at the time of the death of the first Lord Louis, Admiral of the Fleet during the First World War.

The churchyard was enlarged in 1897, taking in a parcel of land to the north called Pond Piece, which belonged to the Queen. New stone walls were built to the north and by the road. To the time of writing this piece of land still has a distinct slope and dip in it, indicating where the old pond was located.

Various local characters are buried here, including Sam Saunders the aircraft builder, John Samuel White the shipbuilder, and Uffa Fox the boatbuilder. Uffa's tombstone depicts the airborne lifeboat he designed which saved so many airmen during the Second World War. Sam Saunders's coffin was shaped like a boat, and regrettably nobody thought to measure the family vault – when the time came to

lower the coffin it was found that it was too long, so bricks had to be knocked out of the vault to allow sufficient space!

The village war memorial stands beside the south door to the church. On the wall of the church is a plaque inscribed with the names of those Whippingham men who gave their lives in the Boer War and two world wars. One of the young men killed during the Second World War was Jack Trusler. He was serving in the RAF when his plane was brought down in North Africa. His mother had been the caretaker at the church for many years. Revd Marshall held a requiem service for Jack, and his RAF cap was placed on the altar. The lad was only 20 years old, and the family had been living at the School House. Two of the Rann brothers are also remembered here. Frank Rann died when the *Royal Oak* went down in Scapa Flow in 1939, and his brother Alfred was killed in action in North Africa in 1943.

The church hall is modern, having been completed in 1991 when the car park was constructed and a garden laid out in the old walled garden of the Rectory. This is a delightful place to rest and is also ideal for church events and social functions. For several years the site has hosted a summer evening of open-air jazz, which has been very successful.

A schoolroom was added to the church in the 1804 rebuild, which may have doubled as a room for the day school and Sunday school. We know that after the church was rebuilt in 1854 Sunday-school classes were held in the village school by Mrs Prothero, the rector's wife. Sunday-school classes were still held at school during the Second World War. In these classes teenagers and young adults were prepared for their Confirmation into the Church of England. There is a 1931 photograph of a Confirmation group, which shows some older ladies, including Mrs Jolliffe. Revd Mostyn Pritchard was the rector then and he intro-duced a number of innovations, many of them with children in mind. Children's services were held twice a month, with special services and 'Children's

## The Whippingham War Memorial

Is to be Unveiled by

### HER ROYAL HIGHNESS PRINCESS BEATRICE

and Dedicated by the

### Lord Bishop of Southampton

at a

### SERVICE OF COMMEMORATION

of

### The Brave Men
### Who Fell in the Great War;

To be held in Whippingham Church,

### On Saturday, September 20th, 1919,

At Four o'clock in the Afternoon.

CLEMENT SMITH,
Rector of Whippingham.

W. H. SMALL, PRINTER, EAST COWER.

Above: *Egg Sunday seagull's nest in the church at Eastertime, early 1930s.*

Left: *A leaflet for the service held at the church for the unveiling of the war memorial, 1919.*

*Jack Trusler entered the Royal Airforce and was killed while flying in Africa during the Second World War.*

*The Whippingham war memorial, photographed in 2005.*

*Sam Saunders's funeral procession passes Truckles in 1933.*

*The boat-shaped coffin at the graveside.*

Surprises' held on feast days. Egg Sunday at Easter saw the children who had chickens bringing eggs, which they took up to an egg nest, their parents hoping the children would not trip on the way. The eggs were later given to the sick or needy in the village.

During the 1930s marching hymns were introduced in Sunday school and a children's banner dedicated and fixed in the church. A boys' club was introduced and goalposts fixed at the school. It was Mostyn Pritchard who introduced the annual candlelit service, and all his services were so popular that the Newport Omnibus Company agreed to rearrange their timetable and route to bring people to the church! Between 1931 and 1937 Revd Mostyn Pritchard took 64 baptisms, 65 weddings and 46 funerals.

In 2006 the Sunday school meets at the new church hall, having moved there from the church rooms at the Rectory. In the 1970s and '80s Mrs Pam Cundall was the driving force behind the Sunday school, with several helpers, and there were three classes of different age groups. Pam Cundall did much for the church, serving as parochial church secretary, followed by a period as churchwarden. She was also a church recorder.

The choir has changed over the years. When Queen Victoria was alive the choirs of St James in East Cowes and St Mildred at Whippingham performed Christmas carols at Osborne House. This tradition returned in the 1980s when the Durbar room was used for carols by the Friends of Osborne. In the 1920s there was only a ladies' choir, but by 1937 there was also a choir of boys.

An old carriage house, once on the opposite side of the road, has been functioning as a teashop for many years. Mrs Margaret Caws was running it before Mrs Pam Tuckwell took over. The little shop finally closed its doors in 2004 and since then teas have been served to visitors in the church hall. An exhibition on the history of the church, local buildings of Whippingham and the Victorian royal children has been on display in the hall since the early 1990s, created by Michelle Richmond. Before there was a shop, Mrs Flux sold postcards, sweets and tobacco from a stall just outside the church gate. Later she started selling teas to visitors in her garden at Truckles.

Visitors have shown more interest in Whippingham Church since Prince Albert rebuilt it. Since 1904, after the Queen's death, parts of Osborne House were opened to the public. Tourism blossomed as excursions were organised to East Cowes, and these frequently called in at Whippingham Church. This continues, with coach loads of visitors arriving daily throughout the season. The church is only open to visitors during weekdays, when a rota of parishioners take turns to act as guides and answer any questions. Visitors arrive from all over the world and the guides have an interesting time showing them the beautiful church and many special items that can be seen.

*The funeral Prince Henry of Battenburg, 1896. He died en route to South Africa to take part in the Boer War.*

*A group of Whippingham ladies and girls on their Confirmation day at Whippingham Church in 1931. Left to right, back row: Marjorie Smith, Annie Speed, Mrs Emily Streets, Mrs Lily Snow, Dene Gregory; middle row: Nellie Owen, Evie Hendy, Maud Brown (?), Mrs Florrie Jolliffe, Alice Andrews, Violet Andrews; front row: Alice Woods, Violet Rann, Edie Whittington, Phyllis Jolliffe, Phyllis Cooper.*

*The church choir was restarted in the 1960s by Revd Deacon. Left to right, back row: ?, ?, ?, Stephen Buckell, Trevor Rann, ? Barton, Peter ? middle row: Phillip McGilliveray, Phillip Mabey, John Hayward; front row: Jonathan Ball, Tim ?, Phillip Jones, ?, Simon Weeks (?), Phillip Underwood, ?, Barry Hayward.*

*The Sunday school in the church garden, 1987.* Left to right, back row: *Helen Raper, Pam Cundall, Gwen Jeager, Gillian Tuckwell in front of Claire Tuckwell, Lucy Pytak, Catherine Mowlam in front of Sally Stapleton, Fiona Higgins, Laura Bradley, Anne Burdett, Michelle Richmond, Stacey Clapp;* front row: *Lynden Clapp, Austin Clapp, Charles Tiffin, Peter Tiffin, Vanessa Harris, Andrina Harris, ?, Stuart Johnson, Melanie Cox, Emma Crawford, ?, Richard Johnson, Paul ?.*

*A 1960s Dixons postcard showing corn stooks in Padmore field, next to the old church shop, which was originally a carriage house. It was moved here from the opposite side of the road.* (REPRODUCED COURTESY OF W.J. NIGH & SONS LTD)

## Whippingham Rectory

Records show that there has been a secular building associated with Whippingham Church for hundreds of years. It is hidden away behind the trees to the south of the church.

The eastern side of the building is older than the rest of it, and is stone-built with flagstoned floors, thick walls and comparatively small windows. This became the domestic area when the western rooms were added, possibly in the early 1800s. The sitting-room had wood panelling that may have been installed before 1700.

It is thought that the building was extended to plans by John Nash. A sketchbook, begun in 1805 by George Repton, who worked with Nash, shows plans for the extension. Revd Ridley occupied the Rectory from 1802–17, and the plans provide a study for the rector by the front door and two large reception rooms. The western of these was built with curved corners, and the dining-room was made octagonal. A spiral staircase led up to Miss Ridley's rooms. The large bay windows to the west are typical of those designed by Nash. Initially, the new extension remained separate from the other rooms upstairs. Later, possibly in 1859, a staircase was built in the hall and a galleried landing added to make all the rooms accessible from it, and the spiral staircase was removed.

In 1828, John Albin in his *Companion to the Isle of Wight* described Whippingham Parsonage as a very beautiful and distinguished feature. Consideration was also given to the grounds. From the house, lawns stretched out to the west and south, where there was an uninterrupted view across the fields and up the Medina valley. This was achieved by the digging of a ditch to keep stock out of the Rectory garden, invisible to the observer in the house. Queen Victoria sketched the view from the Rectory on 15 August 1864, during one of her visits to Canon and Mrs Prothero.

Behind the house, to the south-east, was a walled garden with fruit trees and sufficient space for vegetables to keep the rector's family self-sufficient. Lord Ernle, Revd Prothero's son, wrote of growing up at the Rectory in the 1850s, and eating all their own produce.

Revd Prothero also had several hunters. His coach-house and stables were next to the church, at what is known as Glebe Cottage at the time of writing. His outdoor staff would have lived there.

An interesting document at the County Records Office relates to some reconstruction work at the Rectory in 1859. It had been decided that a damp-proof course should be inserted in the walls. This was made of 'two courses of slates bedded in cement to be carried round all the walls at the level of the underside of the stone plinth.' Some plumbing was also carried out. A new seat of one-inch-thick Honduras mahogany was fixed to the water-closet, and a five-inch brass bolt fixed to the door! The plumber was to 'refix the present water-closet seat to one of the servants' closets,' and to 'lay on water to the housemaid's sink with proper drain from same.'

The 1863 map shows a well to the south of the house. The position of the domestic quarter may have changed over the years. Tennis was not played by the Prothero boys when they were growing up at the Rectory, but was introduced by Canon Clement Smith when he became rector in 1895, and tennis-courts are shown on the 1898 OS map.

In the 1930s Revd Mostyn Pritchard was one of the last rectors to be in residence at the Rectory. He had come to the Island from a rich Kensington living and was given furnishings for his new home by his grateful parishioners as a wedding present. Carpets on the floor in the hall included tiger skins! Mrs Mostyn Pritchard took in lodgers to help with expenses and to help heat the house, as it was very cold in winter!

We know that the rector held 'At Homes', which involved afternoon tea on the Rectory lawn for as many of his parishioners as could attend. There was no church hall or meeting room in the village.

Sam Saunders, living at Padmore, had Whippingham Community Centre built in 1932 and offered it to the Parochial Church Council. The Church Council could foresee expenses in running such a building and regretfully refused the offer unless an endowment of £5,000 was included in the gift. This was not forthcoming.

Following the Second World War, the rector of East Cowes became the rector of Whippingham as well. Whippingham Rectory was no longer in use by the rector and his family. The two main reception rooms of the Rectory, linked by folding doors, became the church rooms, where meetings were held. A kitchen was fitted in a third back room. These rooms were available to rent. The bedrooms of the west wing were converted into a flat, and the rear part of the house was let separately.

By 1980, Revd Snape and his wife Evelyn were living in the flat above the church rooms. Mrs Snape ran dancing classes for children in the two reception rooms downstairs, where many young children had their first experience of dance. Productions were sometimes staged at the Town Hall in East Cowes.

Once the new church hall was completed in 1991 the old Rectory was sold. The building was split into two homes. The incumbent, serving both St James' Church and St Mildred's, had been living at East Cowes Rectory in Old Road for some years. That rambling building was sold in 2001, and now the rector of Whippingham and East Cowes lives in Victoria Grove, halfway between his two churches.

## Life at the Rectory in the 1850s and '60s

Rowland Prothero was born at Whippingham in 1851. His father was the rector of St Mildred's and chaplain to the Queen at that time. Rowland became Minister for Agriculture during the First World War and then, as Lord Ernle, wrote about his life in a book entitled *Whippingham to Westminster*. He remembered the Rectory as a roomy, comfortable home, with sunken fences separating the garden from the fields and view of the river.

Whenever the Queen visited the Rectory the children would be sent for. Her presence inspired awe in young Rowland, and she exuded a simple kindness. The church was being rebuilt and Rowland had been reprimanded by the builder for playing in the mortar. One day Rowland saw the builder on the tower with another man and took a shot at the builder with his catapult. Unfortunately the builder's friend received the missile in the back; he turned around to reveal his identity – it was Prince Albert. Rowland felt very guilty the next time he was brought before the Queen, but nothing was said!

The household was fairly self-sufficient. Bread was baked weekly – a major event. When it was fresh it was delicious and the crust was unforgettably crisp and sweet. By the fifth day the bread was tough and dry. Milk, butter, eggs, poultry, fruit and vegetables came from their own resources. They brewed their own beer. Rowland remembered always having his own silver mug of beer with dinner as a child. The butcher came once a week for orders, and fish was fetched from West Cowes. Pigs were kept and the elderly village postmaster was the pig killer.

Rowland's mother did have some groceries sent specially from London, and sometimes he would accompany a villager on a trip to the market in Newport. This excursion would be on Hollis's passage boat – which called twice a week at The Folly hard. Embarkation at high tide was easy, but more of a problem at low tide. Hollis was a red-faced, hoarse-voiced mariner, with rings in his ears and a blue jersey. The stern of the boat would be filled with a dozen apple-cheeked chattering women all carrying baskets.

They made their own soap and pomatum at the Rectory, using old-fashioned recipes, perfumed with a variety of scents. Wax candles were used downstairs, but the nursery only had tallow candles. If the boy's nose or lips were chapped by the wind then his nurse applied tallow. It smelt musty.

There were some regular callers at the Rectory. Rowland remembered the postman coming every day. Sometimes the pedlar would come to sell his wares, his pack a miracle for the variety of its contents. He was a cherry-cheeked merry fellow. The organ grinder visited with his marionettes dancing in a glass case on top of the organ. One figure stood with a hand out holding a tray for money. If Rowland added a penny to the tray the puppet bowed and added it to the pile. If Rowland gave it a stone this would be thrown out! Between 1857 and 1860 a 'little shrivelled man' from Southern India made an annual visit to sell Madras curry powder.

During the hay harvest Rowland and his two brothers were allowed to go and help in the fields. The grass was cut by a gang of five Irish labourers who came from Cork to Southampton on the 'pig boat', and then crossed to the Island. As the crops ripened the labourers travelled further north, through England. The domestic staff at the Rectory would tend the hay, and when the harvest was complete there would be a feast.

*The Rectory in about 1993, with the Darling family – Heloise, Robert, William and Robin. The fence is in the ditch or 'ha-ha'.*

*The rector's 'At Home' tea afternoon, probably in 1931. Left to right, seated on chairs: ?, Mr Rogerson, ?, Mrs Mostyn Pritchard, Mrs Pitman, Mr George Shedden, Revd Mostyn Pritchard, ?, Mr Birch, Mr Kellaway, Mr Foakes; also included are: Mrs Gregson (standing on right behind Mr Foakes), Mrs Warne with young John in her arms (standing right), Mrs Rann (top back right); children seated on grass, left to right: Vi Rann, Peter Marshall, Jack Trusler, Les Maskell, ?, Arthur Loader, ? Thorne, Joan Marshall.*

*The Sunday school gathered outside the church rooms at the 'Old Rectory', 1984.* Left to right, back row: *Fiona Higgins, Claire Tuckwell, Francesca Parker, Melanie Parker holding Christina Froud, Helen Raper, Sally Bradley, Laura Bradley, Michelle Richmond;* middle row: *Gillian Tuckwell, Carolyn Jefferies, Lucy Pytak, Tracey Heath, Charles Tiffin, Andrew Heath, Aileen Jerome, Anne Burdett, Margaret Heath;* front row: *?, Peter Tiffin, Lynden Clapp, Richard Johnson, Jo Froud, ?, ?, ?, Stacey Clapp, Alex Cook.*

Rowland and his brothers enjoyed only formal relations with their parents. As a young child Rowland would be deposited in the drawing-room at six in the evening to spend an hour with his mother. He had been washed and put into clean clothes for the occasion. As the boys grew older, their mother took on their education. She herself was a linguist and Latin scholar. While living at Whippingham Rectory she clung on to two luxuries – parcels of books from Rolandi's Foreign Library, and a London dressmaker!

From the age of six, arithmetic and writing were taught to the boys by the village schoolmaster, who came three evenings a week. Rowland remembered using quill pens. He also had the pleasure of his father's servant reading to him between the intervals of answering the bell. When he was ten years old Rowland was sent to boarding-school, but the next year was so ill that he was sent home. Another year was passed at the Rectory before he was sent to school at Marlborough in 1864.

Rector Prothero was a hard-working man, running the parish single-handed. Sundays were of course a special day. First there would be family prayers. Then at quarter to ten Rowland would walk with his mother to the village school where she held a Sunday-school class for the older village boys. Each boy would say by heart the collect for the day, and then would be questioned by Mrs Prothero on the meaning of what he had learnt. At 11 there was morning service at the church.

After morning service, Rowland's father would go into the servants' hall and carve a sirloin of beef into dinners for the half dozen or more old people who had been unable to come to church. A daughter or grandchild would come to collect the food with a basin tied up in a handkerchief. Rowland would add a baked potato to the dish.

In the winter, evening service was at 3p.m. and in the summer at 6p.m. After evening service, Rowland's mother held a Women's Club. Some 20 women paid three pence a week, and Mrs Prothero doubled the fund. These savings were paid out at Christmas.

On Sundays the boys had dinner and tea with their parents. At tea there would often be visitors from Osborne, perhaps members of the household and guests, sometimes a famous politician or a clever preacher. Officers from the barracks at Parkhurst, or if the tide and season was right, regatta goers from Cowes, also visited the Rectory for tea. The visits were arranged beforehand by correspondence. All the guests would go to the church service. The children were not allowed any outdoor games on Sundays and only a small range of suitable reading books. Spelling games were allowed, but only biblical names could be used! Newspapers were not allowed and *The London Illustrated News* remained in its wrapper until Monday morning.

Rowland remembered that at Christmas the Rectory had a decorated tree, but cards were not sent.

*The old Mother's Union banner from the church. Mrs Prothero's Women's Club would have been a forerunner of this organisation.*

*Rowland Prothero watched the church tower being built in 1861.*

*Rowland would have been familiar with this view, c.1910, looking down the fields towards the river. East Medina Mill can be seen in the distance.*

*Looking across the peaceful gardens of the crematorium in 2005.*

*Springtime by the woodland walk in the crematorium gardens in 2005.*

Christmas plays were dying out, but a party of young fishermen from East Cowes acted out one of the old mummers plays at the Rectory. On New Year's Eve a wooden silver-banded punch bowl was decorated with holly. The children walked round the table three times and received gifts from all the diners. On 6 January there was a twelfth-night cake and a children's party. Pictures of different characters were drawn and put into a hat. Each child drew out a card and those receiving the cards for the king and queen would sit on a made-up throne and preside over the party. On Valentine's Day, 14 February, the post bag would be full of messages. When Shrove Tuesday arrived, all the village children trooped down to the Rectory, singing a song asking for food.

Rowland remembered going to Southampton with his parents on the *Gem*, at that time a vessel of the Isle of Wight Steam Packet Company, later to become Red Funnel. Or rather, his parents went on the steamer – the carriage and horses, held by a groom, went in a low-sided 'horse boat' towed behind the steamer. Inside the carriage sat the children and their nurses. At the Brambles Bank the seas were choppy and lopped over into the 'horse boat', splashing the carriage. The horses began to plunge about. Once around the corner the seas calmed down, but it must have been a very frightening experience for all concerned. This trip took place in 1855, when Rowland was four.

In 1856 Rowland watched ploughing taking place at Arreton, just a few miles from Whippingham. What made this special was that three teams of oxen were being used, a rare sight for those days.

Looking down from the Rectory towards the river young Rowland saw the boats passing. There were sturdy brigs arriving laden with coal from Cardiff and other vessels carrying goods of all descriptions. He saw the many brown-sailed barges carrying cement on their way to the mainland, or returning empty. The cement mills on the west bank of the Medina, already operating in the 1850s, were generally wreathed in a cloud of smoke.

Rowland's childhood memories give us a rare insight into what life must have been like at the Rectory in Whippingham, and glimpses into a different world of 150 years ago.

## The Isle of Wight Crematorium

The crematorium was built in 1961 in the parish of Whippingham. Prior to this there was no such facility on the Island and any cremations of Islanders had to be carried out on the mainland.

In the first year 308 cremations were carried out – this number has steadily risen to an average of 1,400 cremations a year (2005). About 80 per cent of the ashes are scattered in the grounds at Whippingham Crematorium. Only 20 per cent of deaths on the Island result in burial, which is slightly less than the national average. Cremation is much the preferred option on the Island.

The seating area in the chapel was increased from 60 to 82 in 1985 and new cremators were installed in 1997 to comply with the Environmental Health Act of 1990. Since 1991 the crematorium has been run by the Isle of Wight Council, who took over from the Isle of Wight Crematorium Joint Committee.

The site covers ten acres, adjoining Palmer's Brook. Initially there were only formal gardens of remembrance, but in recent years a children's garden has been opened and the delightful woodland walk created by the stream.

The gardens are a beautiful place to visit. In the spring wild flowers abound, bluebells carpet the woods and the trees echo with the song of birds. The sun warms the gardens, and planting provides colour. There is space to be alone, if need be, and seats to rest and contemplate. While the crematorium can provoke sad memories, it is also a place which is striving to give users the opportunity to remember the good times in life. If you have not already done so, visit the gardens on a sunny, warm day, walk by the stream and enjoy memories of those good times.

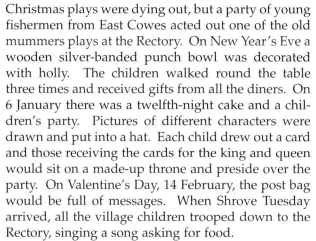

Above: *An engraving of the reconstruction of Barton Manor house for the Queen and Prince Albert, 1846.*

Right: *A picture of the farmyard at Barton, taken in 1867 by A. Disderi. (THE ROYAL ARCHIVES © 2005 HER MAJESTY QUEEN ELIZABETH II)*

## Chapter 4
# Barton Manor & Farm

The recorded history of Barton dates back to medieval times. In 1275 an oratory was founded here at a house owned by John de Insula of Wootton, then rector of Shalfleet and Thomas de Winton, rector of Godshill. This oratory was planned for the retreat of six priests and a clerk, following the rule of Saint Augustin. They were to choose an archpriest from among their number, and this man would be ratified by the Bishop of Winchester. Otherwise, they were an independent body. Copies of the charter of the foundation still exist at Winchester, with their ornate seals attached.

Strict rules were laid down regarding what they should wear – rusty black habits and hats, and a new cloak lined with lamb's wool each winter – and what they should eat – one main meal with a second course and on feast days a third course if the resources of the house allowed. The clerk was to read something edifying to them while they dined. Their old clothes were to be given to the poor, and they were to supply 13 poor people with bread, beer and soup every day. Cridmoor Farm at Carisbrooke was purchased specifically to provide funds for the alms. The priests were all to sleep in one dormitory, unless illness prohibited this, and to follow all the many religious services of the day, including prayers for their founders and benefactors.

The oratory was endowed with numerous parcels of land, farms, grazing land, two mills in Newport – one of them being Cross Mill – and a warehouse in Southampton. It is surprising to see that these lands were owned all over the Island, even as far south as Chale. Over £625, a massive sum in those days, was expended in setting up the oratory. This must have brought in sufficient annual revenue for the priests to live quite comfortably. Lay brothers would have done the day-to-day work of the oratory, leaving the priests to spend their time in study or meditation. From 1321 Barton was given the responsibility for maintaining the oratory at St Catherine's Down, where a light was kept burning at night for the safety of seafarers.

In the reign of Edward III, 1327–60, a list of landholders on the Island who were required to supply men to defend the Island included the prior of Barton. Two bowmen or archers were to be provided by Barton.

Perhaps because of their independence, discipline became lax, and there were complaints to Winchester in 1365. In 1389 William Love, the archpriest, was found guilty of several misdemeanours, and did not take proper responsibility for Barton oratory.

We next hear that in 1390 William Love had been captured and carried off to 'parts beyond the seas', and that the buildings were in a state of dilapidation.

Somehow, he must have been returned to Barton, perhaps a ransom having been paid! He obviously had better intentions, as in 1403 a formal contract was entered into between Love and a mason, Richard Lathbury, to undertake the necessary repairs and continue in the service of the oratory as required. The oratory continued to function until 1439.

That year, Winchester College was running short of funds. Perhaps by then there were not enough priests remaining at Barton to keep it functioning, but we do know that all the Barton lands were given to the college by the archpriest of Barton, Walter Trengof. He left Barton and became an archdeacon in Cornwall.

Barton was owned by Winchester College for the next 400 years and the lands were leased out to a variety of tenants. Winchester continued with the duty of maintaining a priest at the chapel at Barton and there was still a chapel there until the first year of the reign of Edward VI. In 1547 an act was passed to abolish all chantries, Barton among them, as Protestant feeling was against them.

The lands at Barton Manor itself include the more workable plateau gravels and a sheltered valley sloping to the sea. This was seen as a good holding to rent, and a substantial Jacobean house was constructed. It included several small lancet windows which may have survived from the oratory building. In 1790 Hassell wrote *A Tour of the Isle of Wight* and commented that Barton had recently been the residence of Lord Clanricarde. Hassell stated that:

*All the sides of the rooms are of wainscot, formed into small panels, in which are fixed a number of representations of the cross. Here was likewise a chapel, but the building is now appropriated to less sacred purposes, being converted into a warehouse for wool. A great sameness runs through the whole house, both in internal and external parts. The mode of construction, with so many gable ends towards the front, gives a great formality to its appearance, so do the tall chimnies [sic].*

When the Queen rented Osborne in 1844 the lease was for one year, to enable the royal couple to assess its suitability as their family home. Obviously they decided it was too small, as a new building was started as soon as they bought Osborne in 1845. The same year they bought Barton Manor from Winchester College for £18,600. The house would

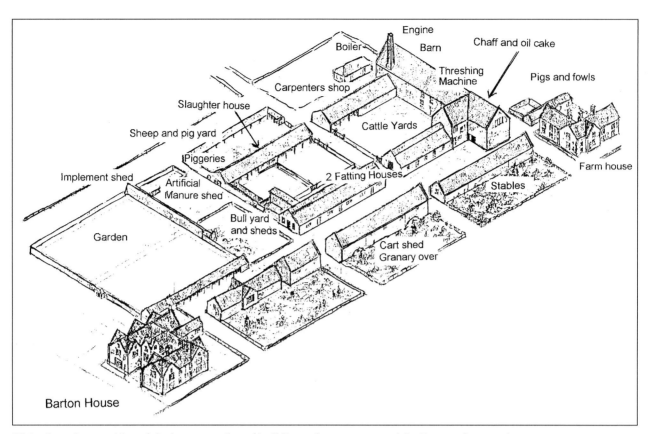

Engine
Boiler
Barn
Chaff and oil cake
Threshing Machine
Pigs and fowls
Carpenters shop
Slaughter house
Cattle Yards
Sheep and pig yard
Piggeries
2 Fatting Houses
Farm house
Implement shed
Artificial Manure shed
Stables
Garden
Bull yard and sheds
Cart shed Granary over
Barton House

*This plan gives an idea of the large complex of buildings that were erected for Barton farmyard.*

provide additional accommodation for the equerries, diplomats and visiting family.

The whole house was remodelled according to Albert's designs. The interior was gutted and the old panelling removed. A suite of kitchens was added that could be used to prepare additional food for Osborne when the need arose. Insulated carts were built specially for the purpose of taking food there from Barton. An historian in 1846 wrote diplomatically about the 'taste and genius that presides over the work,' but also commented:

*It is difficult to forget that, with its destruction, the associations attached to the time-hallowed and hoary dwelling of a distant age are passed away, and however much we may admire the new creation, still we must regret the old and familiar.*

However, much of the external walling and chimneys of the house were carefully repaired with matching bricks and masonry made at their own brickyard. Albert may have been one of the first conservationists!

Albert had the old farm buildings to the east removed. In their place he designed gardens that would enhance the view from the house. He planted many new trees, including a *Cupressus lambertiana* on his 27th birthday on 26 August 1846. This new introduction from America grew to a great height, but unfortunately came to grief in the hurricane of 1987, along with many other trees on the estate.

Barton Farm was run as the 'home farm', without a tenant. It was to supply the royal needs in addition to being run as a commercial farming enterprise. Prince Albert created a 'model' farm, not so much as to set an example to his neighbours, but to give them more ideas that they could freely copy if the new techniques proved useful.

To the west of the house Albert had an extensive range of modern stone and brick farm buildings constructed in 1852, with quarry tiles or slate roofs. The stone and tiles were used on elevations of the buildings that were visible as you approached the complex, and the cheaper materials used inside! These buildings incorporated the latest innovations. The main building housed two steam engines – one was used to pump water up to Osborne for the house and fountains, and the other to drive a shaft that ran the length of the building to belt-drive a chaff cutter, a mill, a threshing machine, corn elevators and other machinery. A hand-operated tramway enabled trucks of prepared fodder and bedding to be pushed easily along to the stables, cowsheds, piggeries, calf-fattening sheds, bull pens and other buildings.

The cart sheds incorporated cast-iron beams to support a grain store above. The floor of the grain store was made from cement to discourage vermin. The carts were another innovation. Sets of axles and wheels were constructed that could have interchangeable beds laid on them. There were cart beds, harvest beds and dung beds. When not required these were stored vertically like plates in a plate rack.

*Slades, the butcher of East Cowes, proudly advertised 'Stock fattened on her late Majesty's farm at Barton', Christmas 1901.*

Metal supports were constructed for the hay and straw ricks. This kept them off the ground, probably keeping the stack dryer. A vast underground reservoir was constructed, with brick barrel vaulting, to collect water from a nearby spring.

The Prince had thousands of drainage tiles made at the Queen's brickyard and these were used to drain the heavy clay fields of the lower pasture. This was the first of the improvements to the estate. The drains were laid 4 feet deep, and from 18 to 40 feet apart, according to the subsoil. The heavy clay soil on the lower ground was greatly improved by adding 30 tons of chalk per acre. This was brought from Portsdown Hill and delivered at Barton Hard, at 2s.9d. a ton. This was one third cheaper than using chalk from Arreton on the Island. Dung for the fields was also brought from Portsmouth at 6s.6d. per 1½ tons.

By 1860 Albert had considerable stock at Barton. There were 31 horses, colts and foals; 10 cows in milk, 54 other cattle; four rams, 422 ewes, 246 lambs, 111 other sheep and 51 swine. The working horses were mainly Clydesdales, the milking cattle Alderneys, the grazing beasts Galloways, and the sheep mainly Southdowns.

The farm accounts were submitted annually to Prince Albert and generally showed a loss, although the woodland was making a profit. In the ten years from 1848 to 1858 the profit on Barton Farm amounted to £857.13s.0d. The land steward, Andrew Toward, pointed out in 1858 that he had expenses not normally incurred on a farm:

*There is the daily expense, not needed by tenant farmers, of sweeping and cleaning about the buildings for the sake of appearance. The coppice wood on the estate will annually become of less value in consequence of the introduction of so many ornamental trees, which causes the undergrowth to be destroyed at an increase in labour with a decrease in profit.*

Barton Farm was visited by the royal children on their walks, and guests would be shown the farm. Consequently everything had to be spick and span all the time.

A total of 400 acres were under cultivation and a further 400 acres were under pasture by 1860. The farm had a Smith's steam cultivator by then, which drew a plough back and forward across a field on wires. However, an observer that year noted that:

*Wheat stubbles are ploughed with four horses 8 inches deep, and other ploughings are with two horses, five inches deep. The harrowing is done by appending four harrows to a pole, covering 14½ feet of land, drawn by four horses, two at each end, in line, walking in the furrows on either side of the land. Thus treading is avoided.*

The royal couple were careful to pay the going Island rate for workers on their estate. They did not want to encourage a rise in pay all over the Island by excessive pay. However, the staff were offered free medical care and received gifts at Christmas. It would be interesting to know if other local landowners were similarly beneficent towards their workers in Victorian times.

The work at the farm continued after Albert's death in 1861. Andrew Toward, who was land agent at Barton, retired in 1871. The stock continued to thrive, and when the Isle of Wight Agricultural Shows started the Queen was a frequent prizewinner. Sometimes she would have a cup made with her cash prizes to celebrate her wins, and at other times she would put the monies into the school prize fund.

Surplus stock was sold locally. After the Queen's death in 1901, Slades, the local East Cowes butcher, had a photograph taken of his Christmas meat display, with labels proclaiming, 'Stock fattened on her late Majesty's farm at Barton.'

From the lodge gates at Barton on the main East Cowes to Whippingham road an avenue of elm trees

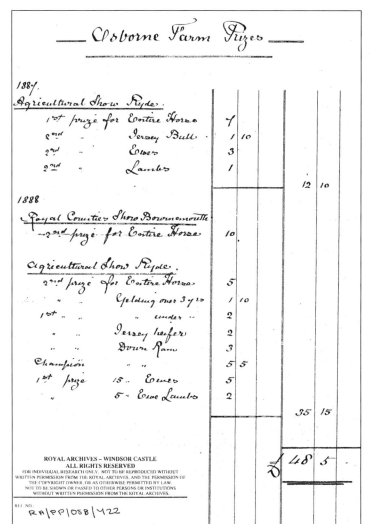

*Prizes won by the stock at Barton Farm.*
*(THE ROYAL ARCHIVES © 2005 HER MAJESTY QUEEN ELIZABETH II)*

*The workmen on Barton Manor Farm take a break from using an elevator to build a stack in 1923.  They include: Mr Mullett the foreman (back row, third from left); Edward Street (second row, far left); Charlie Snow (later foreman) (second row, far right).*

was planted leading to the house. An avenue of elm and Scots pine was also planted from the Alverstone Lodge towards Barton. These elms died in the Dutch elm disease epidemic of the 1970s. Albert had a large Cork oak plantation made to the north of the house, and many of those trees survive to this day.

At Barton a pond was built that could be used for skating if the winter weather permitted. This was first constructed in 1861 and enlarged and made more watertight in 1872. This facility was much appreciated by the royal children, and grandchildren. However, Victoria would not allow mixed skating by the adults – it was much too unseemly should a slip occur!

When Queen Victoria died in 1901 her son Edward soon gave Osborne House to the nation, and much of the building became a convalescent home for officers. However, he retained Barton as a holiday home on the Island. He continued the work that his father had originally started on the gardens, building the terraces leading down to the lake and the walled garden. More trees were planted. King Edward used the house for entertaining, one of his visitors being his cousin the Kaiser of Germany.

In 1909 the Tsar of Russia, Nicholas II, and his family paid a visit to Barton. The King and the Tsar reviewed the fleet on 2 August at Spithead, and the next day watched the racing at Cowes. They visited the Naval College at Osborne on 4 August and took tea on the lawn at Barton.

Mount Cottages were built between 1901 and 1907. They are a pair of semi-detached cottages built of stone in the style of Barton Manor itself. After King Edward's death in 1910, royalty appeared to lose interest in Barton Manor, and in 1922 the Barton estate, with Barton and Woodhouse Farms, was sold. Crown Estates continued to own the outlying farms.

The Tillett family were the next owners of Barton Manor. Mr Tillett continued to run the estate in much the same way as had been done during royal owner-ship. The farms provided an occupation for many people, as the photographs taken in 1922 show. Families had worked for generations on the estate, and several still live there in 2006. In the early-twenty-first century, however, with mechanisation, the farms no longer need large numbers of workers.

In 1922 the estate was profitable and the house a pleasant place to live. Princess Beatrice, the Queen's youngest daughter, visited Mrs Tillett several times. The Princess related the story that the Queen would put up families with young unruly children at Barton, rather than having them running riot at Osborne. Mr Tillett created a billiard room, and one of the coach-houses was turned into a motor car house. The chauffeur lived in one of the lodges.

The remainder of the farm buildings were still in their original use in 1922, including Albert's dairy. It had tiled floors and walls to keep the milk cool on the stone shelves and an elaborate central fountain cooling the air in the summer.

*Barton men working on the hay in 1922 – Charlie Snow is on the left.*

Mrs Grace Davison (née Snow) wrote about growing up as a child at Barton, where her father, Charlie, became farm manager for the Tillett family:

*As a child in the 1930s, I thought that every farm looked like Barton, with its stone and brick outbuildings. It was only later that I learnt that it was Prince Albert's model farm, and rather special as farms go.*

*I remember the dairy well, with its tiled floor and tiled walls. In my mind I can still see the cooler and the vast vats of cream. I stuck my finger in one of these while Miss Thorpe, the Dairymaid, was not looking but discovered it was sour cream for butter. So I just had to swallow it before she turned round! Admission tickets were sold from the dairy when Barton Manor was open to the public in recent years.*

*The main stone barn used to house a threshing drum and in that area there was a grinding drum and mangolds were chopped for feed. There was a chaff house with a granary over the engine house.*

*The cow sheds could house 65 animals and had tram tracks along the floor for ease of feeding. There were two bull boxes with feeding passages and open yards. Eleven horses could be stabled and there were six pigsties. The range of buildings on the north side included a hayloft.*

*The Tilletts housed their Daimler in a shed at the far end of the yard, nearest the manor house. The field nearest the farmhouse had wrought-iron hayrick stands, which I understand were quite unusual.*

*Mr Tillett's herd were lovely Guernseys and we were allowed so many pints of milk a day. As children we drank pints of rich creamy milk and mum made us big rice puddings. The skimmed milk was fed to the animals.*

*The head cowman was Mr Brown who lived in Alverstone Lodge. When Tuberculin testing came into being, the cowmen had to wear milking hats and smocks and wash the cows' udders thoroughly before milking. My father had to impress the importance of this to the older cowmen as their previous less stringent methods were hard to break. The milk was taken to Sandown to the Isle of Wight Creameries.*

*As children we were always interested in picking up bits of cork from the cork oak trees. There were always*

*The Barton farmhouse was used by the farm manager.*

Left: *Charlie Snow and the old Ford at Barton, early 1930s.*

Below: *Charlie Snow with the new Bedford lorry at Barton, mid-1930s. There were still 20 working horses on the farm in 1950.*

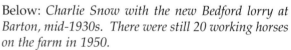

Above: *The yard from the Barton farmhouse, while still in use before 1987.*

Above right: *Ern Bull in the rotary milk unit at Barton Farm in 1975.*

Right: *The new dairy unit at Barton in 1974.*

*The end of an era – the last day of milk churns being collected by lorry at Barton, July 1974.*

*The milk tanker arrives to collect the milk from the dairy's refrigerated tank, July 1974.*

*The 'V' and 'A' entwined symbol featured on many of the estate gates.*

*swans on the pond below the farm. We also used to play on the beach and in the creek at King's Quay with other estate children. We would be sent off for the day with a bag of jam sandwiches. Once the boys lit a fire and cooked a very elderly dead rabbit which they found. It made them ill! We would collect cuttlefish bones for our chickens, and eat wild strawberries. We swam in King's Quay above the sluice and had mud ball fights across the stream. King John's treasure was said to be buried in the creek, but we never found it.*

*Old Mrs Tillett at the big house was a small dainty lady who always dressed perfectly, with her white hair back in a neat bun. She was very kind and looked after my mother for several days during a severe illness. She took calves' foot jelly and so on to Lily Snow at Matthew's Cottage when she was ill. Mrs Tillett visited all her cottagers and helped them all.*

Mr Ablitt came from Newtown to manage Barton Farm from 1936–41, with children George and Sue. In 1942 they moved to Heathfield Farm.

During the Second World War life at Barton changed. Officialdom visited and said that all the iron railings around the Osborne fields rented by the Tilletts, and the ornate gates, were to be taken for scrap. This would have caused considerable inconvenience to the farm, and the loss of the 'V and A' embossed gates would have been sad. So Mr Ivor Tillett offered the authorities the boiler and engine from the engine house at Barton instead. This had not been used for several years as the coal consumption had been enormous, and the only man who could work the engine had died! The old flywheel stood about five feet. The men agreed and carted it off, thus saving the railings and gates, which can still be seen in 2006.

Barton Manor was host to several visitors during the war. German officer prisoners of war were quartered at Barton while undergoing treatment at Osborne Convalescent Home for Officers. Orderlies carried the stretchers the half mile between the buildings. On one occasion, a German plane came over firing its machine-guns as a German officer was being taken to Osborne. The orderlies unceremoniously dumped the stretcher on the road and dived for cover. Fortunately nobody was injured! There were FANYs (Female Auxilliary Nursing Yeomanry) at Barton. Parts of the farm were occupied by Canadian soldiers for a time. These soldiers left in June 1944 with the D-Day invasion.

In 1952 the Tillett family moved to Devon and Barton Manor was sold and the estate split up into its constituent farms.

Barton Manor house had a variety of owners after the Tilletts left. The first was Peter McDonald, MP for the Island. For a short time after his ownership Barton Manor was a school, and then it was owned by Miss Holt and later by Lady Price.

In 1976 Anthony Goddard and his wife Alix bought Barton Manor and set about planting a vineyard on the warm sunny slopes – just six acres to begin with. They also threw open the grounds to the public and people found that the Barton gardens were well worth visiting. In the spring millions of daffodils and primroses carpeted the slopes beneath the trees on the far side of the lake. In the summer the huge herbaceous borders provided exuberant colour and the old skating lake had been turned into a delightful secluded garden with a stream running through it from the lake. The middle lake itself was home to a black swan and numerous enormous hungry carp. The 'secret garden' was full of the scent of roses.

The wines themselves, bottled on the premises, also attracted much attention. Gold medals were won by the Goddards in national competitions, and Anthony became the president of the British Vinegrowers Association. The wine was drunk at Buckingham Palace and the Houses of Parliament. The vineyards were extended to 15 acres. Barton was firmly on the Isle of Wight tourist map, with visitors leaving with their wine-tasting glass and perhaps a bottle of wine to take home.

In 1987 the Barton farm buildings came up for sale. These adjoined Barton Manor house and were no longer needed for farming. The Goddards 'had' to buy them, not only because the size of their vineyard and tourist business had expanded to bursting point, but also because they were itching to restore the old buildings to something of their former glory. The buildings were ideal for expanding facilities for the visiting public.

The Goddards employed an enthusiastic three-man team, as well as working on the project themselves. They created an award-winning restoration development from the old farm buildings. Four out of five of the buildings required re-roofing. By luck, 12,000 second-hand tiles were purchased just a day before the 1987 hurricane, which tripled their value overnight! The former two-storey granary had been used to store 150 tonnes of fertiliser on the first floor. Despite massive iron beams and brick arches, this weight had caused one end of the building to subside,

*Mr and Mrs Anthony Goddard in the farmyard after their excellent restoration of the buildings, 1988.*

*Hospice leaflet for four open days a year at Barton, 2002.*

OPEN ON FOUR DAYS ONLY THROUGHOUT THE YEAR

**SUMMER EVENTS AT Barton Manor**

**Sunday 2nd June 2002**
CELEBRATION OF THE QUEEN'S GOLDEN JUBILEE
Join us for a Giant Tea Party 3pm
Shanklin Town Brass Band ~ 1pm to 2pm
Fashion Show ~ 2.30pm
Salvation Army Band ~ 4pm to 5pm

**Sunday 7th July 2002**
ALL DAY CRAFT FAYRE & AFTERNOON AT THE PROMS
*featuring*
The IOW Youth Concert Band ~ 3pm to 5pm

**Sunday 4th August 2002**
**ANTIQUE FAYRE**
The Largest Antique Fayre on the Island
Over 70 Stalls

**Sunday 1st September 2002**
**JAZZ DAY**
*featuring*
Toco Bonito ~ 11am to 1pm
Tim Saul's Modern Jazz Sextet ~ 1pm to 3pm
Unity Stompers ~ 3pm to 5pm

Many guest charities throughout the four events.
Hospice Shop, Café and many, many stalls
for your enjoyment.
**Open 10am to 5pm**
Entrance: Adults £2.50, Children £1
Free Car Parking   No Dogs – Guide Dogs Only

**FOR THE**
**EARL MOUNTBATTEN HOSPICE**
*The Island's only Hospice caring for people with life shortening illnesses.*
*The Hospice needs to raise over £2,000 each day to ensure the*

*The combine harvester making light work of the harvest in 2002.*

*Harvest time on Barton Farm, 2002.*

requiring a complete rebuild. Parts of other buildings and walls were taken down to provide the necessary 'VR' or 'C' bricks – 'C' for Cubitt who carried out Albert's designs. The lathe and plaster work was in a sorry state and had to be removed, but the original pine rafters were in good condition. The original sliding-door gear was still in excellent condition, and the doors still hang on it at the time of writing.

Of the old buildings, the cart shed and granary became a kitchen, restaurant and function room. The stabling became the toilets and shop, and the dairy became the ticket office. The old farmyard became a very pleasant place to sit, enjoy the sun and eat. Excellent use was made of these redundant old farm buildings.

Barton Manor Vineyard was all set for many more years in Goddard ownership, but then came the Lloyds crash. Mr Goddard was a Lloyds name and funds had to be found to shore up Lloyds. So regretfully the Goddards had to sell Barton Manor in 1993.

Robert Stigwood bought Barton that year for £1.15 million. He had arrived in Britain from Australia with £3 in his pocket in 1959 and soon became an agent for various pop stars. The Bee Gees and Cream were among his clients, and he worked with the Beatles and Brian Epstein. His first pop musical was *Hair*, closely followed by *Jesus Christ Super Star*, then *Evita* and *Grease*. Mr Stigwood made his millions, bought a yacht (with a crew of 28), and a Bermuda home.

The Isle of Wight and Barton Manor captured his interest – the house, the gardens and initially the vineyard. However, within a few years the vines were taken out, and the manor grounds were no longer open daily to the public. Robert Stigwood entertained his friends and spent much of his time quietly at Barton, flying in and out by private helicopter to his own landing pad.

For several years the grounds have been given over to the Island Hospice to use for a fund-raising event four times a year, and many availed themselves of the opportunity to enjoy Barton and have the chance to see a wonderful old house set in superb gardens. Mr Stigwood could be seen hospitably moving amongst the crowds. But otherwise he is rarely seen around the Island. However, with a house like Barton and superb grounds, why go anywhere else!

After the Barton estate was split up in 1953, when the Tilletts left, Barton Farm itself had a series of managers and owners. One family to own Barton Farm were the Grists, who were strict Plymouth Brethren. Even if a storm was forecast for the Monday, with hay waiting to be gathered in, they would not do any work on the Sunday.

Mr R.J. Billings bought Barton Farm from the Grists in 1964 and John Broughton came from Dorset to become farm manager. The farm soon included Woodhouse as well, and several fields were rented from Osborne. The farm covered a very large mixed acreage. On one occasion, Mr Billings wanted a corn drier put in, which involved digging a 12-foot pit. Unfortunately, the plans for Albert's entire drainage system had been mislaid during the war, so everywhere the men dug they broke through more drainage pipes and the proposed pit flooded. Water had been pumped from the large underground reservoir across to Osborne. It took the men 12 weeks to dig the pit and mend the pipes!

In 1971 Richard and Ann Orlik bought Barton Farm from Mr R.J. Billings to add to their Kingston Farm holding and managed it themselves. In 1973 they built a new rotary milking parlour to replace the two obsolete existing dairy units. It was capable of milking 300 cows, although it started in 1974 with 200. The number had increased to 300 by 1985, all from home-reared stock. They were milked three times a day on a shift system and production increased by 20 per cent. Three full-time herdsmen and two students were employed. In late 1984 the EU introduced milk quotas and a system that depended on increasing production became uneconomic. The herd was sold in 1985.

Since 1985, Barton Farm has been farmed as an arable farm growing cereals and oil-seed rape. Hay is also produced for horses. In 1987 the farmhouse and original farm buildings at Barton were sold to Mr Goddard and the farm was renamed New Barton Farm, with a new farmhouse built near Mount Cottages. Heathfield farm land has been included into New Barton Farm since 1996.

# Chapter 5

# Padmore, Little Padmore & George's Field

## Padmore House

Padmore House is a large house near the church. One would imagine that it might have been a manor house, but there is no justification for this. It is not mentioned in Domesday records, and probably developed as a simple farmhouse, which may have been improved to make it a better proposition to rent out. The excellent views from the house looking up the Medina valley would have been a strong contributory factor for 'gentry' to lease the property. There have been only two families – the Balls and the Jolliffes – who have owned and lived at Great Padmore for 40 or more consecutive years since the 1600s.

In references from 1637 it was called Great Padmore, to distinguish it from Little Padmore, the farm at the top of Folly Lane. By that date, the two Padmores were rated separately for tax. Little Padmore Farm paid 13s.11d., while Great Padmore, rented by Mr Takes, paid only 8s.6d. By comparison, Osborne House paid £2.8s.9d. at that time.

In 1640 Robert Baker, heir to Robert Standish of Whippingham, sold Great Padmore to William Turgis, a merchant of London. He died a couple of years later and it passed to Thomas Turgis. His descendant, William Turgis, sold Great Padmore to Revd Benedict Ball in 1673, who became the rector of Whippingham in 1655. The hearth tax records of 1673 show that Padmore House paid tax on four hearths. The hearth tax was a money-raising venture created by the government to pay for expensive wars.

It would appear that improvements may have been taking place around 1700, after Revd Benedict Ball purchased Great Padmore. Certainly, the earlier stone-built house was enlarged at some time and a Queen Ann style frontage was added. This classical style of architecture shows in the hipped roof preserving the heavy horizontal line of the cornice at the eaves, dormer windows to the second floor and a canopied front door. The Island was always behind the mainland in styles of architecture and the beautiful bay windows, with their view up the Medina River, may be of a later date. They could have been added in the early 1800s when John Nash was rebuilding the church and adding to the Rectory.

Great Padmore stayed in the Ball family for at least 63 years. Revd Benedict had a son, Benedict, who also had a son called Benedict. It appears that all were clergymen, and the second of the Benedicts married Elizabeth Cumberland, the daughter of the Bishop of Peterborough. The third Benedict Ball had eight children, two of whom died young. It would appear that they all lived at Great Padmore, until 1736, when he sold the house to Mr Brooke of Portsmouth.

By 1742 Mr Blachford of Osborne was the tenant at Great Padmore, the owner being Mr White of Newport. Mr Blachford was paying rates of £1.10s. for Great Padmore, for the relief of the poor, and £7.10s. for Osborne. Perhaps he required additional accommodation for a relative, so rented the house.

Two decades later, in 1762, Doctor Benjamin Cook was living at Great Padmore. He was a surgeon at Newport and leased out the farm land belonging to Great Padmore to William Cheek. In 1780 William Cheek was a churchwarden and soon rented Great and Little Padmores. In 1780 James Jolliffe and Matthew Jolliffe were also paying rates for houses and gardens in Whippingham parish.

Mr Tovey Jolliffe was a curate at Whippingham in 1780. He may have been related to William Jolliffe of Wolverton, described as a gentleman, who was the first of the Jolliffe family that we know of to live at Great Padmore. William Jolliffe rented Great and Little Padmore from William Cheek in 1790. Between 1791 and 1809 the Jolliffes may have bought both Padmores, as they leased out Little Padmore and some closes of land belonging to Great Padmore in 1810. By this time it was William's son James who was at Padmore. James Jolliffe senr died at Padmore in 1816 aged 59 and was succeeded by his wife Elizabeth and his only son James. Young James had gone into the Church, and by 1820 was the rector of Barton Stacey in Hampshire. He let out Great Padmore to various people, including Charles M. Smith and Charles Bassett Roe.

Between 1841 and 1851 Revd James Jolliffe returned to the Island and took up residence at Great Padmore with his three daughters. They were Frances, Mary and Emily, but may have been known as Elizabeth, Mary and Ellen! Their father, James, died in 1864 and his three spinster daughters remained at Padmore until at least 1914, aged 87, 85 and 81 by then. The youngest had arrived at Padmore in her teens. Frances Elizabeth was buried at Whippingham in 1915 and her sister Mary in 1919. The family tomb, which is on the left by the Queen's door to the church, also mentions a son who died while at Oxford. The Jolliffes had owned Padmore from 1790 to 1915.

Mrs Louisa Smith, a widow with a young daughter, had come with the Jolliffes from Barton Stacey as their cook. She stayed with them, latterly as housekeeper, until she died, in the 1890s. Her daughter was the housemaid.

*A 2005 view of the original front of the house and the rose garden created by Sam Saunders.*

*Padmore House in 2005. The bay windows were possibly added in the early 1800s and a new entrance created to the south.*

The Misses Jolliffe must have enjoyed walking by the ponds. The stream that rises in the field below the house was dammed at some stage to make two ponds. The weir between the ponds was decorated with shells set in cement. This has become overgrown and the ponds have silted up over the years.

We know a little of their way of life in their old age from the book *Arreton All My Days* by Hilda Alice Moore. In 1913, at the age of 16, Hilda had answered an advertisement for a 'between maid' at Padmore. She was interviewed, with her grandmother, in the ladies' waiting-room at Newport Railway Station, by Miss Mary Jolliffe. Miss Mary must have been about 85 at the time. Hilda was told she had to have a cotton-print dress for the mornings, and a black dress and white apron for the afternoons, and these had to be found for her by her grandmother. Hilda's salary was to be £10 a year, and after six months she would be allowed every other Sunday afternoon off.

Hilda found that the 'between maid' had a wide variety of tasks. The Misses Jolliffe liked their own butter, so Hilda had to skim the milk daily and then two or three times a week had the back-breaking task of churning the butter. Once made, the butter had to be put into round pots and stamped with a wooden mould for decoration.

Daily tasks included cleaning out and making up the fires in the bedrooms so they could be kept going all day, and cleaning and filling the oil-lamps and trimming the wicks. There was no gas or electricity. She collected the large stone hot-water bottles from

*The front of Padmore House in 2005. The tower to the right houses a water tank to give pressure for the fountain in the rose garden.*

each bedroom, emptied them and filled them with fresh water. These were placed, unstoppered, in the kitchen oven where they remained for the day, so that in the evening Hilda could stopper them and take them upstairs. She could only carry one at a time as they were so heavy!

The drawing-room and study were cleaned each day, and the stairs with their red felt were brushed. The walls and doors were white, and Miss Elizabeth had painted attractive pictures of flowers in the panels on the doors. Hilda's favourite job was to check over the Misses Jolliffes' court clothes. These were the dresses, tiaras, ostrich plumes, shawls, stockings, gloves and shoes that the three young ladies had worn for their 'coming out' when they were presented at court. Each was arranged in a separate compartment, and had to be checked for moths, then the dresses taken down to the pantry and ironed with the flat irons. It would take her a day, between her other jobs, and had to be done once a week.

Her least-favourite job was cooking up the offal that was brought three times a week by the butcher so she could feed the cats. There were 16 indoor cats and several more outside. The smell of the food was so disgusting that the cooking had to be done in the brewhouse outside, and the cats were very demanding! So too were the donkeys. These had to have two brown loaves cut in strips and numerous carrots, also cut in strips. If Hilda was late with their food they would start braying very loudly!

The donkeys were kept to pull the low four-in-hand coach in which the ladies travelled on the few occasions when they went out. Mr Downer was the coachman and he also helped around the house, carrying coal and so on. The gardener was Mr Shaw, who also looked after the cow. He lived in the small lodge on Beatrice Avenue.

A washerwoman came in on a Monday to do the laundry, and on Thursdays the ironing. She was a Mrs Downer, but not related to the coachman, and she was paid a couple of shillings a week. The servants

*Sam Saunders and his wife at the door of Padmore House in 1927 on the occasion of their golden wedding anniversary celebrations.*

*An advertisement for Padmore Hotel, dating from the late 1980s.*

*The funeral cortège leaves Padmore with the boat-shaped coffin of Sam Saunders, 1933.*

*Padmore Hotel became popular in the 1980s.*

ate in the kitchen and enjoyed the same food as was served to the Misses Jolliffe. It was very plain, such as cold brisket of beef with baked potatoes. The sisters disliked puddings, eating fresh fruit instead, much of which came from the Padmore garden, including green figs.

Hilda was expected to attend St Mildred's Church every other week and sit in the family pew in line with the rest of the servants. After two years at Padmore she felt that she was rather missing out on life as the Misses Jolliffe did not entertain much. They were very kind to Hilda and in many ways she was quite happy with her job, but it was time for her to move on to the bright lights of West Cowes.

In 1915 Sam Saunders bought Padmore House and moved there in 1920. His daughter Ethel had already died from meningitis and his family consisted of his wife Kate and son Hubert. Hubert was a director of the Saunders Company. Sam Saunders had moved from his home in East Cowes, where his boat and plane workshops had been expanding. He sold the land by the river belonging to Padmore to his company for seaplane workshops.

Sam Saunders retired in 1929 and devoted the last four years of his life to planting an 800-tree apple orchard at Padmore, and an extensive rose garden. He was active in doing things for the village, such as having the Community Centre built. He regularly left a basket of apples outside his gates for the schoolchildren to help themselves! Walking around the village one day in the 1920s he encountered Tom Jolliffe (no relation to the Padmore Jolliffes), who had recently been made redundant from Whites shipbuilders. Sam

*Mrs Ursula Hummel, granddaughter of Sam Saunders, seen here in the late 1930s.*

commiserated with Tom and chatted, and when they parted, pressed some money into Tom's hand.

Sam Saunders had 'The Chalet', now known as 'Malacca', built for his granddaughter Ursula, daughter of his son Hubert. She married Guy Hummel and they lived at 'The Chalet'. Grace Davison, at the age of 14, did cleaning for her (and with her!) in 1936, and described her as a very kind, sweet woman.

In November 1933 Sam Saunders became very ill and was taken to a nursing home in Nettlestone, where he died on 17 December. His funeral took place at Whippingham Church, in dense fog, the boat-shaped coffin leaving from Padmore drawn by some of his devoted staff. His wife was at the same nursing home and died there six years later.

Padmore House was sold by Hubert Saunders in 1935. Mr and Mrs Ball and their sons lived in Padmore after 1935 and then we know that Mrs Barclay was there during the early part of the Second World War but left after her son was killed.

Mr G. Bainbridge had the house for some years and when he put Padmore on the market in 1974 the house was bought and converted into a delightful hotel. Padmore had three different owners during its phase as a hotel. A swimming-pool was constructed in the garden and changing facilities erected nearby. The building was later turned into staff accommodation. Regrettably the hotel closed in the late 1980s and has since become a private residence.

## Little Padmore

Little Padmore appears to always have had close associations with Padmore House. Once Padmore was upgraded into a gentleman's residence, there needed to be a farmhouse for the tenant farmer to occupy. Sometimes the land of the big house was farmed by the tenant farmer, and at other times the land was let off in smaller pieces. It provides a very confusing picture to us now. At one time much of the Padmore land was owned by Winchester College, as was Barton Manor.

Various forms appertaining to the Court of the Manor of Barton exist, recording the changes in ownership, tenancy and personnel at Little Padmore. Because the land was held 'copyhold', each time there was a change of name in the tenancy the owner was paid a fee. New copies of the agreement had to be written up for each of the parties named to hold, hence 'copyhold.'

Various names appear in the eighteenth-century records – Robert Searle in 1766, with John Brookman as tenant before him. In 1790 there was an agreement to sell Little Padmore for £500. This was by Mr James Mallet to Mr William Cheek. Mary Searle married Mr Maberley, and a Joseph Maberley appeared as one of three names in the copyhold of 1858. In fact, James Jolliffe of Padmore House set his solicitor to try to find Joseph Maberley, presumably to buy out the Maberley interest in the estate at that date.

Sam Saunders bought both Padmores in 1915 from the Jolliffe sisters. Hubert Saunders, son of Sam Saunders, lived in Little Padmore House at the time of his father's death in 1933. Although this had been built as two cottages, it had been turned into one large house in 1930. There was a 'pretty rock garden with lily pond and streamlet, miniature waterfalls and splashes' that featured in the sale document of 1935. The house was offered for sale with only a small paddock beside the road.

The farm buildings were sold separately with the farm land, which had been operated as a mixed dairy farm by Mr Oatley. The 75 acres of land were bought by a building firm, who intended to develop the site. The sale document had suggested that there were some very fine sites for building on Folly Road with views southwards. However, nothing came of the venture, and Miss Pinner took over ownership of the farm buildings and land.

In 1936 Frank William Thomas took on the tenancy of Little Padmore Farm from Miss Pinner, and soon obtained the farmhouse as well. He continued the farm as a mixed dairy farm during the war. There was a gravel pit west of Folly Road at the top of the hill, and this was roofed over as a large air-raid shelter during the war. Mr Hummel (Saunders's son-in-law) had suggested this, but eventually it became a machinery store.

The Thomas family bought Little Padmore Farm in 1948. Mrs E.V. Thomas (Eleanor Violet) and her three sons (Trevor, Viv and Don) continued the farm, mainly as a dairy farm, after Frank's death. In post-Second World War days the farm provided a living for them all. Gradually the brothers extended their holdings and ran three farms in partnership – Alverstone Farm, Binfield Farm and Little Padmore. Don Thomas stayed on at Little Padmore.

In 1964 the dairy side of the business was concentrated at Alverstone and the grazing beef cattle, some corn, and pigs were concentrated at Little Padmore. When Don died in 1997 some of the land east of Whippingham Shute was sold to Alverstone Farm, and in 2006 Little Padmore concentrates on 'horsiculture'.

## George's Field
### Also known as the Pony Club Field

The field between Padmore House and Whippingham Church was known as Wall Mead in around 1900. It was part of the Padmore estate, and the only walled field in Whippingham.

Children who walked to and from East Cowes to school at Whippingham told tales of running along the top of the wall on their way home from school. The slower children would be pushed off by those catching them up! Uffa Fox was one of the boys involved in the early 1900s. They never played the game on the way to school as it was an uphill run that way!

*The carefully tended ponies at the horse lines, munching their hay in the 1980s.*

In March 1975 Wall Mead came up for sale. Padmore House was for sale at around the same time. The Isle of Wight Pony Club, part of the National Association of Pony Clubs, had been having difficulty in obtaining a field for use for their summer camps. They thought it would be an excellent idea to have their own facilities and the 8½ acres of Wall Mead would suit their requirements perfectly.

It was just off the main road, but in quiet attractive rural surroundings with good pony-proof boundaries in the form of stone walls on all four sides. Mrs Lacon of Norris Castle was in favour of the idea, and offered to put up some of the purchase money in memory of her son George, a keen rider, who tragically died at the age of 21 in a car accident.

A grant was sought and received from the County Education Department for the remainder of the purchase price of £4,300, and planning permission gained for the change of use.

The next task was to erect toilet and changing facilities, and a kitchen. At first, permission for this building was turned down by the county planning committee, much to the dismay of the pony club. The County Education Authority had even promised them the money to build these very necessary facilities! But on 30 December 1975 permission was granted for 'the pavilion' and the pony club members heaved a sigh of relief!

Ken Gill was the district commissioner for the Isle of Wight branch of the pony club, and was a great driving-force behind the project to obtain the field. He was honoured when he came second in the Hampshire and Isle of Wight Sports Council 'Services to Sport' 1976 Award.

At this time there were 280 members of the club on the Island. Their ages ranged from 6 to 20 years old. George's Field was to become the venue for their working rallies, instructional camps, horse shows and various annual camps.

The annual camps were held in two sections. The senior 8-day camp was for those youngsters aged 12–15, and the junior section was for those aged 11 and under. Each camp averaged 75 people,

*In around 1980 the jumps are set out in the upper part of George's Field.*

*Club members let their hair down as St Trinian's extras at the Ryde Queen paddle-steamer at Island Harbour, late 1970s.*

including staff. There was also a camp held for disabled riders and their helpers.

At the camps, instruction was given in the care of horses, grooming, cleaning tack, first aid and, of course, riding. The youngsters did not all own ponies. Many came from riding schools around the Island with borrowed mounts. Following the purchase of the field, membership of the pony club on the Island gradually rose to a peak of about 500.

An open shed was erected that could be used for the storage of the jumps and other equipment, and in inclement weather at camp this was also used as a dining shelter and classroom. Permission was also given for the storage of a couple of caravans that could be used as offices for the judges and scorers during competitions.

Hundreds of young people have made use of George's Field since it was purchased. Apart from seeing horseboxes arriving and departing on summer weekends, and the bright jumps appearing in the top of the field, the club activities have little impact on the village, screened as they are by those old stone walls. The pavilion and shed are over by the Padmore walls, and for the summer camps the tents are usually near them, away from the road. The horse lines are set out in the bottom third of the field, a net of fresh hay set hanging for every pony with a bucket of water provided by his rider.

In the early days of the camps at Whippingham, villagers may have been surprised occasionally by

the sight of 50 ponies and their riders in police-escorted convoy. These would have been on their way to Norris Castle, the home of Mrs Lacon. The pony club members were able to ride in the castle grounds, which was also the venue for the Island hunter trials. Mrs Lacon was involved with the pony club for many years.

In the 1990s at George's Field a fenced ménage has been constructed of a washed grit surface over a compacted chalk base. Now dressage can be taught, and competitions in this discipline held.

A lot of voluntary work has gone into the work of the pony club at Whippingham. Initially the field was treated to remove many of the weeds and new grass seed was sown. However, dock plants continued to be a problem, and there was a time when Mr Gill aimed at digging up 100 of these in an hour of work every evening in an attempt to clear the field of docks, with considerable success at the time. Many others have put time and effort into organising the events and camps, giving very useful instruction and pleasure to the young people using the field.

At about the same time as the opening of the pony club field, some of the members had an interesting experience when they were invited to provide the 'extras' when part of a St Trinian's film was made at Island Harbour using the Ryde Queen.

A more recent highlight in the history of George's Field was the visit of Princess Ann. This was in the 1990s to visit a camp run by 'Riding for the Disabled'.

*Members of the pony club at the end of one of their summer camps, c.1980. The kitchen and shower block are behind them.*

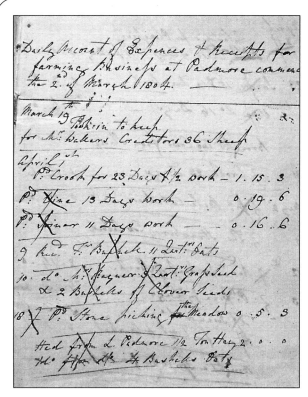

Daily Account of Expenses & Receipts for farming Business at Padmore commencing the 2nd of March 1804.

| March 19th. | | |
|---|---|---|
| | Took in to keep for Mr. Walker's Creditors 36 Sheep. | |
| April 1st. | | |
| | Paid Crook for 23 Days & ½ work - | £ 1-15 - 3 |
| | Paid Line 13 Days work - | £ 0-19 - 6 |
| | Paid Joiner 11 Days work - | £ 0-16 - 6 |
| 9 | Received Farmer *Buckell?* 11 Quarters of Oats. | |
| 10 | do *Mrs Rayner?* 3 Quarters Grass Seed & 2 Bushells of Clover Seeds. | |
| 18 | Paid Stone picking the Meadow | £ 0 - 5 - 3 |
| | Had from L. Padmore ½ Ton Hay | £ 2 - 0 - 0 |
| | Do from do 4 Bushells Oats | |

Above: *The transcription of the first page of the 1804 Padmore Farm accounts book.*

Left: *The Padmore Farm accounts book was started in 1804.* (REPRODUCED COURTESY OF THE COUNTY RECORDS OFFICE, NEWPORT)

*Old Alverstone Farmhouse in the late 1990s. At the time of writing this half is known as April Cottage.*

## Chapter 6
# Agriculture Before 1845

Whippingham developed from its medieval system into several reasonably prosperous farms by 1800.

We know that in 1681 there was still a common somewhere in the village, but this was not for everyone to use. Animals found straying there were rounded up and taken to the village pound, where their owners would have to pay a fine. The following comment comes from the Worsley Accounts: 'To two bailiffs and a boy for driving the beasts in Whippingham common (and ought not to go there) to pound.' Today no trace of the pound remains. However, the one at Brading is still in existence – quite a small walled enclosure by the road at the far end of the churchyard. In Whippingham the clues to the site of the pound lie in a couple of field names halfway along Alverstone Road on the south side behind Six Cottages. These are called Pound Field and Pound Close on the 1841 inventory that goes with the tithe map of the area.

Several interesting documents are held at the Isle of Wight County Records Office. An early estate map exists of Osborne Farm – approximately the present Osborne House estate. It is dated 1734 and shows all the field boundaries, with little drawings of various animals – sheep and cattle. A granary on staddle stones is also drawn in as part of a range of farm buildings, and the house is shown with an Elizabethan style of architecture.

The Board of Agriculture for England was formed in 1793. In 1802 a survey was carried out on the Island, to check up on the amount of land that had been enclosed. The Enclosure Acts were at their height between 1760 and 1810. Agriculturalists had realised the advantages of breeding stock more carefully to improve quality, and improving crops by various methods. Few of these improvements were successful where just three fields existed in each village and all the stock roamed together. One person may have been trying to hoe carefully while his neighbour let the weeds spread, and new rotations of crops could only be practised by all or none.

Several general comments were made about the Island by Mr Bell, the surveyor of the Island, in 1802. Most of the Island was now enclosed, apart from Niton, where 1,000 acres were still farmed in the old way. He found, elsewhere on the Island, that before a crop of wheat, the land would be left fallow for a year. Wheat was cut and then left to dry on the ground – 'It is not bound into sheaves until the day before it is carried to the barn or rick.' Barley and oats were mown and put into cocks.

Men took no part in the weeding of crops. 'Weeding with small hooks (or rather cutting up the thistles, for no other weeds are thought of) is performed by women and children.' 'Hoeing is a system quite unknown, or at least never practised, on the Isle of Wight.'

Mr Bell regretted that so much emphasis was being put on growing grain crops. However, with the French wars underway, grain-crop prices were high and the Island was close to Portsmouth and the great victualling demands of the Navy. 'It is much to be lamented that the cold clay lands to the north are not more generally adapted to grass.' But the landowners in Whippingham were cashing in while they could!

Already the Whippingham farmers were trying to improve their clay soil for grain crops. Farmer Rolf of Barton 'carries 3 tons of chalk to a load and puts 20 loads to an acre costing £10.6s.' Mr Walker of Kingston Farm said that less chalk an acre would be sufficient. 'He thinks 10 loads an acre would answer sufficiently to ameliorate the soil,' not to enrich it but to lighten it, 'and thereby to allow it to be more easily tilled.'

Lord Seymour at nearby Norris was experimenting with a variety of manures including seaweed. Andrew Bell commented 'I trust ere long the barren soil of Norris Farm will by its produce open the eyes of his neighbours!' 'At Barton Farm a field had 30 loads of sea sand carried upon an acre, and the amazing improvement will amply repay the farmer.'

The cattle most frequently seen in 1802 were Normandy or Alderney breeds. The cart-horses were of rather too large a size, pulling wagons in line. Only Mr Nash at his Hamstead Farm and Lord Seymour had fine teams of smaller Suffolk horses. Presumably Nash had still to purchase North Heathfield at this date, but when he did his Suffolk horses may have been introduced in Whippingham.

The poultry was deemed to be very good, and although often very dear was frequently in demand by travellers. The general food for servants was pork or mutton. Mr Bell found that there was a food called Dunch – a pudding made of flour and water – that the labourers seemed to prefer to bread. They would down two quarts of very strong beer at a meal and as much 'small' beer as could be drunk. No brown bread was seen, only white. Most farmhouses also had a half-acre of orchard, so there was plenty of fruit.

The woods at Barton and Osborne were remarked on as being 'extensive' by Bell. A survey carried out 20 years earlier in 1782 for Worsley had put the value of the timber on Woodhouse and Alverstone Farms at £1,327. The coppice wood on Woodhouse was valued at £215.

Bell went on to describe the gates that he saw in 1802: 'Except on Public Roads and Gentlemen's seats [large houses], hurdles made of oak with a couple of slender posts and four withy bands are substituted for gates.'

While he was doing his general survey, some of the landowners paid Mr Bell to do a more specific survey of their property. One of these was for Revd Dr Worsley, owner of Alverstone Farm at Whippingham. Of 20 fields, 16 were arable, and only four pasture. Bell's first observation was somewhat damning:

*This farm consists of various soils, all of which have been impoverished by bad management, but are capable of Improvement by Chalking* [provincially called marling] *and Draining.*

He suggested a rotation of crops should be implemented; fallow, turnips, barley, clover, wheat, or, as an alternative; fallow, wheat, clover, pease or beans, oats or barley. There should have been two ploughings after the clover, and a winter fallow after peas or beans. Proper drainage was also suggested for the farm, which Bell mentioned 'seemed deficient in stock'. He suggested that more profit could be made from the dairy and from a flock of sheep.

Another suggestion that he made was that some Alverstone Farm land should be considered on the Newport side of the farm 'for the purpose of erection of small villas upon.' Bell was possibly ahead of his time in suggesting housing development on the poor land!

Where 'chalking' is suggested, this did not mean throwing lumps of chalk rock on the ground. The chalk had to be burnt in a kiln and the resultant lime powder applied to the soil. Here in Whippingham an old limekiln was discovered on the lower slopes of Heathfield Farm near the marina creek when Southern Water were putting in their sewage pipeline in 2000.

*The remains of the limekiln found at Heathfield Farm near the marina creek while Southern Water were putting in a major pipeline in 2000.*

At first it was thought that the kiln was Victorian, but the bricks date from an earlier period, possibly soon after Mr Bell's observations about the necessity to put more lime on the fields to improve them. He said that the land could be improved and that the tenant should 'chalk within his lease every acre of arable land with 15 loads an acre.' It is probable that the landlord had the kiln built. It was of the 'flare' type and the bricks were laid using the surrounding clay, rather than mortar. The chalk would probably have been brought from Shide chalk quarry at Newport using boats on the Medina River. In around 1800 any prosperous farm owner wishing to improve his soil would have had a small kiln on his land to make lime. The acid soils usually resulted in poor crop yields so liming was needed regularly to neutralise acidity. The upper part of the kiln had been destroyed by 2000 and the kiln is not shown on maps.

The field name 'limekiln ground' appears in the 1841 tithe map survey book in several places. Henry Flux and his father John Flux both had part of 'limekiln ground'. This field was next to Palmer's Brook by the Ryde Road Lodge.

Padmore Farm was not mentioned at all in Bell's farming survey of 1802. However, at the Island's County Records Office there is a little gem of a book relating to 'Padmore'. Started in 1804, the notebook is described by the writer as a 'Daily account of Expenses and Receipts for farming business at Padmore.' The book is like a child's exercise book in size and is difficult to read. However, perseverance pays off, revealing that the leases of Padmore cost £66 and the property tax was £8.5s.5d. The quarterly poor rate was £1.14s.0d., and later the second highway rate was paid at £1.7s.6d. The occupier also had to pay window tax for Padmore in 1804, costing 15s.

It was recorded in this book that two ricks of hay were valued together at £18.8s. The mowing of the next crop of hay and clover grass was done by Vine, who was paid 2s.6d. an acre in June. Farmer Gladdis was paid 15s. a day for ploughing, which makes it probable that Padmore did not have its own team of horses nor a plough. One field, Short Close, took him seven days. The molecatcher, Mr Bull, was paid 12s.6d. The weeders, Messrs Joiner and Bridle, were paid 9d. per man per day. Their task lasted eight days. Joiner's daughter received only 6d. a day for weeding.

By 1808 Joiner was being paid 7s. a week, or 1s.2d. a day. The other agricultural workers at Padmore were Jeffrey, Crook and Bridle, who was paid £2.7s. for threshing the wheat, and for ten days' work and six rats he received 16s.9d. Some of the threshing was carried out in March and some in May. At haymaking time Mary Hollis was paid a shilling a day for her casual work, while Ned Ralph had 2s.6d. a day for reaping. Once the rick was made it cost 10s.6d. to get it thatched.

Livestock details are included in the notebook. For example, Padmore acquired three pigs from Farmer Smith, who was paid £2.2s.0d. for them in June 1804. An entry on 4 July reads 'N.B. White faced cow took the Bull the beginning of June or latter end of May.' A later entry notes that the Strawberry Cow calved. In 1808 seven calves were sold for £17, so there must have been quite a number of cattle on the farm.

In the winter Padmore land was used for grazing other farmers' sheep. Mr Jolliffe sent 21 more sheep on 12 December, removing them in April. The previous year £2.14s. had been received from sheep pasturing.

Looking at the book, it is fascinating to see the farmer's handwriting, his corrections, and his checking of the accounts. 'Omitted last reckoning £0.8s.6d.' shows on one page! It is good to note that he paid for his workers' beer when they went to market for him – 'Beer for both (Vine and Joiner) 1s.6d.'

## Tithes

One thinks of tithes to the parish as being an expenditure that the landowners had to pay in medieval times. However, the tithe map of 1841 and its accompanying survey is one of the earliest detailed records of the last 200 years. All the landowners are listed, along with their tenants, together with details of all the land and whether it was arable or pasture. So tithes were paid in 1841, based, since the 1836 Act of Parliament, on the price of grain.

Looking at an inventory of 1853, it shows that the tithes paid to the rector of Whippingham amounted to £685.18s.1d. However, less than half this sum was received by the rector. He had to pay property tax, financial tax, and land tax on it, pay the curates their stipend, pay for repairs to the Rectory and church, subscribe to the East Cowes school, pay for stamps (five) and printing receipts, and pay to have the accounts audited.

It was surprising to hear that when Fred Blackman took over North Fairlee Farm in 1957 he was still paying tithes of £12.3s.7d. to the church every two years. In 1964 the option was granted to end the requirement to pay tithes, so £200 was paid as a final payment. Looking at the sale document of 1956 for the Osborne estate we see in the initial remarks that 'Tithe... [payment is] believed to have been redeemed'.

Acts of Parliament reflected changes in circumstances and in 1936 it was decided that all tithes should cease by 1996, and landholders were able to redeem their tithes with a lump payment. In the 1980s those still paying tithes were told to stop.

## Old Alverstone Farmhouse

In 1716 a new farmhouse was built at Alverstone. Some maps label the area as Elverton, and this was the name used in 1718 when an account was paid to

'James Dennett and partners... building a new house in Elverton Street in 1716... £35.8s.6d.' This account was recorded in the Worsley estate steward's account book. Alverstone Farm was part of the Worsley estate from 1620 to the early 1800s. The main seat of the Worsley family was Appledurcombe House at Wroxall. Alverstone Farm was quite large at 360 acres, but parts were gradually sold off and by 1840 it had been reduced to about 75 acres.

The house itself is one of the oldest in Whippingham. Its history is well documented and the house has the date 1716 in the lintel over the front door. It is a good example of an early brick-built Island farmhouse. It was built with an eastern central doorway and a bay, or room, each side of this. These rooms both had fireplaces in the centre of the building and the staircase went up to the first floor beside the fireplace. There were two rooms on the first floor and an attic. By 1783 additional storage rooms had been added to the south, and later extra rooms were added to the west. All of these matched the rest of the house, with a stone lower course below the ground-floor-window level, stone quoins (corners) and Flemish bond brickwork above. The front elevation of the house has a horizontal row of chequerboard bricks.

When Queen Victoria and Prince Albert bought Alverstone Farm in 1845 the house was one of only three on the estate that was not demolished and rebuilt. Alverstone Farmhouse was one of the better buildings that the Queen was able to visit immediately.

A new Alverstone Farmhouse was constructed at the bottom of Alverstone Road in 1854, an impressive building with a range of 'model' cowsheds and barns. Old Alverstone Farmhouse was made into two

*Old Alverstone Farmhouse in the late 1990s, with a plan of how it was first built in 1716, with a central fireplace.*

*A belt badge of the North Whippingham Volunteers, probably from the 1790s. Actual size is about three inches from top to bottom.*

cottages for the farm labourers. Two new cottages with gable fronts were built in the old rick yard.

In 2006 Old Alverstone Farmhouse is still two cottages. The building is one of the most charming in Whippingham and holds nearly 300 years of history within its walls.

## The Militia

At Barton Oratory the archpriest, as landholder, had to provide two bowmen or archers for the King's forces. Edward III embarked upon the Hundred Years War with France in 1338 and, similarly, the other landholders in the area were called upon to equip men who would go and fight for the King.

Situated next to the sea, Whippingham was always at risk of attack in times of war. The coastal landowner was the first in the line of defence on these occasions. There were French raids on the Island in the fourteenth and fifteenth centuries, and again in 1545. The Spanish Armada was seen from the south of the Island as it passed up the Channel. Militia units were mustered, and these met twice a year for training during the reign of Queen Elizabeth.

In 1625 there was a military muster of 2,020 volunteers on the Island. Whippingham men were combined with Wootton, Arreton and East Standen, and commanded by John Urry, lord of the manor of East Standen. He had 11 officers, 80 musketeers, 22 'corselettes' or pikemen and nine 'bare vickes'.

In 1681, the Worsley estate included Alverstone and the land towards Woodhouse. The following was recorded in the accounts:

*Paid by the order of Mr Dowdeing for*
| | |
|---|---|
| *A musket and bandoliers* | *9s.* |
| *Two swords* | *15s.* |
| *Two belts* | *5s.* |
| *And a pike* | *5s* |
| *To send to Clavells there being none there* | |

Obviously it was up to the landowner to protect his own property!

By 1782 a full-time militia of 60 men was based on the Isle of Wight. They were marched from area to area and billeted where space could be found. In October 1782 they were in East Cowes. They were disbanded the following year, but re-formed in 1794.

In 1795 worry about invasion by the French caused the formation of 13 Volunteer Militia Units on the Island. There were units in North Whippingham and South Whippingham, probably based on the parish boundary. Again in the Worsley accounts there is an entry for '15 gallons of beer for the Vollunteers [sic] of South Whippingham.' Training to be a volunteer soldier was obviously thirsty work. At a review of troops in Parkhurst Forest in June 1799 3,000 Island militia volunteers were present.

A North Whippingham Volunteer belt badge was found in the village during the 1990s. 'GR' stood for George III in this case. The original owner was probably severely reprimanded for losing it!

When Queen Victoria bought Osborne, troops were stationed in East Cowes for her protection. It is believed that 20 soldiers were sometimes billeted at New Alverstone Farm. At one time there was a rumour of a Fenian attack on Osborne, and these troops were called in to search the grounds. (The Fenians were the Irish Republic Brotherhood, formed in the nineteenth century and well known for revolutionary activity against the British.) By this time the troops were regular soldiers, not volunteers.

# Chapter 7

# Queen Victoria's Estate:
# *Brickyard, Roads, Racecourse & Farms*

## Queen Victoria's Estate

In the same year as buying Osborne House and Barton, Victoria and Albert spent another £13,000 on adjacent land. They bought Woodhouse and Alverstone Farms, Four Cottages from John Tiley and Three Cottages from Joseph Cross and Joseph Hearn. The following year, 1846, North and South Heathfield Farms, Six Cottages and gardens at Brook's, Brook's Copse and Matthews' Cottage were purchased. The name 'Brook's' very soon became written as 'Brock's' in all the records.

More small portions of land were acquired in 1847, including six acres of glebe land from the rector of Whippingham. This marked the boundary of the Queen's estate for some years, and it was not until 1862, the year after Prince Albert's death, that Truckles Farm was purchased, with Kingston Farm shortly afterwards. The popular belief is that Queen Victoria shut herself away at Osborne after Albert's death and did nothing except grieve. However, her journals show that she still carried out many activities, and enlarging and improving her estate was one of them.

In 1873 J.W. Hill wrote in his *Historical and Commercial Directory of the Isle of Wight*:

[The Osborne estate] *now extends from the high road between East Cowes and Newport to the wooded shores of King's Quay, bounded on the south by the highway between Newport and Ryde, and on the north by the Solent. Thus from north to south it extends about two miles and a half, and from east to west nearly two miles, embracing every variety and charm of scenery, the woodland, valley, hill, brook and lea; the sheltered cove, the village church, the leafy copse, and the broad sweep of undulating plains.*

He omitted to mention that much of the western boundary of the Queen's land was the River Medina, providing yet another attractive type of scenery!

Albert and Victoria had acquired a mixture of farms south of Osborne, some of which had been improved a little, but most were still of a poor standard. The first necessity was to drain the fields and for this Albert needed drainage pipes.

## The Queen's Brickyard

In 1845 a tilekiln and drying hacks were put up at the junction of Ryde and Newport Roads. Mr Cubitt, the master builder employed by Prince Albert to build the new Osborne House, also began building a brick-kiln on the same site, to make the bricks which were used for Osborne House and all the estate lodges, cottages and farm buildings. The building work at the brickyard site in 1845 cost £133.15s.3d.

In 1846 621,500 drainage tiles were made, and between 50 and 60 acres of land were drained in different parts of the estate. In 1847 the length of covered drains laid was more than 35 miles! This work went on for several years, with the labourers digging narrow ditches an average of four feet below ground level, in which to lay the tile drains, and then back fill the ditches; 33 miles were completed in 1848, 29 miles in 1849, 46 miles in 1850, 13 miles in 1851 and so on, until all the estate was drained to Albert's satisfaction.

While this was new to the Whippingham area, field drainage was not an unusual activity amongst enlightened landowners at this time. It provided work for several men and boys here, but just how many were employed at the brickyard we do not know.

The Ordnance Survey map of 1854, a prototype for that produced in 1862, shows the brick field in great detail. The round circles would have been the pugmills for mixing the clay to a suitable consistency for working. The clay was dug on site, and when each brick was made it was set out to dry in the hacks before firing in the kiln. The hacks were open-sided sheds, clearly shown on the OS map. The clay turned a red colour when it was fired, and these bricks can be seen in buildings all over the estate. In Osborne House, of course, the bricks were rendered to resemble stonework.

The bricks made at the Queen's brickyard all had the initials 'VR' in the frog, or dip. Ridge tiles were also made and imprinted with 'VR'. Occasionally the bricks or tiles became imprinted with the paw marks of cats or dogs. These may have been hunting mice around the hacks while the clay bricks were still soft.

Not only regular bricks were made. When Albert was having Barton Manor restored, elaborate moulded bricks were made to the exact design and size of the originals to recreate the chimney-stacks, only one of which remained in 1845.

In 1846 William Pierce was recorded as being a brickmaker at the Queen's brickyard. He gave 49 years' service to his Queen, retiring in 1894 at the age of 78 as foreman of the brickyard. He was granted a pension of £11.14s. quarterly, which was the same as the foreman of the Queen's pleasure grounds, and higher than any other pensioner of the estate at

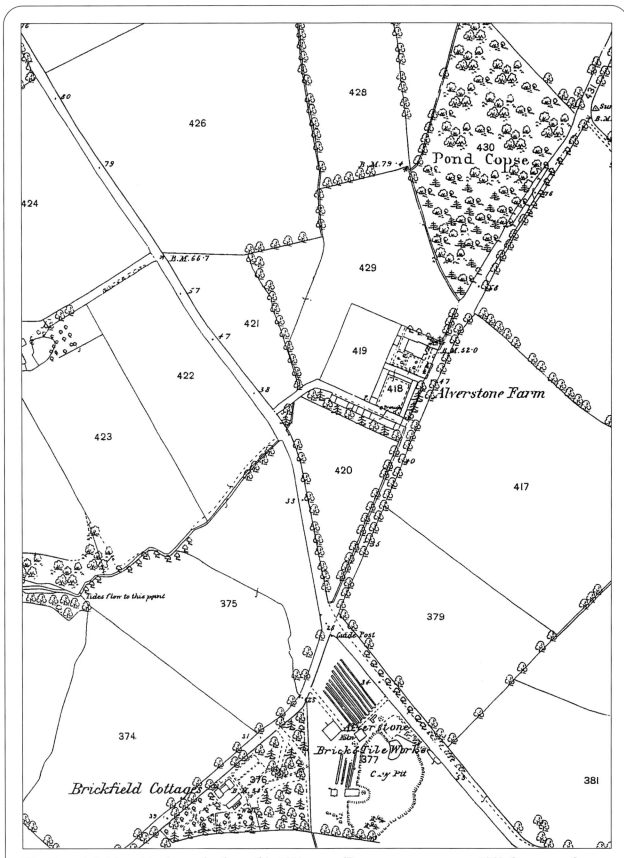

*The Queen's brickyard is shown clearly on this 1863 map.* (Reproduced from the 1863 Ordnance Survey map by kind permission of the Ordnance Survey)

*The northern end of Brickfield Cottages.*

that time. William was living at the Brickfield Cottages from at least 1860.

The brickyard took the name Alverstone Brick and Tile Works and continued to function until the First World War. Decorative pots were made for the tourist market, with an Osborne House medallion on them in clay.

## Brickfield Cottages

Three tenements were constructed adjacent to the brickyard in 1853 and are still known as Brickfield Cottages in 2006. They were built in the 'Old English' style to a design by Prince Albert and were constructed of red brick with buff dressings. The upper storey is contained within the roof void, so the cottages have dormer windows. Those to each side also have windows in the gable-end beneath decorative barge-boards. The porch across the front centre of the house has the same detail as the Woodman's Cottage at Barton. It is thought that Prince Albert may have been present at the 'topping out' ceremony for the cottages, as something very like his signature was discovered in the lead flashing by the ridge.

On the Ryde Road two more tenements for brick-yard workers were built the same year, known then as Ryde Road Cottages and later as Point Cottages. These were almost on the site of the present cremato-rium roundabout and were completely destroyed in the major air raid of 1942. They were also occupied by brickyard workers. In design they were similar to Mount Cottages on the estate, but built of red brick.

## The Estate Roads

The Queen and Albert had bought a peaceful retreat. They wanted somewhere that they could walk unhindered by the local people, and found that they could do so at Whippingham. They would walk to church along the public roads, or drive in their carriage in inclement weather. Local people respected their desire to be private, although there were occasions, such as the Queen's arrival in her royal yacht at Trinity Pier, when the local population would turn out to greet her and welcome her back to the Island. In fact, the school in East Cowes had such a problem with truancy on these occasions that they

decided to call a half-day holiday whenever the Queen was expected, otherwise the attendance figures took an unhealthy dip!

The royal couple set about improving the roads within their estate. Being on top of 'plateau gravels' it was easy to have new gravel pits opened up for use in road construction. A report in *The London Illustrated News* of 1858 extolled the virtues of the Osborne estate roads:

*... roads, which, for solidity, width, and uniformity in appearance, cannot be surpassed. Well made roads are the first essentials for good farming; and in this instance their value is of more than ordinary character, for they extend over many miles, intersecting the estate in those parts most convenient for farming purposes, and yet forming ever-varied drives and scenery through which Her Most Gracious Majesty can pass unmolested and unnoticed in the pure enjoyment of rural life.*

In fact, by 1900 there were over 20 miles of private drive in the estate. Some of the roads that had previously led straight through farmyards were re-routed. The new roads now decorously bypassed the yards and skirted cottage gardens. Albert was also particular about hedges being kept cut, which was relatively unusual in the mid-nineteenth century. While this was good for thickening up the hedges and making them stock-proof, it would also have enabled Victoria and the children to see over hedges into fields from their carriage while out driving.

New roads were created, such as the Ring Road around Osborne House itself and also the drive to King's Quay and the Boundary Drive. The latter required so much construction work to stabilise the cliff that it must have been one of the more expensive works carried out at Osborne. The route was not a farming necessity, but instead provided attractive glimpses of the Solent through the trees. The roads led through woodland, which would have provided shelter, avoided the need for numerous gates to be opened and closed, and provided access to the woods for rough shooting.

The section of road between King's Quay and Barton Wood was seriously damaged during the war years when tanks were drawn up under the trees prior to embarkation for D-Day.

Mount Road on the estate was re-routed in 1858 – a road was inserted between the site of Coburg Cottage and the Alverstone Gate. This passed behind Whippingham Cottages, known as Primrose Cottage at the time of writing. All along Mount Road Guernsey elms and *Pinus Austriaca* were alternately planted as an avenue. The ditches beside all the roads were always kept clear to allow for good drainage, and the surface of roads kept smooth and pothole free.

The road from the Barton Lodges to Barton Manor was planted with Guernsey elms, creating a

*The avenue of Guernsey elms at Barton. Mr George Jones talks to two young children, late 1960s.*

magnificent avenue. Unfortunately, these, like the other elms on the estate, succumbed to Dutch elm disease in the 1970s and had to be felled. This particular road has been replanted with trees, including some eucalyptus by the recent Australian owner. Already, in 2006, the avenue of trees is almost touching overhead.

When the Queen was driving around the estate outriders would precede her. Cottagers would be alerted of the impending visit, and would hurry to remove their washing from the line. Any children would be whisked inside and put into clean smocks, ready to be at the gate to curtsey or bow to the Queen as she passed. Any workers beside the road would bow to Her Majesty. (This information has been passed on by word of mouth and is placed here third hand!)

Outside the estate, Prince Albert made one notable alteration to the public road system. Alverstone Road from the Forge eastwards made a bend to the left before Six Cottages and continued on towards the site of Coburg Cottage. Albert closed this road, replacing it with the present footpath on the line of the old road. Instead, he had the old pack-horse track across Alverstone Farm land widened and straightened to meet up with the previous road system at Alverstone Lodge. This was in 1858. Traces can be seen of the old field system on the maps and ancient pre-Victorian hedgerow oaks still mark the truncated old hedges.

## The Racecourse

Thousands of people drive along the road known as 'The Racecourse' every week on their way from Ryde or East Cowes and Whippingham to Newport. Many are oblivious to the name, but others may wonder what lies behind it. It passes through land that once belonged to the Queen.

According to Brettell, writing in his 1848 edition of the *Handbook to the Isle of Wight*, horse racing was

carried out here. After passing Whippingham, going towards Newport 'To the left is the new racecourse: the races are held generally in the month of July, and are well supported.' His edition of 1841 did not mention the racecourse.

So horse racing took place here, and on the 1841 tithe map we can see the track marked out in double dotted lines. Crossing the racetrack are the lines of the present road, which do not appear on earlier maps.

The race card of 1842 showed that the races were held on 2 and 3 August, with four races on each day. In 1843 there were only three races held each day, when the meeting was held on 19 and 20 July. The Hon. Mr Holmes was the steward that year. In a newspaper report the attending gentry were listed, and it was noted that the colt 'Little Wonder' did not win, he only gained third place. Presumably he had been the favourite!

Prior to 1845 the land was owned partly by Lord George Seymour and partly by Mr Holmes and these gentlemen may have created the racetrack. The Queen bought in this farm land in 1845 as part of Alverstone Farm, and it was farmed by George Whitmaich and William Bull. So far we have not established when racing stopped, but perhaps it was soon after the Queen bought the land. Other guide-books of the time do not mention the racecourse, apart from its appearance on a Brannon map in an 1847 *Guide to the Isle of Wight*.

In 1865, 140 acres of this outlying southern portion of the estate, including 'Mount Misery', were sold from the Queen's estate to Henry Pinnock for £2,500. This would have included the racecourse land.

## Queen Victoria's Farms

Woodhouse was incorporated into the estate almost at once and run with Barton. The following year, 1846, North Heathfield Farm was purchased from Mrs Nash for £1,000, copyhold for three lives, and South Heathfield from John Whitmaich for £100, copyhold for his life. These farms were enfranchised in 1853, so then the Queen held the freehold.

### Alverstone Farm

The Queen bought the freehold of Alverstone and Woodhouse Farms in 1845 at a cost of £12,000. The vendors were the trustees of Mr and Mrs Holmes.

In 1854 Prince Albert set about having a new farmhouse and farm buildings constructed at the lower end of Alverstone Road. The old farmhouse at the top of the hill was made into a double cottage in 1861 and in 1862 a four-gable cottage was completed on the site of Old Alverstone Farm rick yard nearby. There was still insufficient accommodation for all the labourers on Alverstone Farm, so a new farm cottage was built at the back of the cartshed near the new farmhouse in 1863, known in 2006 as Ivy Cottage.

*Brettell's 1848 map with the name 'Race Course' printed on it. A recently purchased copy of the book, Brettell's* Handbook to the Isle of Wight, *had the circle of the track drawn on in pen. It may be that the first owner, using the book in 1848, added this!*

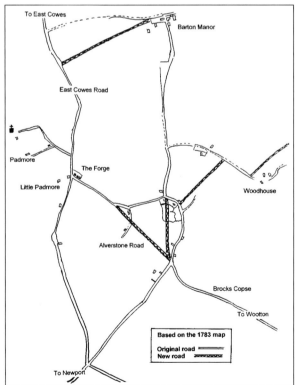

*A plan showing how Prince Albert had the roads re-routed to make the estate more private around Alverstone and Whippingham Street, and the public road straighter.*

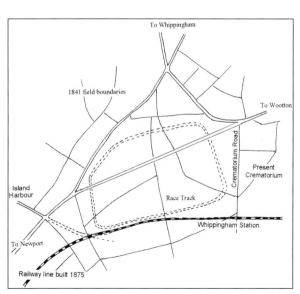

*A redrawing of the 1841 tithe map showing the racecourse, with the later railway and station added.*

*The 1854 date plaque on the wall of Alverstone Farmhouse, photographed in 2005.*

The new farmhouse was a very large and impressive building, perhaps built 'for show' in such a prominent position. It is in the somewhat Italianate style, built of brick with rendered dressings. The arch windows of the ground floor have exaggerated architraves, which are lacking on the first floor. Both gable walls have large plaques bearing the garter ribbon and the date 1854.

An additional wing was soon added to the rear of the farmhouse. It is believed that 20 troops of the Queen's Lifeguard were billeted here, although no written proof has yet been found. This would account for the size of the accommodation, more than twice the size of any other farmhouse on the estate, and the two very large additional ground-floor rooms.

The cottage to the south of the farmyard was built in a similar style, although with the gable turned to the front. This red-brick house is considerably smaller than that built for the tenant farmer.

The whole complex at Alverstone has a unity which epitomises the early-Victorian ideal model farm.

The farm buildings consisted of a U-shaped range of buildings with a cowshed to the east, a separate long range of stabling and cartsheds to the south, barns to the west and a large walled rick yard. The buildings were originally single storey and built of the red bricks from the Queen's brickyard just across the road. In 1877 the straw barn was altered and the west range given a second storey. This enabled loaded carts to enter. A granary was created on the first floor in the north-west corner.

The Victorian buildings have changed very little. The old cowshed has become the stables, and the stables are used as calf sheds in the winter. The original troughs, many of the roof vents and the wooden hooks for hanging up the harness remain. In 2006 hay and straw fill the barn, and the granary is empty of grain. However, in the granary the original wooden partitions where the grain was stored loose, the hatch and chain for the pulley for lifting the sacks, and a grain chute to the mill below still exist, together with a small winnowing machine on the ground floor.

In 1873 a 12-year lease was drawn up between Her Majesty and Thomas and Henry Knighton. They were described as butchers of Northwood. Their yearly rental was to be £130, with the Knighton brothers to be responsible for adding bone manure to the fields annually. In the valuation of the farm that year the land was said to be in a fair state of cultivation. The arable land was mostly strong clay with some gravel, a very weak soil. The pasture land was mostly poor with weak clay and gravel. It was suggested that the lessor should pay for more chalking, with the tenant paying for the carting and spreading of it. Only four cottages would go with the farm. The value of the farm produce in 1873 was:

| | |
|---|---|
| *Corn – standing crop* | *£279* |
| *Tillages, including grass seeds and* | |
| *superphosphates* | *£91* |
| *Hay in whole and part rick* | *£135* |
| *Wool from 100 teg sheep* | *£27.10s.* |
| *Livestock* | *£475* |
| *Dead stock* | *£311* |
| *Total* | *£1,320* |

The surplus dead and livestock were sent to auction by Queen Victoria's land steward, together with some from Barton, and realised £858.

Mr and Mrs Knighton were to move into the farmhouse, but there was some discussion with the Queen's land steward as to the condition of the decoration in the house. The land steward sent a letter to the Keeper of the Privy Purse asking that before the Knightons moved in 'The walls usually papered in such a house might be thus furnished instead of being coloured with distemper as usual – of course with cheap papers.'

After the death of Queen Victoria in 1901 Alverstone Farm remained part of the Crown lands until 1956, at that time being rented by Don Cheshire for £649 per annum. It was auctioned with other parts of Queen Victoria's lands in Whippingham. By that time the tied cottages for the farm were Ivy Cottage and numbers 1 and 2 Brickfield Cottages. The land being sold was 237 acres, of which 73 acres were pasture and 133 acres were arable. There were 25 acres of woodland, the timber being valued at £687.10s.

The farmhouse had hot and cold running water laid on, even to the bathroom, and had eight bedrooms. The outbuildings had been extended by a four-bay Dutch barn and the yard had been improved by concreting.

A red-brick shed for milking some 40 cows with electrically-driven machinery was installed in the 1950s by either Arthur Cheek, or Don Cheshire who had bought Alverstone Farm in 1956. Mr Viv Thomas bought Alverstone in 1964 from Don Cheshire.

Alongside helping with the farm, Mrs Cheshire had been running bed-and-breakfast accommodation in the enormous farmhouse, and Mrs Thomas continued, for a time, letting out the front of the farmhouse.

Right: *View of the farm buildings from a bedroom window, 2003.*

Left: *Grain sections in the granary with a sack chain and hatch in the floor, 2005.*

Below: *The old cowshed, used as stables in 2005.*
Bottom left: *Alverstone Farmhouse in 2003, showing the large extension at the rear of the house.*
Bottom right: *The granary, photographed in 2005, is the tall brick-built building with an upper door, which was used for unloading carts.*

Above: *A new tractor in the early 1970s with,* left to right: *Don Thomas, ?, Ginger Knight, Trevor Thomas.*

Above: *Another view of the farm buildings from a bedroom window, 2003.*

Left: *Old wooden hooks for harnesses in one of the original stables. Photograph taken in 2005.*

*Each section in the granary was for a different type of grain which was stored loose. Photograph taken in 2005.*

*The small mill below the chute from the granary above. Photograph taken in 2005.*

Above: *The 'new dairy' ten years after the last cows were milked on the farm. Photograph taken in 2005.*

Right: *Redundant milk churns in 2005.*

*Colin Thomas, Ginger Knight and the bale wrapper, pictured in 2003.*

*Alverstone Farmyard full of steers in the winter of 2003.*

In about 1983 her daughter Helen started running dancing lessons at the farm, using one of the large back rooms. Helen, now Mrs Bull, still teaches dancing in 2006, at Whippingham School amongst other venues, with her mother at the piano.

Mr Thomas started at Alverstone Farm with an 80-strong Guernsey herd, and with one cowman to help. An average of 18 10-gallon churns were filled each day and were collected from the wooden stand next to the dairy by lorry every morning and taken to Isle of Wight Creameries, as it was then, in Newport. With the milk only collected in the mornings, Mrs Thomas was always worried in the hot summer nights that the evening milk would go off, even though it had been through the cooling system. She even tried standing the churns in a bath of cold water! Then Isle of Wight Creameries changed to the tanker system. The pipes went straight from the dairy to a refrigerated tank, and thence to the tanker lorry. Lorries collected milk from 300 farms on the Island in 1964.

In March 1996 Viv Thomas changed from milk to beef production. The price received for the milk was going down, health tests and paperwork were increasing and milk production became uneconomic.

By 2006 the farm is still about the same size, 230 acres. However, the majority of the land, 188 acres, is under pasture. The owner is still Viv Thomas in 2006, and the farm is run largely by his son Colin, with Peter Bull coming in one day a week. The farm keeps 200 beef animals, about 50 cows and two bulls, as well as young stock and calves. There is also stabling for eight horses and a sand school for riding.

The old farm buildings are a Victorian time capsule. So much of Prince Albert's original structure has been retained. Also, behind the new dairy door are the complete remains of the milking system – a 1980s time capsule!

### Heathfield Farms

Both Heathfield farms were among the land which had been given to Barton Oratory, and thence to Winchester College in 1439.

North Heathfield Farm no longer exists. In the early 1800s it was rented by John Nash who lived at East Cowes Castle. When he died in 1835 it passed to his wife. She sold the copyhold to Her Majesty in 1846 for £1,000. In 1853 the Queen purchased the freehold from Winchester College.

The farmhouse and yard were on the left as you go down Whippingham Shute, just south of the copse and opposite the present Heathfield Farm Cottage. In 1853 the entire site was levelled, but in dry summers the outline of some of the buildings is visible in the discoloured crop or grass growth. The extent of the farm was from the river up to the top of the copse and halfway to South Heathfield, and along Tobacco Pipe copse, halfway down to Alverstone Farm.

The North Heathfield land to the east of the main road was combined with Alverstone Farm, and that to the west into South Heathfield Farm.

South Heathfield Farm was run by the Whitmaich family for many years until the Queen bought the copyhold from them in 1846 for £100. The Queen

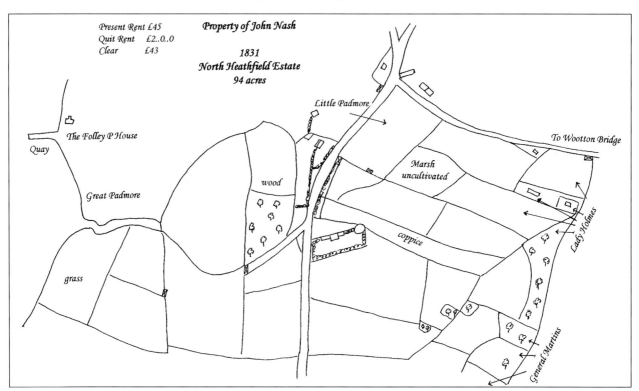

*A redrawn plan from 1831 of North Heathfield Farm.* (ORIGINAL COURTESY OF THE COUNTY RECORDS OFFICE, NEWPORT)

bought the freehold from Winchester in 1853. John Whitmaich continued to rent the farm, which since 1846 had been enlarged with part of North Heathfield, until his death in 1874.

The farm was in poor condition in 1874, and the outbuildings dilapidated. Canon Prothero, the Queen's chaplain and rector of Whippingham, pleaded on behalf of Whitmaich's 73-year-old sister for her to be allowed to stay in part of the house, which was permitted, while new building work was carried out. Until this time the farm had rarely covered the rent paid! There was a cottage on the estate that the officer of health considered to be unfit for human habitation, and it was pulled down. Could this have been the original poorhouse? We know that in the eighteenth century Whitmaich was the overseer for the poor, and there was a poorhouse rented from him, but its location is not clear.

The land was taken into the estate management for improvement and was then let to one of the Knighton brothers from Alverstone Farm – Thomas. The Queen did not want to unite Heathfield and Alverstone Farms into one unit. Miss Whitmaich was allowed to stay for a further 12 months, but she had to 'get rid of her cow and poultry'. Thomas Knighton also asked for 'spouting around the yard to catch rainwater off.'

There were two wells at Heathfield and both were analysed in 1881. The first well, which had been dug in 1870, was found to contain unacceptable levels of organic pollution, which could have been due to a cesspit sited only a few yards away! The second well had just six feet of mud at the bottom. So a one-inch galvanised wrought-iron pipe was put in to bring good water from the well at Alverstone. The steward wrote 'It is considered that it would be a waste of time digging for good water at Heathfield.'

It would seem that there were several bad harvests, and the Queen kindly remitted a half year rent in 1893 and again in 1896. It was on Heathfield Farm land that Sam Saunders built his first sheds for constructing aeroplanes, and a small airstrip was created in 1914.

Fred Charles Warne took over the tenancy of Heathfield Farm, followed by his son Fred Henry Warne until 1940. Fred Henry's son John remembers that the terms of the Crown tenancy were very strict – 'Not even a nail could be put into a tree, let alone cut one down.' The Warnes had a dairy herd, and bottled their own milk on the farm. In a drought summer in the late 1930s they were permitted to cut branches for cattle feed.

In 1956 Heathfield Farm was sold by Crown Estates. This included 159 acres of land and the farm buildings with a cowhouse for 31 cows. Messrs G.H. Ablitt and son were renting the farm at £315 per annum, having come to the farm in 1942 from Barton. Also sold were the two Heathfield Farm cottages that had been constructed in 1872 at the bottom of Whippingham Shute.

*Sheep dipping in Heathfield Luck with George Ablitt in the 1960s. Marks of 9/10 for diving style!*

In the 1960s George Ablitt was running a flock of sheep on the land and had a novel way of dipping his sheep. Between Heathfield Farm and Twenty Acres (Medina Park) is a small stream, Heathfield Luck, which the riverside footpath crosses by a bridge. With the assistance of a few hurdles and helpers, George would persuade his flock to jump, or dive elegantly, off the bridge one by one into the water below, and swim to the shore!

George Ablitt left Heathfield in about 1990 to return to Newtown. For some years in the late 1970s there was a move afoot to turn the farm into a golf course. However, this did not take place and instead Mr Orlik bought the 150 acres of Heathfield Farm in 1996, and the farmhouse was sold off separately. The old farm sheds were converted into a dwelling.

In 2006 the land is farmed with Barton and Kingston, Heathfield having been re-drained to improve the fields for arable crops. For all these three farms, just two men were employed in 2002, a very different scenario from 80 years ago.

### Kingston Farm

While Kingston Farmhouse is the southern boundary of East Cowes in 2006, the farm land belonging to Kingston once reached from Victoria Grove in East Cowes to south of Whippingham Church.

In 1864 Kingston Farm came up for auction. The owner was Sir Hamilton Seymour, who had inherited the Norris Castle estate in East Cowes. Letters held at the Royal Archives show that the Queen's land agent, Andrew Toward, went to some lengths to keep secret the fact that the Queen was interested in buying the land, for fear of the price rising. Toward did not want the farm 'falling into the hands of a stranger'. An unknown agent stood for the Queen at the bidding, and after two other bidders had raised the price to £5,400, he bid £5,450 and was successful. Andrew Toward recorded that the other bidders had intended 'to try to let it off in small plots for building, which would not have improved the respectability of the neighbourhood.'

Above: *An aerial view of the farmhouse and farm buildings at Kingston in the late 1960s.*

Above left: *Kingston Farmhouse in the late 1960s.*

Left: *In 1966 triplet calves were born at Kingston. Ern Bull holds the cow, with David Morey, Peter Bull and young David Orlik on the tractor.*

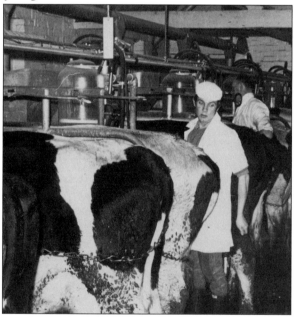

Above: *Derek Cooper milking at Kingston in the 1960s.*

Left: *The churns being filled with milk at Kingston in the 1960s.*

The building of a new Kingston Farmhouse began in 1866 and work there finished in 1869, when the two labourers' cottages were completed. These two cottages were built on the road down to Halliday's boatyard, now Cadets' Walk.

The farmhouse was constructed of red brick with much decoration, but in a more 'countrified' style. The outbuildings were numerous and carefully arranged. Prince Albert would have been proud of them!

In Queen Victoria's time the southern boundary of East Cowes was Victoria Grove, abutting Kingston Farm land. She gave land from the farm for a cemetery by the river in 1875. The road leading to it was called Kingston Road. From this time the size of Kingston Farm continued to decrease. The Victoria Recreation Ground was created on Kingston Farm land given by the Queen in 1898. During the First World War this was ploughed up for cereals.

When the Royal Naval College Osborne was developed in the early 1900s, fields of Kingston Farm, as part of the Osborne estate, were given to the Admiralty to allow training engineering works to be built by the river. After the college closed in 1921 the gasworks and electricity power station were built on this land and additional Kingston fields.

An early Crown tenant of Kingston Farm was William Drudge, followed by Edwin Harvey, whose son carried on after him until 1944 when Mr Starke took over. Older people in East Cowes remember going on annual Sunday school picnics to Farmer Harvey's fields, each carrying their mug tied on to their clothing with a ribbon or string. The picnic was an exciting day for the children in the 1920s. The name Harvey is remembered in Harvey Close, now built on land near Kingston Farm. Even before the Second World War, Kingston land was being sold for a council-housing estate and a large area was given over to allotments during the war. In the 1950s the council estate was extended.

In 1956 the remainder of Kingston Farm was put up for sale by Crown Estates. The size of the farm at that time was 158 acres. Mr Starke bought it in 1959, and in 1961 Richard and Anne Orlik bought a reduced Kingston Farm of 120 acres with 60 cows and all the machinery and outbuildings. The cropping for the first few years was around 35 acres of cereals with the rest in grass for hay, silage and grazing. By 1970 there were 100 cows and cereal production had been reduced. However, by 1973 the milking system at Kingston was obsolete and it was decided to build a new dairy unit at Barton.

The part of Kingston Farm south of Crossways Road as far as East Cowes Vic's Football Club had been sold to the council. Part of this was used for Osborne Middle School. More of Kingston Farm was sold for housing in the early 1970s and Greenlands Road was built.

In the 1990s permission was given for housing on the two fields south-east of Kingston Farm. After the public inquiry into the 2001 Unitary Development Plan, permission was given for development as far south as the East Cowes Vic's Football Club in Beatrice Avenue and west of the Osborne Middle School, which had been constructed on the Kingston fields in 1973. The decision to develop East Cowes south of the Kingston Farm road boundary was unsuccessfully fought by local environmental groups. One of the objections was the contraction of the green belt of farm land between Whippingham and East Cowes. They claimed that the two settlements should remain visibly separate and the Conservation Area that now surrounds the church should be protected. At the time of writing planning permission is being sought for housing on the fields west of Beatrice Avenue.

When the Kingston Farmhouse was sold the outbuildings and a nearby field were bought by the electricity company who were building the new power station. The outbuildings were demolished as the company saw them as a public liability. Consequently, those farm buildings at Kingston were the first of Queen Victoria's to disappear from the Whippingham map. The remaining land at Kingston is farmed from Barton by Mr Orlik in 2006.

The loss of Kingston Farm land continues at the time of writing, as the southern boundary of East Cowes marches relentlessly southward. It is threatening to remove the open green belt separating the two communities until the character of the rural village of Whippingham is buried in the industrial and residential sprawl of East Cowes.

**Truckles Farm**

This farm was bought freehold from Admiral Sir George Seymour in 1862 for £7,000. The land was incorporated into Kingston Farm in 1874. In this year the farmyard was levelled so the Almshouses could be built there, and shortly afterwards two new outhouses were built for the use of the 'cottagers' living at Truckles old farmhouse.

The thatched farmhouse had large brick chimneys on the outside walls. However, thatch is always a vulnerable building material, and on 26 July 1890 there was a fire at Truckles, which resulted in the destruction of the cottages. It was not until 1892 that the two cottages at Truckles were completely rebuilt and occupied.

The first tenant in the rebuilt Truckles west cottage was Henry Cooper and his large family. He had been working as a carter on the estate since 1846. His daughter Eva married Albert Thorne and they continued to live there. Subsequently their son Ray took on the tenancy, and together with his wife Audrey looked after the 'family' cottage until 2002 when they moved next door to the Almshouses.

In around 1910 the Russell family were living at the Truckles east cottage. Mrs Flux lived there in the 1930s and '40s and served teas for visitors to the

Above: *Truckles Farm, c.1875. (The Royal Archives © 2005 Her Majesty Queen Elizabeth II)*

Above left: *Truckles seen through the elm trees, which succumbed to Dutch elm disease in 1974.*

Left: *'The Truffle'. Many of the early postcards like this one, pre-1910, were printed in France, which resulted in a few spelling mistakes!*

*The fire at Truckles in 1973.*

*The wedding of Phyllis and Alan Jerome, 5 July 1941. This photograph was taken in the garden at Truckles east, where they had their reception tea.*

church, and catered for parties such as Phyllis and Alan Jerome's wartime wedding, when, thankfully, the big guns nearby did not fire all afternoon!

The roof had been thatched again, which was to result in yet another fire in 1973, when sparks from the chimney set the roof ablaze. It was six months before the repairs were complete. Bob Rann, the village blacksmith, and his wife Una moved back into Truckles east, which they bought later when council-houses started to be sold off.

Truckles must have been one of very few thatched houses on the Housing Association stock on the Isle of Wight and, with the Almshouses, makes a very picturesque corner of Whippingham.

**Woodhouse Farm**

Woodhouse was the most easterly farm of the lands purchased by Victoria and Albert. It stretched down to the sea and King's Quay, and in 1841 many of the fields still had the name Clavell, e.g. Clavell's Meade and Clavell's Heath. The original manor of Shoflet may also have been part of this land.

In 1846 Prince Albert combined Woodhouse Farm with Barton as the 'home farm' for Osborne. The present farmhouse was built as labourers' cottages, and converted later into one house for a tenant farmer. The lower fields were damp and made ideal pasture.

The Tillett family bought the Barton estate in 1922, which included Woodhouse Farm. During the Second World War the Ministry of Agriculture instructed that some of the fields were to be used for growing potatoes. The farmer said it wouldn't work, but the 'Min. of Ag.' were adamant. So seed potatoes were planted. However, when the time came to lift the crop the ground was so wet that it was impossible. To this day the odd potato pops up in the field, a growing relation of that failed wartime crop!

In 1953 Barton and Woodhouse Farms were sold separately when the Tilletts left the Island.

In 1967 Roy Richards sold Woodhouse Farm to Eric Taylor and his wife Carol. They employed four

people, working full-time on the land, and used contract workers when the farm was silage making.

A small amount of wheat was grown but most of the fields were laid to grass for a flock of about 150 sheep and a prizewinning herd of Friesian milking cows. Initially, during their time there the milk was still put into churns, until later milk tankers started collecting the daily milk and taking it to Newport.

Eric and his daughter Barbara, who was the herdswoman, had considerable success with their cattle. They were very good milk producers and in 1989 one of the Woodhouse cows was the supreme champion at the I.W. County Agricultural Show.

From 1984–94 Mrs Carol Taylor ran 'Country Produce', a greengrocers in East Cowes. The farm provided the potatoes for the shop.

In 1994 the Taylor family retired from farming and sold Woodhouse to Nick Johnson, who came from Sussex. He continued the herd until 2002, when the declining fortunes in agriculture made it no longer viable to continue as a traditional dairy farm.

The number of dairy farms on the Island had decreased from about 60 in 1993 to 20 in 2003. Prices paid for milk made small units uneconomic. The farm was sold in 2003 and the live and dead stock put up for auction. The milking equipment, which would have cost many thousands of pounds to install when new, fetched only £100, such was the lack of demand by a dairy sector in depression. Woodhouse Farm has started a new phase in its story.

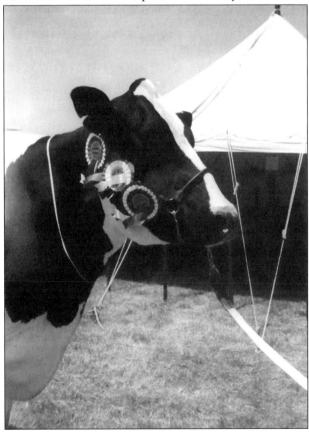

*The Isle of Wight supreme champion of 1989 – Taybar White Lilac 2.*

*The gates to Barton Manor, c.1875, photographed as part of a series of pictures taken all around the estate by Jabez Hughes.* (THE ROYAL ARCHIVES © 2005 HER MAJESTY QUEEN ELIZABETH II)

*The Alverstone Road Lodge, c.1875, photographed by Jabez Hughes.* (THE ROYAL ARCHIVES © 2005 HER MAJESTY QUEEN ELIZABETH II)

# Chapter 8

# Queen Victoria's Estate:
# Entrance Lodges & Cottages Inside the Gates

When Victoria and Albert leased Osborne in 1844 it was for one year, with an option to buy the property if they found it suited them. It did, and having bought the estate and Barton they found that they were responsible for the lives of the people in the 31 cottages that were sold with the estates and the extra farms that they bought.

The Queen wrote in her journal at Christmas 1848:

*I take such an interest in all our labourers and people here, also their children, and hope that when their cottages are in better order, I may be able to go and see them, which, with two or three exceptions, I cannot easily do now.*

Most of the cottages were occupied by farm labourers and were in a very bad state of repair. Families of six or seven people were crammed into two rooms in 'miserable' cottages – very small and uncomfortable according to the Queen. It was Albert who set about improving his farm-workers' homes as he aspired to become a model agriculturalist. He had master builder Cubitt instructing his men to mend pumps, kitchen ranges, windows and leaking roofs. Walls were repaired, replastered and repainted.

Many of the cottages were simply torn down and rebuilt, with no record of what the originals looked like. Some of the new cottages were built on exactly the same sites, but others shifted to new positions. One interesting field is that to the north of Primrose Cottage. On the 1841 map various small enclosures and dwellings are shown next to the track along its northern edge. In dry summers the outlines of small structures can still be seen there. Queen Victoria had these 'miserable' dwellings flattened as soon as new cottages were constructed. This was the settlement called variously Alverstone, Elverton Street or Whippingham Street on the old maps.

Two other areas exist in Whippingham where cottages have completely disappeared. One place was on the west side of Brock's Copse halfway between the Ryde Road and Brock's Copse Road. Here there were four tenements and another cottage owned by Richard Whitmaich and James Taylor. This is another possible site for the original poor-house, given up in 1759, which had been rented from Richard Whitmaich. These cottages, later on the Queen's land, were demolished in 1895. In a dry summer the outlines of the buildings can be seen, and Colin Thomas 'found' an old well when his tractor wheel got stuck in it in the 1990s. Pryor's

Cottages are mentioned in *The Works of Albert* and the adjacent field is known as Prymore in 2006.

Another area now returned to pasture was to the north of the churchyard where Church Cottages existed by the old gravel pit. They were demolished after having been used by soldiers practising house-to-house combat before embarking for D-Day. They were told they could use these cottages for practise and they used them to destruction!

The Queen enjoyed visiting her people on the estate. She knew them by name, and all about their circumstances. Visits were not only made in summer weather as an excursion, but whenever Victoria was in residence. The Queen wrote very frequently in her journal about these drives, or walks. For example:

*6 February 1864. Walking with Lenchen and Katherine to Whippingham Church... Walked about the lovely church, my beloved's own design, the churchyard and visited some of the cottages close by.*

*17 February 1864. After lunch drove with Louise and Katherine B., visiting some of the cottages, most of which I found very clean and tidy.*

The work of improving the cottages continued for a number of years until there were eventually 36 cottages divided into 61 separate dwellings owned by the Queen in East Cowes and Whippingham. Although the new cottages were a considerable improvement on the old, they were still primitive in their facilities compared to the modern day. The toilets were simply earth-closets in the shed at the end of the garden, and in many cases these continued in use for a long time beyond 1901.

However, at certain points around the estate some of the cottages were provided with a Queen's rest room. This comprised of a private sitting-room and a proper water-closet toilet specifically for her use.

Each tenant on the estate was allowed to keep a pig and to work a garden or allotment. This supplemented their wages, by providing fresh fruit and vegetables and pork.

## The Royal Estate Lodges

### Barton Manor Lodges

South Lodge was built in 1848 and North Lodge in 1850. Their style copies that of the manor house itself, using similar stone and features. The design originated from Prince Albert, and his drawing for the proposed lodges is in the British Museum. However, slight alterations were made to his first draft, as a porch was added and the rear wing became T-shaped. The chimneys were grouped in one large stack and the overall appearance is rather more impressive than Albert drew. Heraldic devices were applied externally recording the connection of the Barton estate with Winchester College, as well as the Queen and Prince.

Across the driveway between the two lodges were three gates, two for pedestrians and a large central one for carriages. This central gate and the two wooden gateposts for it were removed in the late 1970s, leaving only the pedestrian gates, which are now constantly opened back into the drive, having nothing to latch on to. All the gates had the intertwined letters 'V' and 'A' as a centre symbol.

Various estate workers lived in these two cottages through the years. Near the end of Victoria's life one occupant was Thomas Foakes, who had been working for the Queen since 1846, when he was just ten years old. He started by weeding the grounds, but by 1888 he was a carpenter on the estate, like his father had been before him. Records show that George Foakes, Thomas's father, was a foreman wheeler and carpenter, receiving £1 a week in 1846. He was the second-most-highly paid man on the estate, apart from the land steward. George Foakes's final position was as estate carpenter for Barton Manor.

Mr Streeter was the chauffer and lived at one of the Barton Lodges while the Tilletts were living at the manor.

At the end of the twentieth century Mary Cox lived at North Lodge. In the 1970s she had developed an apple tree in the garden which bore fruit that was both good for eating and cooking, and with

*Mary Cox, who lived at North Lodge, developed her own strain of apple tree there. This photograph was taken when the trees, called Mary's Millennium, went on sale in 2000.*

excellent keeping qualities. A nursery took it up and the trees were produced commercially in 2000 under the name Mary's Millennium.

The cottages still look much the same in 2005 as when they were built, and still proudly guard the entrance to Barton Manor from the main Whippingham Road. Despite the loss of the main gate, on entering the driveway visitors still feel that they are entering a special Victorian estate.

### Alverstone Road Lodge

The lodge at Alverstone Road was constructed in 1858, at the same time Mount Road was extended from the site of Coburg Cottage to the lodge. Previously the only road to the estate had been to the east of the new lodge, past Dallimores.

Consequently the lodge had two gates to attend to on the east and west sides. Each gate had brick-built piers using red brick coursed with bands of buff brick, and screen walls to further piers on the west side, creating a strong visual feature that can be seen in 2006. The gates themselves were of a slightly more countrified style than that at Barton's main road entrance, but still sported the entwined initials 'V' and 'A' in the centre. Each of the gates is still there, although in rather a sorry condition in 2006.

The building itself formed a pair of lodges with a central chimney stack. It is built of red bricks from the Queen's brickyard, coursed with bands of buff brick. A striking feature is the deep band of a diamond-pattern frieze made of the bricks below the eaves. The quoins and window and door surrounds are of dressed stone, as are the piers that support the porch roof. Two attractive first-floor bay windows feature in the end walls, overlooking the driveways and gates. These were carefully restored when work was done to the building in the 1990s. However, the tall chimney-stacks were removed then, leaving a truncated capped-off stack. At the same time the original clay tiles were replaced by modern machine-made tiles.

The Jabez Hughes photograph (see page 68), probably taken before 1875, gives an idea of how pristine the estate entrance was kept. The gravel road is perfectly smooth, with just a few narrow tracks of carriage or cartwheels and faint horse-hoof marks. The hedge around the lodge looks as if it has been measured with a ruler, the top is so exactly level. Ahead through the gates stretches Mount Road with its avenue of pine and elm trees and hard, level, neatly-edged gravel surface. Certainly it was an entrance fit for a Queen.

In 1860 Henry Hurst and Eli Jenkins were occupying Alverstone Lodge. Henry had a young family with Victoria and Morris both at school four years later. Victoria received both a dress and a doll as a Christmas present from the Queen that year, but Morris, who was older, was given a book. The same Christmas Mrs Hurst and Mrs Jenkins both received a Christmas gift of a petticoat from the Queen. Presumably the task of gate opener fell upon them while their husbands were working on the estate.

In the 1880s Mrs Gallop was the sick nurse on the estate, and lived at Alverstone Lodge. She asked if it would be permissible for her to have her elderly mother to live with her. Her mother, Widow Cooper, was on poor relief in the parish of Wootton Bridge. She was told that it was not approved of on the estate, especially as she was a pauper of a different parish. However, as Mrs Cooper offered to forego parish relief and her friends were willing to supply the same amount for her keep, the steward thought it might be permissible in this instance.

By 1888 Henry Hunt and George Lock were living as tenants at Alverstone Lodge. George Lock had been working for the Queen for four years, but Henry Hunt had retired as foreman of the pleasure grounds at Osborne three years earlier. He had been working as a gardener for the Queen from the beginning of their ownership of Osborne in 1845, and retired on a high pension of £11.14s. a quarter.

Also in 1888, estate steward Andrew Blake noted in a letter to the Queen that there was a considerable number, 16 in total, of her elderly pensioned estate workers still occupying cottages on the estate. A total of 11 more men living on the estate were either nearing retirement, or were invalids. He feared that able-bodied workers would have to be sought from outside the estate if this continued to be the case.

The east end of Alverstone Lodge showing the bay window and gatepost.

*Princess Alice leaves Osborne with her new husband, Prince Louis of Hesse Darmstadt, 1862. (REPRODUCED COURTESY OF THE COUNTY RECORDS OFFICE, NEWPORT)*

This was despite the Almshouses having been opened for a dozen years for pensioners.

Mr and Mrs Billy Snow started their married life at Alverstone Lodge in 1894. Billy Snow was foreman of the pleasure grounds, roads and avenues of the Osborne estate, which included Barton Manor. He was made foreman in 1885 when he was 25 years old, and had a gang of 11 men working under him.

When Queen Victoria came through the gate on her official drives, Mrs Snow had to open the gate for her. The outrider would ride ahead and call out, 'Gate, gate!' giving the signal. She received a shilling a week for doing this. Mrs George Snow took on this gate-opening task later.

Alverstone Lodge was occupied by Mr and Mrs Williams for many years in the early-twentieth century and the western lodge by the Misses May and Maud Brown in the later half of the twentieth century.

### Brock's Copse Lodge

Continuing downhill from Alverstone Lodge towards Wootton one passes through Brock's Copse. The original name for this area was Brook's Copse, bought by the Queen in 1846, but the name soon appeared as Brock's.

In 1864 Brock's Lodge was built just above the bridge, at the same time a driveway was created through the copse to the south towards the main road between Ryde and Newport, called the Boundary Drive. The south side of the Brock's Copse road has just the remains of a 'V A' mono-grammed gate, but traces of the drive have disappeared. A similar lodge was built on the Ryde Road at the southern end of the drive.

Brock's Lodge in 2006 is often in the shade of the surrounding trees, although when the Queen's drive was in existence through the woods there were fewer trees and less shade on the lodge itself. It is built from the estate red and buff bricks, but in this lodge the buff bricks form the major part of the building with red banding. It has ornate timber bargeboards. Crossed-brick decoration is used on the chimney-stack and side of the house, together with the same cross pattern on the buff-brick gate piers. The gate matches those at Alverstone Lodge, but this one is in a much better state of repair, showing its entwined monogram and rosettes.

At the time of writing the building is still largely intact and has been little altered. It still has its original Elizabethan-style chimney-pots and the crests mounted on the gable-ends. It presents an excellent example of the estate architecture.

Mr and Mrs James Hollyer (or Hollier) were tenants of Brock's Lodge in 1864. They had moved into the new lodge from Primrose Cottage with their three children – James, aged 12, Lucy 10 and Harriet 7. James senr had been working on the estate since 1846, when he was described as a farm labourer, and earned 12s. a week. By 1888 'young' James Hollier was 35 years old and had been working on the estate for 20 years and the family were then living at Six Cottages at the top of the hill along Alverstone Road.

Like many of the cottages, Brock's Lodge was reliant upon a well for water. In 1888 a new well was dug, but it was found to be rather brackish and failed completely in the summer and autumn. When this happened the lodge had to be supplied by water cart. In 1900 a piped water-supply was laid on to the lodges at Alverstone and Brock's Copse from a supply found 14 feet down behind Six Cottages in Alverstone Road.

### Ryde Road Lodge

This impressive lodge opposite Palmer's Brook Farm was the southernmost of Queen Victoria's lodges. It was built in 1864 and the drive led north to Brock's Copse Lodge. Built mainly of red estate bricks, made just a 400 yards away, it has buff bricks used as banding and wonderful decorative diamond patterning around the upper walls. It is the most ornate of all the lodges, and still has some of its decorative chimneys and the brick-built gateposts with the iron mounts for the gate, which can still be seen. The design is reflected again in the lodge in Brock's Copse. Heraldic arms and a plaque on the gable confirms the date of construction.

It has been said that the lodge was built for the Queen to use when she went to catch a train at Whippingham Station. Unfortunately, this myth is untrue as the station and railway line were not constructed for 11 years after the lodge was built, in 1875. Even if this was true, it is believed that Victoria only used the train once at Whippingham. However, the lodge did give access to the estate for those arriving from Ryde by train, as a carriage would be sent to meet them.

William Cooke was resident at Ryde Road Lodge in 1888. He had already served the Queen for 14 years.

*The gate to the Queen's drive at Brock's Copse Lodge, 1990s.*

Dotty Wilson (née Cooke) lived there as a young girl, walking to school at Whippingham along the quiet roads in the 1930s. Her father worked as a gardener at Kent House in East Cowes. The lodge was sold by Crown Estates in 1956, and was called Palmer's Lodge in the sale document.

## The Cottages Inside the Gates

### Coburg Cottage

Perhaps one of the most ornate and unusual cottages on the estate is Coburg Cottage. Prince Albert had come from the principality of Saxe-Coburg, which in present-day Germany is near the old East German border. Queen Victoria had visited Saxe-Coburg several times, including three times after Albert's death in the 1860s. When further cottages were necessary on the estate in 1870 she may have suggested that something in the Coburg style might be suitable. Hence, we have in Whippingham a building that faithfully copies this Germanic style.

Coburg Cottage was built as a pair of cottages and was completed in 1872. They are a unique architectural expression on the estate, and possibly in the whole of England. The building also contained a sitting-room and flush toilet for the Queen's personal use. The toilet was in a small room almost two stories high and was illuminated by a window set in almost the second floor. This afforded extra privacy for the Queen. Nobody would be able to accidentally look through that window at their monarch! Her sitting-room was part panelled and had a large marble fireplace.

Externally, the ground floor has decorative dark-wood beams with white render, giving a slightly Tudor impression. All the first floor, the central balcony over the wide porch and the third-floor gable-ends are hung with slate. This slate has been decorated with white-painted garlands and ribbons, crowns and a 'V' motif for the Queen. It is a beautiful and stunning decoration, which was restored in the 1990s by the present owners, as the white paint was fading. The decoration is signed 'Louise', the

*Coburg Cottage, c.1875, was built in the Saxe-Coburg style after Prince Albert's death. (THE ROYAL ARCHIVES © 2005 HER MAJESTY QUEEN ELIZABETH II)*

name of Victoria's artistic sixth child, but this signature is not visible on the photographs of 1875. It is quite possible that the design for the painted decoration could have been produced by Princess Louise.

On the rear elevation of the house the slate roof becomes a 'cat-slide' roof to cover the ground-floor rooms. There was a washhouse and privies built in the garden to the rear, but at right angles to the house, away from the Queen's room. The earth-closet was still in use in 1953, although the northern cottage had the use of the Queen's water-closet by then.

The ridge of the cottage has a distinct dip in it, and this odd-shaped roof can be recognised across the fields from the main East Cowes Road.

On the occasion of Queen Victoria's golden jubilee, one of the soldiers firing the Royal Salute at Portsmouth was killed when the canon blew up. The Queen heard about the accident and offered accommodation to the soldier's widow and children in Coburg Cottage.

Harry Sheath was living in Coburg Cottages in 1888, and Widow Land. Mr Land had been the gamekeeper until 1878. During the Tilletts' time the Barton shepherd, Mr Speed, lived at Coburg.

When Barton Manor was sold in 1953 the cottages remained as accommodation for the farm labourers.

Since then there has been no need for the cottages so they have been sold.

### Dallimores Cottage

In 1859 a new gamekeeper's cottage was constructed near Alverstone Gate on the site of Dallimores Cottage. The building looks continental, with a low-pitched roof and open gables. It is built of brick with a rendered first floor and a slate roof with a porch under an attractive first-floor balcony, in the centre of the front.

The same year a range of kennels was constructed to the west of the keeper's cottage. These have changed greatly, now forming a bungalow. Once the keeper's dogs would have been kept here, ready to help him in his work and to provide retrievers for the shooting parties, or just for Prince Albert's use. In 1953 the sale catalogue described them as 'a very useful range of buildings providing three Boxes, two with large runs enclosed by iron railings and Fodder Room with copper and ovens...'

In 1953 Dallimores was still in the Barton estate, and was still in a very basic condition with only an earth-closet, but mains water and electricity were laid on. There were, however, three rooms downstairs and three rooms upstairs, proving that the keeper's

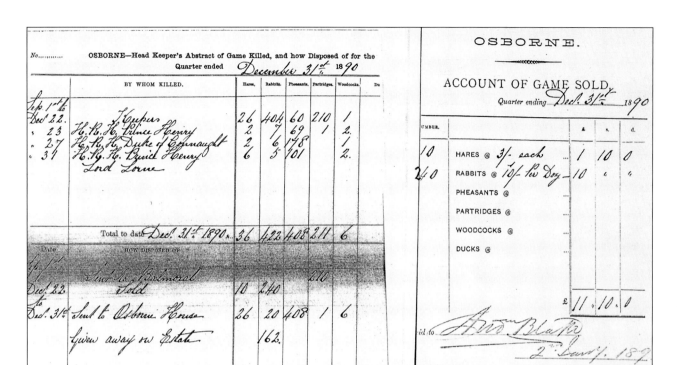

*These documents show who shot the game on the Osborne estate and how the game was disposed of. Many of the rabbits were given away to estate workers. (THE ROYAL ARCHIVES © 2005 HER MAJESTY QUEEN ELIZABETH II)*

position was a cut above the average estate worker! Since then the house has been carefully extended, but to the casual observer in 2006, it looks little different from how it looked in Queen Victoria's time.

Mr Land was the head gamekeeper living at Dallimores until his sudden death in 1878. *The Isle of Wight Press* reported that:

*Mr Land had won for himself a character of the highest kind, and was esteemed and respected not only by those on the estate but also by the farmers and others with whom he came in contact.*

He died the day before the Queen's arrival at Osborne, and the Queen visited Mrs Land an hour after arriving on the Island. Mrs Land was given a pension of £45 as she had no children, and she moved into Coburg Cottage to make way for a replacement keeper in Dallimores.

In 1885 another new head keeper had to be appointed. His name was Wheeler and he was described by the land steward as 'a nice looking pleasing man who must keep the rabbits down.' He was to start work on 15 October. Four years later, in December 1889, Andrew Blake told the Queen in a letter 'Wheeler says there are 30 per cent fewer rabbits than when he first came here.' Wheeler was also of the opinion that the present keepers could keep the numbers down, and they were not in need of any outside assistance. He mentioned that the keepers also killed the rats – 1,200 in 1889. No, that is not a misprint, 1,200 rats were killed that year.

*Dallimores, c.1875. This cottage was home to the game-keeper, at this time Mr Land. (THE ROYAL ARCHIVES © 2005 HER MAJESTY QUEEN ELIZABETH II)*

*The hunting beagles walking along the road, 1908. (REPRODUCED COURTESY OF THE COUNTY RECORDS OFFICE, NEWPORT)*

*Cadets from the Royal Naval College strung out across the field with the beagles ahead. (REPRODUCED COURTESY OF THE COUNTY RECORDS OFFICE, NEWPORT)*

The Queen replied to Blake on 28 December 1889: 'I wish that the keepers should be told by you that I wish the rabbits to be kept down, but not entirely destroyed... And that the rats should be <u>exterminated</u>! VRI.' The underlining was done by the Queen herself, probably horrified at the thought of those 1,200 rats! But she had a soft spot for fluffy rabbits!

So in all probability some of the dogs kept at the kennels would have been terriers to catch the rats. Others would have gone out with the keepers when summoned from the house to attend gentlemen intending to shoot. We know that a gamekeeper also lived at King's Quay, and at one time there were kennels there as well. While the keeper had his own dogs, these were trained to behave where game was concerned. In 1874 the keeper had complained about the hounds of the local hunt disturbing the game in Osborne Woods when they hunted at Palmer's Brook that November. The keeper asked the Queen if they should be stopped from hunting. Letters were sent to the master of the hunt, John Harvey of Marvel, near Newport, informing him that the Queen refused access to the hunt over her land at Palmer's Brook.

Numerous records exist of the shooting on the Osborne estate. Shown on page 74 are those for the last quarter of 1890, when His Royal Highness Prince Henry of Battenburg, Princess Beatrice's husband,

shot 69 pheasants, one partridge and two woodcocks on Christmas Eve, and even more on New Year's Eve with Lord Lorne. Prince Arthur, the Queen's seventh child, was the Duke of Connaught, and he went out shooting on 27 December, bagging 178 pheasants.

It is notable that the keepers had been keeping the rabbits down since September, shooting 404 of them, and had shot 210 partridges, leaving few of these for the royalty. However, the pheasants had been left. These would have been bred on the estate especially for the sport.

It is interesting to see that the 210 partridge shot were sent up to Balmoral, but the total of 408 pheasants shot that quarter were all consumed at Osborne, as were six woodcocks, 26 hares and just 20 rabbits.

Of the rest of the rabbits, 162 of them were listed as being given away on the estate, and 240 of them were sold. The keeper had a separate book to record the amount of game sold, probably to the local butcher in East Cowes. Rabbits in 1890 fetched 10s. a

*The kennels, pictured here in 1908, were built next door to Dallimores. (REPRODUCED COURTESY OF THE COUNTY RECORDS OFFICE, NEWPORT)*

*Barton, or as they became known, King's Cottages, 1980s.*

dozen, but hares 3s. each. This money was passed to the land steward for the estate accounts.

After the Queen's death a letter was sent to the King on 5 November 1901 by the land steward, asking: 'What are his Majesty's commands as to the shooting of the pheasants in the Osborne Covers? About 150–200 might be shot.' The reply was 'The King has given Princess Henry of Battenburg's son permission to shoot a few pheasants and as many rabbits as he likes.' Some of the birds were to be sent to Princess Henry (Beatrice) and the others sold. This side of the business of running the estate is often forgotten today.

Later, certainly in 1908, it would appear that a pack of hounds were kept at the kennels. The naval cadets from Osborne Royal Naval College went out on foot with these beagles on the Barton estate.

### King's Cottages (earlier known as Barton Cottages)

In 1848 three tenements were built just north-east of Barton Manor on the Barton Hard road. This leads down to Osborne Bay. They were the first of the new cottages on the estate and still stand in 2006, appearing to have changed externally very little since 1848.

They are similar in design to the Brickfield Cottages on the East Cowes Road, being built of red brick with buff banding, but the design is perhaps a little simpler. The central cottage has a projecting gable to the front and a small porch. The cottages either side have their doors at the ends of the building. The windows have small diamond-shaped panes.

By 1864 William Jackman, James More and Arthur Shepherd lived at Barton Cottages with their families. William Jackman had started as a carter on the Barton estate in 1845, at a wage of 12s. a week (£31.4s. a year). He retired in 1890 with a quarterly pension of £6.10s. (£26 a year). The Jackmans were chosen as foster parents for the two Bulgarian children that the Queen was looking after. (More details of this can be found in Chapter 10.)

The Barton Cottages gained the name King's Cottages at some stage after the Queen's death, and are known by this name in 2006 as King Edward VII and King George V had retained Barton for their own use until 1922. In 1953, while mains water was laid on and water-closets provided, these were still in the original washhouse outside, and there was no electricity. It was at this time that Dorothy Wilson moved in with her husband.

### King's Quay Cottage

King's Quay Cottage was in existence before Victoria bought Osborne. A building and quay are shown on the 1783 map, and by 1809 a cottage ornée appears on the site, possibly built by a Mr Cox. The cottage sits near the shore of the Solent with land running down to King's Quay.

*Keeper's Cottage at King's Quay, c.1875. (THE ROYAL ARCHIVES © 2005 HER MAJESTY QUEEN ELIZABETH II)*

The virtues of King's Quay are extolled in Englefield's writing about the Isle of Wight in 1799:

*The mouth of the little inlet called King's Quay has some pretty scenery about it. The inlet itself runs a winding course through... overhanging woods for above half a mile.*

It was in 1809 that artist Charles Tomkins completed a series of 58 watercolour scenes of a tour around the Island. This may have been at the request of the lord of Yarborough. One of his paintings was of 'King's Key and Barton Point, Wootton.' This delightful view shows not only the cottage ornée on the rise just above the shore, but also the fishermen with their net and a lobster fisherman with his pots and boat. The cottage has solid brick chimneys, with ornate brick tops, a dormer window is visible and the roof appears to be tiled. It is reminiscent of similar cottages designed by John Nash, who was living at East Cowes Castle at the time, although there is no record of him having built King's Quay Cottage.

A stone-fronted dam and sluice were constructed across the inlet in Albert's time, presumably to help with drainage. There was also a footbridge across the sluice-gate. The inlet is now a Site of Special Scientific Interest for wildlife, and the silting creek has changed considerably since Tomkins painted his picture in 1809.

The Queen had purchased the property and in 1862 the old King's Quay Cottage and its outbuildings were pulled down. A new cottage was erected on the site and dog kennels built close by.

The new cottage was of three stories in brick, with the top storey hung with tiles. In 1867 rooms were added to King's Quay Cottage for Her Majesty's use. A separate porch-covered entrance was constructed leading to a sitting-room, a retiring room and lavatory. The addition did not do a lot for the appearance of the cottage, when looking at it from the sea, but gave the Queen a good view from her simple sitting-room! A carriage shed was erected in 1868, but removed and reconstructed at Swiss Cottage seven years later.

Another name used for the cottage was Keeper's Cottage, and one of the keepers can be seen in the photograph on page 76, which was taken in 1875 by Jabez Hughes. Frank Cook was living there in 1888.

In 2005 the cottage, now a private home, looks much the same as it did in the Queen's day, but the drive that had been created along the seashore and through Brock's Copse is no longer the feature that it was. The sea is eroding the shore and eating into what may have been the original pre-Victorian quay, and Albert's dam and sluice are no longer serviceable. Because of its SSSI classification there are difficulties in restoring the shore to its original Victorian configuration, and so the land will continue to erode.

Despite these problems, King's Quay remains a peaceful, private and quiet place, and every effort should be made to keep it so.

## Ludham's Cottage

There is a private gravel lane that runs from Mount Road to King's Quay. Along this road lies Woodhouse Farm and beyond that is Ludham's Cottage. It was workers' accommodation for the farm.

This cottage is one of the few that Victoria did not have completely rebuilt. It is constructed of rendered brick and stone, white painted, with a thatched roof, and was originally a pair of cottages. Additions were made to it in the 1900s. It remains an example of the Isle of Wight vernacular style and is quite different from anything else on the estate. The only other thatched building in Whippingham is Truckles Cottage by the church, although the Post Office Cottage opposite the Forge was thatched until 1961.

Mr and Mrs Basil Matson lived at Ludham's in the 1940s. When Ludham Cottages appeared in the Barton Manor sale document of 1953 they were part of the labourer's accommodation for Woodhouse Farm at that time and to be sold in the same lot. They are described as 'excellent cottages set in large gardens'. Each cottage had two rooms up and two down, with an outside washhouse and earth-closet. Water was procured from a well, and lighting would have been by candle or oil-lamp.

It would appear that these cottages were sold off before the next sale took place, as they were not included on the inventory for Woodhouse or Barton Farms after 1953.

## Matthew's Cottages

Some 200 yards along the gravel lane from Mount Road to Woodhouse are Matthew's Cottages, facing east across the valley of Palmer's Brook.

These cottages were built after 1908 by the East Cowes firm of W.H. Brading. In the Barton sale document of 1953 they were described as 'a pair of very superior modern brick and tiled cottages, substantially built and in good order.' Each had three bedrooms, a sitting-room with fireplace, a kitchen with a tiled floor, a kitchener and a pantry. There was an outside washhouse with a sink and a copper, with water laid on, and an earth-closet. No. 1 also had a sink in the kitchen.

The original Matthew's Cottage probably had none of these luxuries, as soon after the Queen bought it in 1846 it was demolished. It had been in the field north of the present Primrose Cottage, and nothing but a few foundations remain beneath the grass in 2006.

## Primrose Cottage

One cottage in particular that still has a vegetable patch that would have been approved of in Victoria's time is Primrose Cottage, along Mount Road. The east garden has changed little, apart from some new modern varieties of vegetable being introduced. The produce keeps Mrs Grace Davison (née Snow) and her daughter in fresh fruit and vegetables throughout the year. Fruit trees still survive from Victorian times.

Built in 1849 as 'Whippingham Street Cottages, four tenements', this was one of the earliest of the sets of cottages to be built on the estate, probably housing the tenants from the cottages in the next field to the north that were then demolished. They were very functional, with little of the adornment that characterised the lodges that the public could see. The building is of red bricks with buff quoins under a slate roof. At that time their 'front' was to the road to the east, and so the washhouse and privies were built to the west, near the present Mount Road which was constructed in 1858.

In 1864 the four cottages were converted to just two, giving the occupants far more space. Until that time each cottage had only two small rooms downstairs and up.

When the Barton estate was sold to the Tillett family in 1922, Nos 1 and 2 Primrose Cottages were sold as well, and were occupied by the same workers, working for a different landlord. Shortly after the Second World War a scullery and an internal toilet were added to each cottage.

*Primrose Cottage in 2005, with the original outhouses to the left.*

By 1953, when the Barton estate was being sold, the Snow family was occupying No. 2 at a rental of 11s. a week. Charles Snow, who had become foreman on the Barton estate, bought this cottage then, having been given a lump sum by the Tilletts when they left. A sale document quotes the cottages as having a bathroom and a scullery. However, the bath was actually in the scullery, which also had the back door! Mr Snow senr bought No. 2, which was later bought by Grace (née Snow) and her husband Tony Davison.

Many schoolchildren will remember an annual Whippingham School outing to visit Primrose Cottage and Mrs Davison for a glass of 'Rhubarb wine' (rhubarb juice!). Goats were sometimes encountered, and now alpacas can be seen in the field next door. Grace helped as the school dinner lady (meals supervisory assistant in modern parlance), for 22 years, and even did a stint as the school crossing warden.

### Woodhouse Cottages

Initially Woodhouse Farm was part of the 'home farm' for the Queen's estate, and consequently farm labourers' cottages were constructed. The main pair of these became the farmhouse in later years.

In 1856 the Queen wrote in her journal 'Walked with Vicky and Arthur to Woodhouse, where cottages are to be built.' The new farm buildings had been completed in 1855, and the summary records that Woodhouse double cottage was finished in 1859.

The design was similar to the Keeper's Cottage at Alverstone, but with entrance porches at each end. Brick was used for the ground storey and the upper storey was hung with tiles. The roof has a low-pitched gable at the centre of the long elevation, and originally there was a pair of chimney-stacks on the ridge.

### Woodhouse Thatched Cottages

There were some original buildings from when the Queen bought the estate called Woodhouse Thatched Cottages. These had probably been patched up in the early days, and in the 1880s it was decided to make some alterations. A proviso was made that the external appearance should remain unaltered, keeping the thatched roofs and low backs. This work was completed in 1888.

These cottages have since disappeared. They do not even appear on the 1908 map.

### Woodman's Cottage

This existing cottage was bought with the estate in 1845. Three years later it was altered and greatly improved. By 1953, in the Barton estate sale document, the house was being described as a picturesque bungalow cottage, situated in a charming and secluded spot between Barton Wood and the Osborne estate. The house was built from brick and partly rendered, with a verandah on three sides.

In 1953 Woodman's Cottage was let to Mrs E. Wiles, who was paying a weekly rent of 11s.2d. At some stage Mrs Wiles bought the cottage, as it is still owned by the family. Mrs Wiles became the district nurse, known to many simply as Nurse Wiles. She got around in a battered old blue Landrover, quite useful as the gravel road between the cottage and Barton Manor deteriorated to a series of puddles.

The garden was large, as it had been designed to feed a family. The local East Cowes Girl Guides would regularly help Nurse Wiles cope with the garden when she was elderly, in the late 1980s.

*Woodhouse Cottages later became Woodhouse Farmhouse. Photograph taken in 2004.*

# Chapter 9

# Queen Victoria's Estate:
# Village Cottages, The Forge & Dashwoods

It was not until 1956 that the agricultural portions of the Osborne estate were put up for sale. This included Kingston, Heathfield and Alverstone Farms, each with their attached 'tied' cottages, Palmer's Brook Lodge and various adjacent individual fields that had been rented to different people. This 1956 sale effectively cut the ties that had bound Whippingham to the Queen.

There were several cottages built for the estate workers situated outside the Queen's gates, but owned by the Queen.

## Six Cottages, Alverstone Road

Six freehold cottages and their gardens had been bought into the Queen's estate in 1846 at a cost of £582.10s. Following the realignment of the public highway on Prince Albert's instructions, a terrace of six new cottages was constructed nearby in 1859 and the original cottages were pulled down. At least two of the old cottages were occupied by members of the Bull family – Sarah Bull in one and William Bull in another. Five other members of the Bull family lived in the neighbourhood and tithes were paid to the parish of Whippingham for all their cottages in 1853 by the Queen.

The cottages that were built in 1859 are of red brick with only buff lintels and a stringcourse which becomes the cill of the first-floor windows. The building has been described by an architect as 'one of the most sophisticated of all the estate buildings.' It is a simple design, with the pairs of dormer windows and three substantial chimney-stacks.

The new cottages were first known as Bull's Cottages, as they replaced the original Bulls' cottages. In 1860 two of the cottages were occupied by families

named Bull; William Bull and Frederick Bull. Both were married and four daughters were at the school. So the Bull family maintained their strong association with the cottages. By 1880 the cottages were described in estate records as Six Cottages, and at this time new outbuildings were constructed. Porches were added at the back doors of each of the cottages in 1898.

Frederick and William Bull were labourers at Barton Manor Farm, and Frederick retired in 1873 with a pension of £3.18s. a quarter, which he was still getting in 1895. In 1885 Widow Maria Bull started receiving her husband's pension, and she moved into the Almshouses. James Bull was also a labourer on Barton Farm and he retired in 1894 with a pension of £4.11s.

The outhouses still survive in 2006 as a tidy block at the rear of the cottages. The two boilers that were used for doing the washing still exist. The ladies of the cottages must have taken it in turns to do their washing. There had been a pump from a well to supply water. In 1953 these cottages were no longer tied to Barton Manor and they had been bought by the council. In 2006 one of the cottages still has its kitchener oven, which is useable, and has just had the original sink removed.

## Four Cottages, Whippingham Shute

These four cottages were probably those bought by the Queen in 1845 from John Tiley, which were shown on the 1841 map. They were quoted as having gardens and land. It would appear that when they were rebuilt in 1855 they were called 'Post Office Cottages' – perhaps because they were near to the cottage used as a Post Office. This causes some confusion. The name 'Four Cottages' was in use on the 1863 map.

*Six Cottages in Alverstone Road were built in 1859. Photograph taken in 2005.*

*Porches at the back of Six Cottages were added in 1898. Photograph taken in 2005.*

*The outhouses at Six Cottages remained intact in 2005.*

*A fireplace in the outhouse in 2005.*

*A kitchener still in situ at Six Cottages in 2005.*

*One of the copper boilers in the Six Cottages outhouse in 2005.*

On the 1854 map there was no building on the site of Four Cottages. This would coincide with the old cottages being pulled down to make way for the building of the new ones in 1855. The cottages are built of the red bricks from the Queen's brickyard. Some of the internal dividing walls use a 'VR' brick that is in the form of a hollow brick-shaped tube, an interesting feature not noted elsewhere as yet. The two outer cottages have their doors at the ends, and all shared the washhouses and privies built across the yard on the uphill side.

There has been a suggestion that some of the women living here could have been laundresses for Osborne, and that linen was brought here for washing and drying. However, Mrs Jerome (née Jolliffe) had never heard of this, and she lived here as a girl in the 1920s. There were extensive laundry facilities at Osborne itself, but perhaps some of the laundry from there or from Barton was given to 'outworkers'.

Whatever their name, Four Cottages at Whippingham Shute were definitely built and were occupied by royal estate workers. The estate office seems to have been using both the names. A new water tank was built for the use of the labourers living in 'Post Office Cottages' in 1869, and 'new piggeries were built at 'Post Office Cottages' in 1880.'

In 1860 'Whippingham Cottages' housed Charles Tucker, James Salter, Henry Greenen and William Rose and their families. In 1864 we know that the same labourers were occupying 'post office cottages' as their wives all received petticoats from the Queen for Christmas that year! Mrs Tucker had three boys at school, the Greenen family a daughter, the Rose family had a girl and a boy, and the Salters two girls at school.

Whippingham Four Cottages were comfortable family homes, with large gardens to provide food. By the 1920s some of the people living there had retired from the Queen's service. One of these was Thomas Foakes, who had been the carpenter at Barton Manor Farm. He used to keep the fences 'up together' there. He was a respected sidesman at Whippingham Church in the 1920s, reading a lesson every week. Also living at Four Cottages was Mrs Ward. Mrs Jerome remembered her as an old lady, who had worked at Osborne House when the Queen lived there. Mrs Ward had the distinction of having helped to lay Her Majesty out when she died.

Mr and Mrs Jolliffe moved to Four Cottages in 1926. Thomas Jolliffe became ill with an aneurism and for seven years he was unable to move from the cottage. He enjoyed singing hymns and one day, when rector Mostyn Pritchard came to visit him, the rector asked if he had been confirmed. Thomas hadn't, so was asked if he would like to be confirmed into the Church of England. Thomas agreed, so it was arranged that the Bishop of Portsmouth should come over especially to confirm Thomas in his own home. Mrs Jolliffe laid out the dining table as if it were an altar for the occasion. This was probably in 1934.

This event endeared Revd Mostyn Pritchard to the family. Mrs Jerome, Thomas's daughter, mentioned that people came from as far away as Freshwater to hear Mostyn Pritchard preach and she regretted his departure from the parish in 1937.

Four Cottages still stand in 2006, at right angles to the road as you drive up Whippingham Shute. The gardens still look delightfully productive, facing south down the slope of the hill towards the copse, where the hazel catkins and primroses are always a welcome sign of spring.

## Post Office Cottage

This is situated on the main Whippingham Road opposite the Forge, and is called Old Cottage in 2006.

A receiving-house was appointed in Whippingham in 1843, and the first cancelling stamp to be used had the inscription 'Whippingham St.' on it. Whippingham Street is at the east end of Alverstone Road, at the junction with Mount Road.

By 1855 the *Post Office Directory* stated that Mrs Jane Groves was the receiver of letters. She lived opposite the Forge. The post arrived at Whippingham at 8.30 in the morning and 6.30 in the evening. It was dispatched at the same times. Letters went through West Cowes, which was the nearest money-order office.

By 1878 it was Mr William Groves who had the Post Office. Letters then arrived at 8.30a.m. and 3.30p.m., and were dispatched at 8.45a.m. and 5.30p.m. In 1889 John Hawkins was the receiver of mails and ran the Post Office at Whippingham. He was also the village blacksmith and was described as farrier to the Queen.

In 1890 a new Whippingham Post Office Cottage was built on the Queen's orders. The Queen received a letter from her land steward explaining that the cottage was in need of repair.

*Mr Blake and Mr Mann fear that the Whippingham Post Office Cottage will fall down if not repaired. But as your Majesty will allow a new cottage to be built here Mr Mann says that this can be done on the lines of the present cottage. But the piece of land for the back yard is very small and Blake suggests that [more] might be purchased from Miss Jolliffe.*

So the new cottage had more land than previously, as a small section of Padmore land was bought. The cottage was thatched, and had a porch to the road entrance. It was this porch which constituted the Post Office, as people still in the village in 2006 can remember. From the photographs we can see that by 1938 it was possible to telephone from the Post Office.

In 1920 Frank Rann took on the Forge and moved into the Post Office Cottage. His wife, Fanny, became the sub-postmistress until she retired in 1946. She also had the job of caring for their family of 12 children.

Above: *Old Post Office Cottage in the snow, 1938.*

Right: *Bill Lee the postman with his bike, c.1920. In the 1930s the next postman was Jack Foss.*

*Post Office Cottage, picturesque in its thatch in the early 1930s.*

The photograph of the Post Office in the snow in 1938 (*opposite*) prompted Mrs Sue Rann to remember the snow of 1963 which started on New Year's Eve. People came out from East Cowes, on foot, for the New Year's Eve dance in the village, but unfortunately the band could not get there! Even the main roads were blocked with snow, and the village ground to a halt. Mr Orlik went around the village with his tractor delivering milk to all the elderly people who needed it. A lorry eventually got away from Folly Works by driving over the fields as Folly Lane was impassable for some time. Supplies for The Folly Inn were fetched by boat.

In 1946 the Post Office moved to Dashwood's, the double-fronted house opposite the Community Centre in Alverstone Road. The west side of the house had a general store and the Post Office. The letterbox was housed in a brick pillar by the entrance path. Mr and Mrs Andrews worked there first, and then Stan Foreman. Dashwood's closed as a Post Office in February 1987.

In May 1987 Maddi Chessell opened a new sub-Post Office combined with a small general store at 8 Alverstone Road, where she continues to serve the community in 2006.

## Dashwood's Cottage and the Forge

The Dashwood family was quite extensive, and many members were involved in carpentry, building houses and coach making, mainly in Newport, Ryde and East Cowes. In 1748 William Dashwood was overseer for the poor rate in Whippingham, a responsible position.

In the 1790s Thomas Dashwood was doing 'carpenters work' for the highways commissioners in Whippingham. Dashwood's Cottage and land were bought into the Queen's estate in 1845 from Winchester College when she bought Barton Manor. At that time Henry Dashwood leased the house and the Forge on adjacent land.

By 1861 William Dashwood, aged 63, was described as a wheelwright and blacksmith living at Dashwood's. In 1881 he was only doing carpentry work, not blacksmithing.

*Looking along Alverstone Road past Dashwoods on the left, c.1910.*

*Dashwood's general shop and Post Office in the 1980s.*

William Dashwood also had another cottage next to the Toll House near East Cowes which he had rented to the previous blacksmith who worked the Forge. When that blacksmith left, Dashwood rented out the East Cowes cottage to someone else. Consequently, when in 1878 blacksmith John Hawkins took over the tenancy of the Forge, there was no cottage for him to rent and he had to walk to and from home in Newport every day. Eventually he managed to rent a cottage on the Padmore estate.

At this time, Canon Prothero of Whippingham Church enquired of the Queen whether Hawkins could have one of the new Heathfield Farm cottages, as he felt that William Dashwood should be under obligation to find a cottage for the blacksmith. However, there was no written agreement stating at the time when the Queen bought Dashwood's cottage that she should provide or keep a blacksmith on the place, nor to give him a house to live near his work. Mr Dashwood remained in his cottage next to the Forge. Prothero felt that really Dashwood's cottage should be occupied by the blacksmith, and it should not be for the blacksmith's customers to find him somewhere to live!

Eventually the solution was found when the blacksmith moved into the Post Office Cottage directly opposite the Forge. Hawkins was described as 'a hard-working respectable man' by Canon Prothero. As he was described as farrier to the Queen, he presumably shod all the Barton horses.

By 1905 Bill Gray was the blacksmith. He lived at Post Office Cottage opposite the Forge, now 'Old Cottage'. His stepson, Percy Hardy, was a messenger at the time the photograph on page 85 was taken.

In 1895 the old blacksmith's shop was in need of rebuilding. It was pulled down and a new workshop put up in its place by order of the Queen. This is the building seen in 2006, which has been extended further westwards in recent years.

*The blacksmith Bill Gray and helpers at the Forge, c.1910.*

*Blacksmith Frank Rann shoeing a horse in the 1930s.*

In 1919 Bill Gray sold the lease on the Forge to the Rann family. However, accommodation was again difficult to come by and Frank Rann walked daily back and forward to Newport. The Rann family eventually moved into the 'Post Office Cottage' in 1920. Frank's son Robert joined him working at the Forge, eventually taking over in 1946. Bob Rann bought the Forge from the Barton estate in 1953.

At that time, the Forge was still shoeing horses, together with making and repairing farm machinery, as it had done in Victorian times. Bob Rann built up the trade in steel fabrication and on-site welding. His son Trevor has expanded this. Michael Augustus came in as a business partner with Trevor, but has since retired. Trevor has a workforce of six producing a wide range of steel fabricated items. These include large items such as fire escapes, balustrades, balconies and railings. Recent clients have included GKN Aerospace and English Heritage, for whom Trevor constructed the new walkway arches in the Osborne House gardens. Boat trailers and cradles are made for the RNLI.

Although Trevor Rann no longer shoes horses, the original furnace is still used and kept alight with hand-pumped bellows for the weekly sharpening and tempering of chisels and points for Island tool-hire companies. Trevor is a member of the Guild of Master Craftsmen and recently gained the Investors in People Award, which he feels has brought the workforce closer together.

Dashwood's Cottage has remained separate from the Forge. In 1946 it became the village Post Office and stores and remained as such until 1987, when it reverted back to being a private home.

*Left: Bob Rann and his father Frank in the doorway of the Forge in the late 1930s.*

*Below: Blacksmith Bill Gray and messenger Percy Hardy at the Forge.*

| Date of first payment for quarter ending | | Name | Amount £ s d | | | How employed previously |
|---|---|---|---|---|---|---|
| June 30 | 1886 | Henry Hunt | 11 | 14 | | Foreman of Pleasure Grounds |
| Sept. 28 | 1894 | W.ᵐ Peirce | 11 | 14 | | " " Brickyard |
| " 29 | 1893 | C. Moore | 11 | 5 | | Fireman at Osborne House |
| March 31 | 1886 | Stephen Day | 7 | 16 | | Cowman - Barton Farm |
| " 30 | 1894 | A. Bennett | 7 | 10 | | Mason - New Barn |
| " 29 | 1890 | William Jackman | 6 | 10 | | Carter - Barton Farm |
| " 28 | 1891 | Henry Cooper | 6 | 10 | | Labourer |
| " 30 | 1892 | James Salter | 6 | 10 | | Carter |
| June 30 | 1884 | Jane Gallop | 6 | 10 | | Husband - Alverstone |
| March 29 | 1895 | G. Bright | 5 | . | | Clerk of Works |
| June 30 | 1874 | Eliza Isaacs | 4 | 11 | | Husband - Barton Farm |
| Sept. 30 | 1876 | Jane Harding | 4 | 11 | | Husband Labourer |
| June 30 | 1871 | Leah Jenkins | 4 | 11 | | Husband Carpenters Labourer |
| December 31 | 1885 | Maria Bull | 4 | 11 | | Husband Labourer |
| March 30 | 1894 | G. Soakes | 4 | 11 | | Husband Estate Carpenter |
| September 30 | 1871 | Jane Cork | 4 | 11 | | Husband Carter at |
| June 30 | 1884 | Fanny Taylor | 4 | 11 | | Husband Labourer |
| March 30 | 1892 | Martha Chambers | 4 | 11 | | Husband Estate Labourer |
| June 27 | 1890 | Burney Bennett | 4 | 11 | | Gardener at New Barn |
| March 30 | 1894 | James Bull | 4 | 11 | | Labourer Barton Farm |
| December 31 | 1878 | M.A. Miller | 4 | . | | Husband |
| March 31 | 1875 | Frederick Bull | 3 | 18 | | |
| " 29 | 1889 | Ellen Rose | 3 | 18 | | Husband Engine-driver Osborne |
| " | | E. Wooldridge | 2 | 12 | | Husband Carter Barton Farm |
| June 27 | 1891 | M.A. Greenen | 2 | 12 | | Husband Labourer |
| September 28 | 1889 | R. Scott Allowance for F. Trott's children | 2 | 10 | | By Order of The Queen |
| | | Beatrice Prisk | 1 | 5 | | Ditto |
| | | | £ 147 | 4 | | X Died 3ʳᵈ May 1895 |

*A list of the pensioners on the Osborne and Barton estate, 1888.  (THE ROYAL ARCHIVES © 2005 HER MAJESTY QUEEN ELIZABETH II)*

*The Almshouses photographed soon after their construction, showing the first of the estate pensioners to live there in 1876.  (THE ROYAL ARCHIVES © 2005 HER MAJESTY QUEEN ELIZABETH II)*

# Chapter 10
# The Queen's Benevolence

## The Poor Rate

The Poor Rate Book for Whippingham dates from 1748 and is held at the Isle of Wight County Records Office. It is shows who the land or copyhold owners were, and how much they paid for the relief of the poor of the parish 'at two shillings ye pound for the year.'

The most paid into the fund in 1748 was by Farmer Walker, who paid £11.9s.6d. for his Barton Manor holding, with Mr Blachford at Osborne paying only £7.10s. Clavells Farm, at £1.15s.6d., was half the value of Woodhouse, but both were held by W. Sheath. The holdings Matthew's and Dallimores were paying 10s. each, and were held by Cooper.

William Dashwood was the overseer for the poor rate for Whippingham in 1748. At this time each parish had its own poorhouse. While we do not know where this was, we do know that it was rented from Mr Whitmaich in 1759 and the rent was £22 a year. Mr Whitmaich was at South Heathfield Farm but the family also had property near Brock's Copse.

Going into the poorhouse was a last resort for villagers. Only those incapable of looking after themselves, and with no home or means of making money to live, were taken into the house. Thus we read that on 17 May widow Odle was taken to the poorhouse by Robert Bartlett, who was paid 8s. for his services. In June widow Odle died. Her funeral was paid for by the parish poor rate, costing 14s.7d., which included 6s.1d. for bread and beer. The coffin, at 10s.6d., was extra.

Widow Young was in charge of the poorhouse and was paid 36s. a year. William Dashwood took an inventory of the goods in the house and spent one shilling.

Expenditure was made on furze faggots and wood for cooking, but what was spent out on food for the inhabitants does not show in these accounts. William Marten and Mary Ratsey were both taken to the poorhouse in the autumn of 1748.

Some assistance was given to the other poor in the village. Andrew Hollis was being kept by Farmer Brading of Truckles, who received 6s. for this. A total of 3s.6d. was spent on a new coat and waistcoat for Andrew. Arthur Weay's family were suffering hard times and clothes and money were given to his wife. Five pairs of stockings for the children cost 3s.4d. in March 1749.

In 1759 the decision was made by the Vestry to give up the poorhouse at Lady Day and notice was given to Mr Whitmaich. This was because the new work house had been opened in Parkhurst, and all the poor of the Island were to be sent there. The poor rate, still at 2s. in the pound, was levied and sent to Parkhurst.

## The Queen's Benevolence

Taking over the Osborne and Barton estates and the neighbouring farms in 1845 gave the Queen a great feeling of responsibility for the welfare of 'her people'. Firstly, the royal couple set about renovating and later rebuilding the estate cottages, so that the people had fit places to live.

In their work the labourers were under similar conditions to those elsewhere in England. The rates of pay were no higher at Osborne than elsewhere, but in other ways the people were much better off. The Queen paid an annual retainer to the local doctor, who then looked after any sick people on the estate without them having to pay for themselves. There was also an estate nurse paid for by the Queen. Mrs Gallop held that position in 1885, and Mrs Critchley was given £25 when she retired as estate nurse in 1898.

If the men fell sick they could expect sick pay until they recovered. On most other estates at the time the men would think themselves lucky to get a few weeks half pay under similar circumstances. If the illness resulted in death, then the Queen often contributed towards the funeral expenses.

When her head gamekeeper Mr Land died in 1878 the Queen was on the mainland. She visited Mrs Land immediately after arriving back on the Island the following day. The Queen then went personally to Whippingham Church and selected the ground for the grave, and on the day of the funeral was at the house and then joined the procession at Whippingham School on the way to the church. A wreath of white camellias from the Queen was laid on the coffin, together with one from Princess Beatrice. It was reported in *The Isle of Wight Press*, from which the above information was gleaned, that:

*The above will, we are sure, be read by our readers with interest, as the kindly acts of Her Majesty, so well known here, show the deep sympathy felt by her for all classes of her subjects.*

Mrs Land moved from the gamekeeper's cottage to Coburg Cottage on the estate with a gift of £45 from the Queen and a pension.

> Alverstone Farm.
> Whippingham.
> January 15, 1893.
>
> Sir,
>
> I respectfully and gratefully acknowledge, on behalf of myself, and my Brother, the kindness, and generosity, of Her Majesty, in remitting us a half-year's Rent, by reason of the late unfortunate Season.
>
> My Brother, and I, have been tenants of Her Majesty over 20 years, and we have at all times received the greatest kindness, consideration, and encouragement.
>
> I cannot express all that we would wish to say, but we are indeed very deeply grateful to Her Majesty.
>
> I am, Sir,
> Your obedient Servant,
>
> Henry Knighton.
>
> Genl. Rt. Hon. Sir H. F. Ponsonby,
> K.C.B.

*A letter from Farmer Knighton thanking for the reduction in his rent because of the poor harvest. (THE ROYAL ARCHIVES © 2005 HER MAJESTY QUEEN ELIZABETH II)*

Pensions were paid to her employees when they could no longer continue to work. These were paid in relation to the pay received, but if a man was fit and healthy he continued to work as there was no automatic retirement at age 65. William Pierce, foreman at the brickyard, retired at the age of 78. His service and knowledge were obviously appreciated. Four men were recorded as being on invalidity payment in 1888 – William Wooldridge, Charles Tucker, William Durham, and John Greenen. Five others in their sixties and seventies that year were expected soon to be receiving pensions and were being given lighter duties.

A school was built at royal expense. It continued to be improved right until the time of the Queen's death. In fact, the Queen took over the entire expenses of the school, paying all the outstanding bills in 1894 and until her death.

Parties were given to the estate children at Christmas and they received gifts according to their age. The older children either received a book or, on alternate years, a dress or material for the girls or suiting for the boys. Children between the age of four and seven received a toy every year. The Christmas list for 1864 was – 17 dresses, eight dolls, 15 books and ten toys for boys. That year all the wives of the estate workers received a petticoat as a Christmas present.

A Knecht Ruprecht Brisque doll was given to one of the children of the estate workers in 1885 by Queen Victoria at the Christmas party. The German legend is that Knecht Ruprecht (servant Rupert) was a little elf who accompanied Santa Claus, often dressed as a furry creature. If the children had been good and thought of the Christ child they would be given sweets by Ruprecht. He also had a big stick, and if the child had been naughty that year there would be no presents. Instead Knecht Ruprecht would chastise the child. This doll was given to the Lilliput Antique Doll and Toy Museum at Brading to look after by the recipient, aged 93 at the time, who had treasured it all her life.

If every girl on the estate had dolls of similar quality given to them every other year, there must have been quite a collection on the estate by the end of the Queen's reign. Probably the fact that there were so many meant that the children were allowed to play with them, and being fragile Brisqueware, accidents happened. But, after all, they were presents for the children to play with!

An interesting letter from the land steward is in the Royal Archives, explaining the Christmas gift situation to His Majesty King Edward VII in the autumn of 1901. It was suggested that action should be taken if the gifts were to continue. A poignant answer is written on the request 'The king does not see any necessity of giving these presents this year.' So although the estate was still in the royal domain, the tradition of gifts from the sovereign ceased. No mittens for the children that year!

It is very noticeable, comparing the school photographs of the children at Whippingham School and those at East Cowes, just how well-dressed the children of the Queen's estate were. There is a verbal story about a little boy splashing in a puddle at the side of the road as the royal carriage passed him. The Queen is reported as saying 'Get out of that puddle young Jimmy! Your mother only bought those shoes last week!' It gives you a feel for the care and interest she took in 'her people', even if the story cannot be verified.

Gifts were not only given at Christmas. Mr and Mrs Chambers celebrated their golden wedding anniversary in 1886 and received a present from the Queen. It made them feel so proud. Mr Chambers had been an estate labourer working on the Osborne grounds from 1845, and his wife Martha was still receiving a pension from the Queen in 1896.

The Queen's concern at those suffering loss in East Cowes is also well documented. When seven local Trinity House men were lost as they attempted to explode a wreck on the Brambles Bank in 1894, the Queen invited all the widows to Osborne and talked to them, offering her condolences. The youngest, Mrs

Snow and Mrs Oatley, had only been married for one and three weeks respectively. Others had children. The Queen found that Trinity House would be providing pensions, but still gave each widow £10.

Another example of the Queen's benevolence occurred in 1893. The previous year had proved a disastrous one for the harvest, and her farmers were finding themselves in difficulties. The Knighton brothers, who by this time were farming both Alverstone and Heathfield Farms, had their rent reduced by half for that year, and the same reduction was given to Kingston Farm. A delightful letter in the Royal Archives from Henry Knighton is reproduced on page 88.

The Groves family lived at Whippingham Post Office. Their daughter, who became Mrs Elizabeth Tuffield, was a deaf mute. As a girl she had been educated at the expense of Her Majesty, receiving her education in the new 'Silent Language'. The Queen took pains to learn the finger alphabet so that she could communicate with Elizabeth. After suffering cruelty from her husband, Elizabeth returned to live at home and was visited by the Queen. Mrs Tuffield died in 1874 aged 34. In later years the Queen recounted the story to one of her chaplains, and mentioned that she was not as proficient in the 'Silent Language' as she used to be in her younger days.

In 1900 William Agnew, who was also deaf and dumb, painted what he imagined the scene would have looked like in the Post Office Cottage when the Queen communicated with Elizabeth in sign language. A copy of the picture was found at the Post Office when the Rann family took over the house in 1920, and remains there to the time of writing.

## The Bulgarian Orphans

In 1855 the Crimean War was at its height. The Queen and Albert had been closely following the proceedings, first watching the troop ships leaving Portsmouth, then hearing first-hand accounts of the death and disease, and writing to Florence Nightingale. After a battle on a beach at Cüstëndje, sailors from HMS *Firebrand* found two small boys lying injured beside their dead parents. They took the boys onboard ship, where the captain Hyde Parker adopted them. Medical treatment for gunshot wounds in the arms of both boys was carried out, a goat was procured to provide milk, and the children were christened John and George Firebrand. They were onboard for two more battles at Sebastopol, where sadly the captain was killed.

The Queen became aware of the incident, and announced her wish to take the infants under her wing. They were the same age as her youngest boys, Arthur and Leopold, aged five and two respectively. She consulted her land steward, Andrew Toward, who suggested that Mrs Jackman at Barton Cottages, wife of one of the Barton carters, would be the best

*A Knecht Ruprecht doll, given to an estate worker's daughter by Her Majesty in 1885. (COURTESY LILLIPUT TOY AND DOLL MUSEUM, BRADING)*

person to care for them, her house being the most spotlessly clean on the estate.

As soon as the boys arrived the Queen went straight over to see them. Despite having the scars of five bullets in his right arm, the Queen described Johnny as, 'very merry and intelligent and speaks English perfectly.' She described little Georgy as delicate and gentle. She visited frequently, and the children were allowed licence beyond the norm. When one of them stole her parasol and galloped off using it as a hobby horse, the Queen just laughed! The boys were renamed John and George Hyde, and remained with the Jackmans until they joined the Navy. George was still at Whippingham School in 1864 and received a book from the Queen that Christmas.

## The Almshouses

In 1875/6 the Queen had the Almshouses built opposite the church for use by the retired employees on the estate, or their widows. The old yard of Truckles Farm was cleared for the purpose, and an excellent terrace of cottages built from red brick with much decoration. There were six apartments and adjoining the southern-most there was a room and cloakroom set aside for the Queen's personal use.

The Queen took an interest in the development of the Almshouses and was a frequent visitor. In her journal for 21 January 1876 the Queen wrote 'Drove with Beatrice to the Almshouses at Whippingham, where I got out and I settled with McPherson where the peoples' gardens and the road is to be.'

On 14 August 1876 the Queen wrote:

*Out to tea with Beatrice, and later went with her to look at the Almshouses at Whippingham which are now furnished and the ground in front laid out which looks very pretty. Old Mrs Isaacs is the only one yet living there. She was so delighted and as usual very funny. Another old woman, Mrs Kingswell is to live with her and I made her laugh by saying old women generally quarrelled, but I hoped they would not.*

Mrs Isaacs continued living at the Almshouses until 1896 when she died aged 88 years old.

The Almshouses were soon fully occupied. In 1877 the land steward queried with the local council whether the Almshouses should be assessed for payment of the poor rate. He understood that in similar cases on the mainland the poor rate had been waived as the owner was providing the service for the aged retainers. However, the arguments were refuted, and there was no exemption for the Queen, so she had to pay the poor rate for the Almshouses in Whippingham.

In 1888 widows Bull, Isaacs, Gallop, Gosh and Harding were living there, as well as George

*Refurbishment of the Almshouses had just been completed in 1980.*

Foakes, who had been estate carpenter. It was the Queen who had the final say in who was to live in one of the Almshouses, after examining the recommendations put forward by her land steward. In 1896 the then steward, Andrew Blake, wrote to the Queen's secretary suggesting William Houndsell be sent there:

*10 February 1896. Sir, I beg to recommend William Houndsell for a pension and the vacant Almshouse. He has been farm labourer [on the estate] for over 50 years and is now in his 78th year. During his service here he has been a very steady and trustworthy man and a thoroughly good labourer. Dr Hoffmeister does not think that he is fit to be about now, as he is subject to giddy attacks and falls down.*

The Queen's secretary added a note saying ' William Houndsell has a wife so perhaps Your Majesty will allow him to have the Almshouse.' The reply comment on the letter is the word 'Approved.'

Various women were engaged over the years as attendants at the Almshouses. Often these ladies were married to an estate worker and would visit the Almshouses daily, checking up on the residents and doing various tasks for them. We think of 'sheltered accommodation' as a modern phenomenon, but Victoria had set it in place in 1875 in Whippingham, on a much grander and kinder scale than the old poorhouse.

It was not until 1935 that the Crown Estate no longer required the Almshouses for old employees of the estate and the criteria for eligibility were widened as the local council took over the upkeep. The Queen's room had been incorporated to form another bungalow in 1889 and in 1952 electricity was installed. In 1980 the Almshouses were completely renovated and bathrooms added at the rear.

Queen Victoria looked after her people from the cradle to the grave, continuing the concern and attention that both she and the Prince Consort had shown from the beginning of their residence at Osborne in 1845.

# Chapter 11
# Whippingham School

There has been a school at Whippingham on the present site since 1848. The land, a quarter of an acre, was given by Lord George Seymour to Revd Bouverie and the Rural Dean of East Medene 'for the education of poor persons of the village.' The first National School was a simple building with accommodation for the school master to the east, and one long schoolroom to the west, which had a gallery at one end with the seats raised in tiers. The National School Organisation was a charity interested in extending education to 'the lower classes'. Local landowners and clergy were encouraged to subscribe to erect a school and pay for a master, and guidance was given as to what should be in the curriculum.

Only the plans and elevation exist. It was in the same style as buildings erected at New Barn on the Queen's estate – brick covered in stucco with rather an Italianate look to it. Prior to 1848 the only accommodation was in 'the school room' attached to the west end of Whippingham Church in 1804. Any earlier schooling in the village would have been carried out in rudimentary 'dame schools', in the schoolmistress's own home.

Queen Victoria probably contributed to the National School fund for Whippingham, as by 1848 the royal couple owned much of the surrounding land. Prince Albert was a paternalistic landowner and in 1850 had a survey carried out of all the young people on the estate to establish whether they could read or write. A total of 26 of the children in the five to 14 age range could read well or fairly well. There were 62 children at the school in 1850, the majority of whom came from the Queen's estate. Of the 34 15–20 year olds on the estate only 14 could read.

This survey also revealed that some children as young as 11 years old had already left school and were in employment; a situation that continued even after the 1870 Education Act had made schooling compulsory. If a child had reached a certain standard he or she could leave school at the age of ten.

James Baker was the school master in 1851 and his wife Elizabeth was the school mistress. However, in 1855 Mrs Baker was dismissed by the management committee because of the lack of discipline and control of she had over her class. Her husband was also given six months' notice, although he was completely exonerated and not implicated in the conduct of his wife.

Because of the need to provide separate accommodation for a new headteacher and a school mistress, and also because of the increasing number of children attending, plans were drawn up in 1859 for a new school. Initially, only the house was to be enlarged, and the plans have little flaps on showing alternative ways of doing this. However, Prince Albert decided on a complete rebuild, which the Queen paid for entirely out of her own funds. Albert died before the new school was completed. The early name for the school on some documents is written as, 'The Queen's School, Whippingham', although it remained a National School.

The new school, which forms the basis of the present building, was erected in 1863 to the north of the original school. The old school was then demolished and became the gardens for the two schoolhouses. Now much of the old site is under tarmac for the infants' playground.

Two acres of land adjoining the school to the north were levelled, enclosed and planted round with a row of elms, pines and laurels. The whole of this was sown with grass seed and became the playground for the children. It is understood that 41 pine trees were planted, one for each year of Albert's life. In 2006 very few of the original pines remain as the top of the hill is very exposed to the wind. Several blew down in the 1987 hurricane, blocking the main road into East Cowes.

The inscription carved into the stone above the entrance informs us that 'This school was erected after a plan of the Prince Consort by Queen Victoria – 1864.' The drainpipes are actually dated 1863.

It was on 4 February 1864 that Queen Victoria officially opened the school, accompanied by Princess Feodore of Leinigen (her half-sister) and four of the royal children and Princess Feodore's daughter. The Queen's journal for that date records the event:

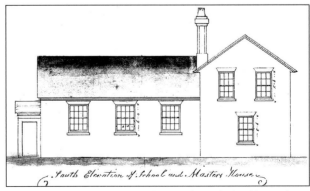

*A drawing of the 1848 school taken from the building plans.*

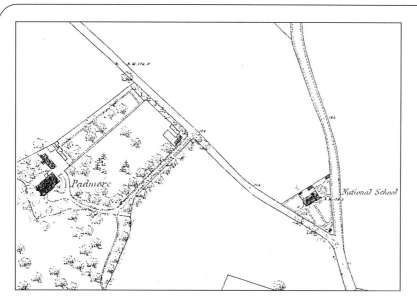

*Maps of the school showing the first school surveyed in 1854 (left) and the second school in 1863 (below). (REPRODUCED FROM THE 1854 AND 1863 ORDNANCE SURVEY MAPS WITH THE KIND PERMISSION OF THE ORDNANCE SURVEY)*

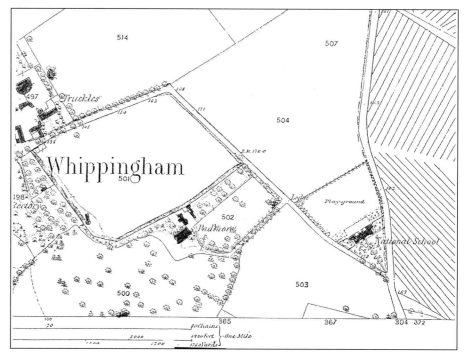

*The datestone over the school's front door.*

*The pine trees in 1984 before several blew down in the 1987 hurricane.*

*Went with Feodore and all the Children (the ladies and gentlemen having gone on), to the new school at Whippingham, which was opened by a tea given to all the school children. They sang a hymn, then grace, after which they sat down to tea, consisting of bread and butter and plum cake, enormous quantities of which they ate, drinking equally as much tea. This over they again sang Grace, followed by 'God save the Queen'.*

The school had one main room, which could be divided by means of two folding wooden screens. This was deemed sufficient accommodation for 195 children, although in 1865 there were only 89 children and by 1871, according to *Hills Directory* there were 47 boys and 39 girls on the registers.

In 1855 Charles Thomas became the headmaster and, with his wife, was living at the schoolhouse. By 1871 Mrs Thomas was recorded in the census as being the schoolmistress, with her husband the schoolmaster. The couple had five children of their own by then. Miss M.E. Hooper was also described as a school mistress. Charles William Thomas was recorded as being a school monitor at the age of 12. In 1881 Mr and Mrs Thomas are still schoolmaster and mistress, but their son had moved on. Instead, their daughter Ida Thomas was a pupil teacher at the age of 19. The pupil-teacher system was a scheme whereby the teacher agreed to continue the pupil's education in lessons after school while the teenager helped teach the younger classes. Her sister Lizzie was a school monitress, aged 16, the next step down from a pupil teacher.

Charles Thomas died in 1886, having been at Whippingham for 34 years. His daughter, Ida Helen Thomas, took over as schoolmistress and Kate Stevens was also named as schoolmistress. These two ladies continued to run the school during the rest of Queen Victoria's reign, being 39 and 38 years old respectively in 1901.

Queen Victoria was a frequent visitor to the school. She popped back again a week after opening the school, for instance. At Christmas she would attend sometimes with Princess Beatrice in order to give gifts or prizes to the children. By 1897 she was visiting with her daughter and grandchildren, as she recorded in her journal for 13 January:

*Went to Whippingham School with B, D and Ena, Mr Clement Smith meeting us there. I got out and went into the infants school where the children all had dolls in their arms and sang and recited little rhymes with actions on the 'Kindergarten' system after which they made way for the bigger boys and girls who went through their musical drill, first together and then separately. They did it wonderfully. The books and work were shown me, also drawings, all most creditable.*

It must have been an ideal teaching situation. One can imagine the teacher's admonitions. 'What would

*A 1865 report of the Whippingham National School. (THE ROYAL ARCHIVES © 2005 HER MAJESTY QUEEN ELIZABETH II)*

the Queen think of that untidy work! Do it again so that it is fit for Her Majesty to see!'

While government grants were forthcoming for teachers training pupil teachers, the capitation grant was dependent on sufficient numbers of pupils being entered for examination, with extra payment if the children passed their examinations. If, for some reason, such as illness, they could not sit exams, then the school received less money. This often resulted in the school having a deficit. The financial statement for 1865 shows this was the case, and also that the children were paying their school pence at 2d. a week per pupil. However, the results of those children examined in reading, writing and arithmetic was excellent, with a 97 per cent pass rate, and the inspector said that this was better than any other school in the neighbourhood.

There were major problems in 1877 when a fever epidemic had resulted in the closure of the school for several months. The school pence income was lost, and the rector Canon Prothero explained to the Queen's secretary that the deficit was £89.9s.11¾d. The Queen's secretary wrote in May:

*I have spoken to the Queen about the school finances... Cannot allow the burden of the deficiency to fall on you, as it has been caused by a misfortune that you could not avoid. If you can obtain no assistance from the Committee for the Council for Education, or from other sources... the Queen is willing to contribute...*

The Queen sent a cheque for £89. In November the school received a £38 rebate from the council, which was sent to the Queen.

The main income for the school was from subscriptions from the few wealthy landowners living nearby. Subscribers gave £65.5s. in 1865. Salaries for staff that year cost £93.10s.10½d.

In 1895 the Queen contributed £45. However, the previous year she again paid off a deficit for the school, and the message was sent that the Queen 'wants to have complete control' [of the finances]. So when the school drainage had problems, it was the Queen who paid the bill. In a letter to the Queen it is recorded that:

*The cost of alteration to the drainage etc. at Whippingham School required by the Education Department will be £130 but Sir Fleetwood fears it is unavoidable and must be done.*

A room for the teaching of cookery was also deemed necessary by the school inspector.

There was a certain amount of confusion about just where the money was to be acquired from. At one time requests were to be made to the Privy Purse, but this was corrected in April 1897: 'The Queen has now undertaken to pay all expenses at School', so the money was to come from Osborne estate funds. Requests were to be made to Andrew Salter, the land steward. Just what happened in 1901 after the Queen's death we do not know, but certainly the new King did not give out Christmas presents like his mother had done! Perhaps at this stage the County Council took over the finances, but the King kept the land and a rent of £1 a year was paid to him.

We do know that in 1902 the school was surveyed for the County Council. There were three partitions in the main schoolroom. Two classes of infants occupied the two west rooms. The surveyor was very scathing about the cookery room that had been added, which he considered entirely unsuited to its supposed use. The headmistress occupied the western schoolhouse. The surveyor also decreed that the present water-supply from the pump was dangerous, as the well water was pumped up to a tank that was never cleaned out.

The infants' and girls' 'sanitary offices' were poorly placed off the main corridor entrance and the staff toilet was in the teacher's house. The boys' toilets were in a detached building next to the poultry house. It was reported to have:

A list of subscribers to the school in 1895. (THE ROYAL ARCHIVES © 2005 HER MAJESTY QUEEN ELIZABETH II)

*... a trough closet with four seats over same; there are no divisions, the boys having to sit in a row. At the end is a small urinal without water to flush; it is badly ventilated, the only opening being the door; when I made my survey it was very foul.*

He suggested that partitions and doors should be installed, and adequate flushing provided. The drains led to a cesspit in the teacher's garden, which then overflowed across Beatrice Avenue! In the 1950s possibly this same cesspit caused flooding actually within the school!

Generally the windows were of opaque glass, which shut out a large percentage of the light. It was suggested that these should be replaced with clear glass, and better ventilation provided.

In 1907 Miss I.H. Thomas was still the head of the school which had 150 children on the roll. Soon after this, according to Uffa Fox, Mr James W. Rogerson became the headmaster. Mr Rogerson was still head in 1914/15 when he had two assistant mistresses, Miss A. Cooke and Miss A. Board.

The early photographs of the pupils at Whippingham School all show a group of perfectly dressed children. While Queen Victoria was alive each child received material as a gift every other year, so there was no excuse for poor dressing. The boys' sailor suits would have been passed from child to child and the white pinafores would have been carefully boiled and starched time and time again. The photos of Whippingham are a great contrast to

*Sailor suits and starched pinafores were the order of the day in c.1905.*

Osborne, Cowes,
I.W.
23 May 1895

Sir –
The Government Inspector has examined Whippingham School, and expressed himself highly pleased with everything he saw excepting the convenience for conducting a cookery-class which he considers to be the most important branch of the education of girls.

The attendance at the School was never so good as it has been since The Queen took the School into her own hands, having increased from 83 to 107; and Mr Burrows says that the cookery-class will have to be discontinued altogether unless something can be done in the way of having a kitchen outside, as it is not wholesome for the whole School house, to continue where it is conducted now, viz:– in the classroom for infants. If abandoned, it would have the effect of reducing the Government grant to a considerable extent.

I have gone through the matter with Mr Thompson, and he says that the probable cost of a new building complete would be about £200.

Awaiting your instructions I have the honour to remain, Sir,

Your most obedient servant,
Aug. Blake

Sir J. I Edwards, K.C.B.
Windsor Castle

*The Osborne land steward's report on the Government inspection of the school, 1895.  (THE ROYAL ARCHIVES ©
2005 HER MAJESTY QUEEN ELIZABETH II)*

Above: *The class of girls at Whippingham School, c.1910.*

Left: *The class of older boys at Whippingham School, c.1910.*

*The girls and their teachers with Mr Rogerson, the headmaster, c.1910.*

photos of East Cowes National School children of the same era.

Uffa Fox (later a famous yacht designer) attended Whippingham School with his elder sister Mahala, walking along Beatrice Avenue with other children from East Cowes, and running along the wall of Padmore paddock on the way back. He started at Whippingham in about 1903. He remembered each older child had their own desk which they could lock up if they wished, and in which Uffa kept his conkers, toffees and pens. They had a break of one and a half hours for lunch, when most children went home. However, those from a distance would eat their sandwiches, often under the pine trees. The resinous smell of these trees lingered in his memory.

Uffa enjoyed playing games on the school field, but the boys were much better at cricket than football. Another school beat them at football 10–1, so the Whippingham boys started their cricket training early in the spring. Mr Rogerson coached his boys until they could bowl accurately and very effectively, and bat steadily. The day arrived for the cricket match against the school that had defeated them at football. Whippingham batted first and made 120 runs. Billy Bullimore bowled first for Whippingham, and took four wickets in the first over; Uffa Fox took four wickets in the second over, so the opposition were eight wickets down, having scored nothing. The Whippingham boys had an attack of the giggles at this stage, and it took three more overs to finish off the other school for 13 runs. Revenge had been taken.

The Education Committee decided that the schoolchildren should be taught to swim when they were ten years old, if possible. Whippingham children were marched down to The Folly for their swimming lessons twice a week with Bob Savage, the Folly landlord, in the River Medina. Uffa and a few of his friends were already known to Bob as good swimmers, so they were allowed to swim across the river while Bob taught the other children. It was recorded in the log book on 24 September 1919 that 'Girls attend for swimming instruction at 11 and boys attend at 1.30 as the tide is suitable about mid day.'

Gardening occurred frequently on the timetable for the boys at Whippingham, especially during the First World War. In the school log book for 3 September 1917 it was recorded that 'Boys lifted one and a quarter cwt of late crop potatoes in the school gardens.' Four days later it was recorded that 'Instruction for boys for two hours, mostly planting out winter greens.' On 14 December it was recorded that 'Boys attended to school gardens getting in a load of manure and spreading it over the beds'! In the photograph (above right) it is interesting to note how well dressed the boys are for the job in hand. Many have proper gardening aprons on, and there is an abundance of tools. Perhaps the lady is Miss Ida Thomas, the headmistress.

*All ready for gardening, c.1905.*

Efforts were made to harvest blackberries and chestnuts for the war effort – '23 October 1918. Nearly 2cwt of chestnuts have been gathered by the scholars, and are being used by the army authorities.' On 9 September 1918 the following was recorded:

*Elder girls went out during the afternoon to gather blackberries, by permission of the L.E.A. and the Government Authorities. They were in charge of the assistant mistress Miss Cooke. Miss Thorburn, supplementary teacher, took charge of the junior girls for sewing. Monitors took charge of the infant class. About 10 lbs of blackberries were gathered.*

After the First World War Miss Cooke was the teacher remembered by many. She ruled by the cane and there were frequent punishments. One sulky boy with a hot temper was sometimes locked in a room at the back of the school by Miss Cooke. He kept shouting loudly and all the other children could hear him, including young Phyllis Jolliffe. It was very frightening for the little children, but then on one occasion the miscreant fell silent. He had managed to escape through the window! What happened afterwards was not recorded.

In 1930 Miss Marion (known as Madge) Moody took over as headmistress of the school. She was only 23 years old and was, as Phyllis Jerome (née Jolliffe) put it, 'full of bright new teaching ideas which we enjoyed'. A different regime ensued. Miss Winter was appointed as assistant mistress.

Children attended Whippingham School until they left to go into employment. There may have been the occasional scholarship to Newport Grammar School, but this was rare. However, in 1934 Whippingham became a junior and infants' school only. The main transfer of senior children was to be on 1 April each year and 'would include all children aged 11 or over, and any others who have spent a year or more in standard IV.'

Whippingham shrank overnight to a school of 39 pupils. Miss Winter had charge of the infants, and Miss Moody had the juniors. The school was remembered by everyone as being a very happy place under

*Whippingham School, c.1931. Left to right, back row: Mrs Jackson, Charlie Hinds, ? McBride, Trevor Thomas, Basil Warrior, B. Owens, Cyril Jupe, Charlie Andrews;* third row: *Myra Clancey, Edna Woods, Thelma Snow, Phyllis Hendy, Evelyn Tewkesbury, Queenie Loader, J. Dixon, D. ?;* second row: *Bill Streets, Dorothy Cooke, Mary Johnson, Peggy Rann, Dorothy Daish, Barbara Snow, Peter Salter (?);* front row: *C. Mills, ? Skinner, ? Smith, H. Smith, George Moody, Pat Clancey, Kenneth Hendy, Bob Rann.*

*Miss Moody with the cat and her class in 1932. Left to right, back row: Bob Rann, Jack Trusler, Eric Thorne, Wilf Groves, John Simpson, Ginger Gray, Glanville Dixon;* second row: *Sybil ?, Edie Haddon, Iris Natten, Emily Bennett, Joan Chapman, Miss Moody, Mavis Natten, Phyllis Jolliffe, Beryl Coffin, Dorcas Natten, Betty Aitken;* front row: *Evelyn Tewkesbury, Joan Tewkesbury, Grace Snow, ? Johnson, Edna (Nin) Woods.*

*Whippingham School in 1936.* Left to right, back row: *Miss Winter, Kathleen Fitzpatrick, June Snow, Pansy Johnson, Jean Hardy, Eileen Cooke, Fay Cheeter, Brenda Cheverton, Ena Maskell, Miss Moody;* fourth row: *Ken Perkins, John Warne, Bill Clancey, John Aitken, Ray Thorne, Alan Andrews, Terry Fitzpatrick, Peter Arnold, John Rann, John Perkins, Ian Garrett, Ray Thomas, Ted Foss;* third row: *Aubrey Allen, Peggy Maskell, Nesta Everard, Florence Allen, Jean Graimes, Sheila Cheverton;* second row: *Joy Mosdell, Violet Guy, Ella Browell, Janet Floyd, Winnie Brewer, Myrtle Cass, Sheila Clancey;* front row: *? Wray, ? Green, ? Dawkins, John Snow, Robert Mosdell, Alan Mosdell, Ray Mosdell, John Green.*

*Whippingham School in 1938.* Left to right, back row: *Miss Moody, Janet Floyd, June Wake, June Snow, Nesta Everard, Kathleen Fitzpatrick, Jean Graimes, Florence Allen, Peggy Maskell, Jeanne Harvey, Miss Winter;* fourth row: *Norman Nobbs, Roy Brinton, ? Green, Ian Garrett, David Felton, John Snow, Bill Clancey, John Rann, John McGarrity, Ray Thomas, Ray Mosdell, Ken Perkins, John Warne, ? Green, Eric Heber;* third row: *Ken Mosdell, Enid Maskell, ?, Joy Mosdell, Winnie Brewer, Myrtle Cass, Sheila Clancey, Ella Browell, Margaret Knott, Sheila Cheverton;* second row: *John Roberts, Audrey Appel, Janet Waight, Barbara Phillips, Violet Guy, Theresa Brewer, Brenda Arnold, Mary Chessell;* front row: *?, ? Green, Aubrey Allen, David Warne, Derek Smith, ?, Alan Mosdell, Robert Mosdell.*

*Miss Moody allowed the children to work at their desks under the trees in the summer during the early 1930s.*

*Welsh holiday in June 1933 with Miss Moody and Mr Upward.* Left to right: *John Simpson, Glanville Dixon, Jack Trusler, Eric Thorne, Dorcas Natten, Grace Snow, Mr Upward, Iris Natten, Joan Chapman, Mavis Natten, Phyllis Jolliffe.*

Miss Moody's command, and the expressions on the children's faces in the photographs reflect this.

In 1933 Miss Moody and a local benefactor, Mr Upward, took ten of the children on holiday to North Wales for two weeks. Each child only had to pay ten shillings, all the rest of the trip was paid for. They had a perfect holiday and Grace Davison (née Snow) was later given the log book that the children kept during that holiday.

The proper school log books provide a fascinating glimpse into the life of the school. The book was to be kept by the headteacher, who was to enter anything that deserved to be recorded. Only facts were to be entered, not opinions. Any reasons for closure were to be entered, and 'any deviations from the ordinary routine of the school!'

Thanks to the log book we know that in 1940 tarmacadam paths were laid to the gates, Nurse King called to inspect the heads of the children, and the rector visited, and, in December, 'Workmen are wiring the school for electric light!'

In January 1940 there was a very cold snap. The temperature only rose to 36 degrees in the classroom on 17 January:

*The children were accordingly taken for an hour's sharp walk, and given a hot drink upon their return. No writing lessons were taken today.*
*18 January. Morning walk as yesterday. Classroom temp. 40 degrees. The rector called.*
*19 January. Morning walk. Temp. 41 degrees. Report sent to the Director of Education.*

Mrs Ella Butler remembers the tall cylindrical container with a plunger that made the hot Horlicks drinks for the children. At lunchtimes those children who brought a packed lunch were able to give their pies or jacket potatoes to Miss Moody for her to heat up. The walks included trips to the field below the church where the children could make slides on the steep hill side, warmed up afterwards by Horlicks!

Mrs Grace Davison remembers being a pupil in another winter in the 1930s when Miss Moody took the children down to Barton Manor pond which had frozen over, and the children tried skating during lesson time! One cannot imagine Miss Cooke, her predecessor, doing that, and it probably could not be fitted into the National Curriculum today. Would present-day health and safety regulations permit it?

Some of the comments written by Miss Moody in the log book during the Second World War make poignant reading. Air raids at night made the children very tired, and sometimes they were allowed to sleep during the afternoon. Air raids during school time were catered for by an air-raid shelter located in the centre of the playing-field. Miss Moody did not teach football, so this didn't matter. The children enjoyed playing rounders with her, and there was still plenty of field for that.

The shelter was half underground and accessed by steps. To the right were bench seats along the walls. The sound of the guns just across the main road at Whippingham Battery must have been deafening. Mrs Ella Butler, who started at Whippingham School in 1935, remembered being taught to knit by the light of an oil-lamp while in the shelter. The first task was bedsocks on size one needles and they progressed to red pixie hoods, which involved pearl stitching, and Ella decided she hated knitting!

On the night of 4/5 May 1942 there was a severe blitz on East and West Cowes. Only five children managed to get to school the following morning, and three of the others were never to return. Mary and Vera Chiverton and Joan Abrook had lived at Point Cottages. Bombing to close the road to East Cowes had destroyed their homes. Miss Moody informed the Education Department and received a kind letter back from the Director of Education, asking her to pass his condolences to the parents if she had the opportunity. There was no chance to do this as the whole families had been killed. Gradually the numbers built up again, and school reopened.

The older children were taken out blackberrying for the war effort in September 1941, picking 20lbs of berries. During the expedition one child was bitten on the chin by a sheepdog while he was playing with it!

Another task carried out by the children was the making of camouflage nets for the guns at the battery. They were given large pieces of open

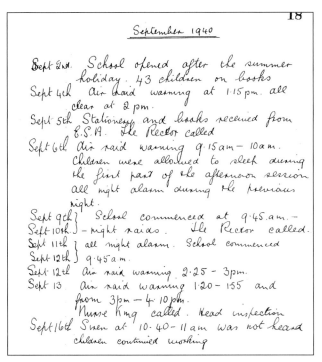

A wartime page from the school log book. (BY KIND PERMISSION OF THE PRESENT HEAD TEACHER)

The Peter Pan play at Christmas in 1932.

Miss Moody 20 years before. Mrs Butler wrote the plays from 1966 to 1985, when she retired. *The Bell that Cried* was performed in 1980, and then there was a play that involved a row of penguins. It had been suggested that they should wear big rubber swimming flippers, but, as they were falling over their own feet anyway as they waddled along, the idea was dropped! The costume mistress at that time was the school secretary, Mrs Bernice Grist, who did an excellent job, even creating costumes for Mole and Ratty in a production of *Wind in the Willows* in 1986. Mrs Butler remembers that one of the best productions was *Jack Frost*. Both she and the children enjoyed doing the Christmas plays, and Mrs Maher has continued the tradition.

In 1950 the present Community Centre was no longer needed by Saunders Roe for their offices. It was purchased from them by the Isle of Wight Council for £3,925 and was used as an annexe by the reception and infants' classes. The kitchens there were used to provide school lunches. The older children were still taught at the 'top' school, and marched in crocodile fashion down to the 'bottom' school at lunchtime.

By 1956 Mr Darrington had joined Miss Moody on the staff. He worked hard on the football skills, and achieved great success, especially considering the small numbers of boys he had to coach compared with some other primary schools on the Island. We have not heard how the cricket got on at this time!

In 1966 Miss Moody retired from teaching at Whippingham School. She had been headmistress for over 35 years. Miss Violet Coull took on the headship, helped in the 1970s and '80s by Mrs Maureen Smith and Mrs Ella Butler.

The number of children in the village or in the catchment area south of Victoria Grove in East Cowes had diminished over the years, and in 1982 it was decided to move all the children onto one site. For a year Mrs Butler taught in a mobile classroom sited in the present Community Centre car park. In 1983 the new extension was completed at the 'top' school and the Community Centre was no longer necessary for use as classrooms. It had been a warm sunny place for the children, with the infants having their own playground. Ted Streets had planted six flowering trees in the grounds to celebrate the Queen's silver

webbing material, and then had to weave khaki and green strips of cloth in and out of the webbing. As soon as each net was completed, two or three children would be sent across the road to the gate at the camp, carrying the net. A sentry would let them in and the net was gratefully received. Then the children would be taken to the sergeants' mess, where there would be a vast array of sweets and chocolate for the children to choose from! There was great incentive for the next net to be completed and a different set of children to visit the camp!

Despite the war, Miss Moody took the children, on foot, to West Cowes Royalty Cinema to see a film.

School plays were written by Miss Moody, who was very keen on theatricals. In May 1960 a pageant was performed. This was to celebrate the centenary of the laying of the foundation-stone at Whippingham Church. The stone had been laid by Queen Victoria, and a message was received by the school on the occasion from her granddaughter, Queen Ena of Spain, who regretted that she was unable to attend.

All the children were superbly costumed. The royal family of Queen Victoria were depicted and then the descendants of each of those children, up to Queen Elizabeth and Prince Phillip. Famous Victorians in politics, medicine, science and literature were depicted, and the history of Whippingham Church, concluding with four of the choirboys who were also pupils. There were no speaking parts as the pageant took place outside in the grounds of the school, with Miss Moody broadcasting a commentary.

The tradition of annual Christmas plays continued. In 1956 Mrs Ella Butler had been brought on to the staff of the school where she had been taught by

*Pupils take part in a nativity play in 1940.* The picture includes: *Norman Nobbs* (Dutch boy on left), *Aubrey Allam and Bruce Carpenter* (two turbaned kings, back left), *Sheila Carpenter* (girl standing between and in front of the kings), *Roy Brinton* (shepherd centre back with crook), *Myrtle Cass* (as 'Mary', seated centre).

*The cast of the 1960 pageant.*

*One of the pageant groups.* Left to right back row: *Diane Hooper (?), Sarah Ball, Jane Charleston, ?, Marcia Lockart, ?, Lindsey Laming (?), Simon Weeks, ?;* front row: *Michael Triggs (?), ?, ?.* *The unknown faces include, Julie Cheshire, Neil Munro, David Johnson.*

Left: *Headmistress Miss Moody on pageant day, 1960.*

Below: *A production of* Snow White and the Seven Dwarfs, *Christmas 1979.* *The group includes: Richard Peters, Ian Dyer and Juliette Allen.*

*The school leavers, summer 1957.* Left to right, back row: *Graham ?, ?, Christopher Matthews, Robin Grist, John Pierce (?), John Saunders, Robin ?;* third row: *Diane Owers (?), Kevin ?, ? Clack, ? Anderson, ? Leal, ?, ?, John Warne, Beryl ?;* second row: *?, Jane Darrington, Miss Webb, Mr Darrington, Miss Moody, Joyce Goodenough, Elizabeth Jackson (?);* front row: *Paul Hutchinson, David Blenkinsop, Brian Chessell, Stuart Needham, Michael Weeks, Roger Nicholls.*

*The football team, 1956/57.* Left to right, back row: *Michael Kemp, Roger Nicholls, David Burrows;* middle row: *Mr Darrington, Brian Gurney, Christopher Matthews, John Saunders;* front row: *Michael Weeks, Ian Wilson, David Blenkinsop, Brian Chessell, Stuart Needham, Kevin ?, John Oakley (?).*

Right: *The 1963/64 football team.* Left to right, back row, standing: *Simon Weeks, Tug Wilson, Tim Cato, ?, ?, Brian Butler;* middle row, seated: *Phil Underwood, ?, Roy Foster, Chris Norris, Steve Trigg;* front row: *Mark Weeks, ?, Barry Hayward, Paul Blenkinsop, ? Denny.*

*The football team, 1965/66.* Left to right, back row: *Phillip Jones, ?, Alan True, Robert Graham, Ken Clack;* front row: *Malcolm White, Chris Smith, Kevin Harris, William Gillespie, Simon Quigley, Mark Weeks.*

*League and cup winners, 1964/65.* Left to right, back row: *Alan Cramp, Lawrence Woodford, Brian Butler, Chris Gardiner, David Morey;* front row: *Chris Smith, Robert Crocker, Paul Blenkinsop, ? Denny, Tim Cato, Kevin Harris, Mark Weeks.*

*The first extension, 1984, with Derek and Helen Burdett.*

*The second extension in 1996.*

*The school from the west in 1996.*

*The ancillary staff in 1987 in Victorian costume.* **Left to right:** *Mrs Grist, Mrs Phillips, Mrs Woodward, Mrs Searle, Mrs Saint, Mrs Davison.*

Right: *The staff and pupils dressed as Victorians in 1987.*

Below right: *Waiting for the Queen to arrive in 1987.*

Below: *Her Majesty Queen Elizabeth II stops at Whippingham School to receive a posy in 1987.*

Above: *Children wearing their golden jubilee crowns.*

Left: *The school staff at Miss Coull's retirement party.* Left to right, back row: *Mrs Joan Crowhurst, Mrs Barbara Phillips, Mrs Joyce Saint, Mrs Bernice Grist, Mrs Woodward;* front row: *Mrs Ella Butler (deputy head), Miss Violet Coull (headmistress), Mrs Maureen Smith (reception class teacher).*

jubilee in 1977, as the oldest of the local 'ex-Whippingham School' pupils. He had left school in 1903, aged 14.

There were great advantages of having the school on one site again, and in a building designed by the county architect, Mike Rainey. The extension copied external features of the original school and provided a completely new classroom for the top class, and new cloakrooms and a new classroom were formed between the new part and the old.

In 1985 Miss Coull retired as headmistress. Her place was taken by Mrs Viv Maher. Over time the numbers on the roll started increasing until three mobile classrooms were in use on the playground. So in 1995/6 major remodelling took place, again sympathetically designed by Rainey Petrie. The major task was to build a new school hall and kitchens, so that the old hall could be divided properly into two classrooms. Another classroom was also added, with a new head teacher's office and secretary's reception area. The result was an excellent extension giving far more space for the children and better working areas. The square hall has many advantages over the old long narrow rectangular one for many activities.

Many interesting events have taken place at Whippingham School since Mrs Maher began in 1983. Several have had a royal theme. One of these was the visit of Queen Elizabeth II to the Island in 1987. The whole school spent a week studying life at school in Victorian times, with all the children dressed in costume. The Queen was scheduled to drive past the school on her way to Osborne House, and agreed to receive a posy. Many past pupils availed themselves of this opportunity to see their monarch stop outside 'Queen Victoria's school', and joined the crowd of Whippingham folk there.

The golden jubilee of Queen Elizabeth II was celebrated in 2002 with a picnic tea at the school, to which many of the village residents were invited. Tables decked in red, white and blue were set out for the children, all of whom wore homemade crowns and

enjoyed waving their flags. An exhibition of old school photographs was set out in the hall and received considerable interest. The children demonstrated maypole dancing and various trees were planted, the first being a red oak, planted by Bill Allcock.

In 2004 the school celebrated the 140th anniversary of its opening by Queen Victoria, and pupils spent time dressing and working as the pupils would have done in 1864, albeit surrounded by modern technological gadgetry. The children found it an interesting experience to have to sit in rows and work silently, stand up when a visitor entered the room, and to see their head teacher walking around with a cane. At least one child was reduced to tears by a simple verbal reprimand! Living history in action! The author was invited to attend as 'Queen Victoria' and, helped by two of the children, planted a maple tree.

The environmental area at school was created soon after the first extension, but like all gardens it needed revamping after a few years. New fencing had to be erected and the pond relined. Additional habitats were added and a class-sized hut erected by the decking overlooking the pool. The whole project was helped by a BTCV grant and opened in 2004.

The annual school fête usually takes place in July. It had a Victorian theme in 1987. This fête, and the

*Maypole dancing for the jubilee celebrations in 2002.*

*Mrs Anne Burdett as Queen Victoria at the school fête in 1987, with Mairie Meek helping, and Heather Meek and other pupils.*

*Two of the remaining school chimneys, symbol of the play centre.*

Christmas Fayre, have always provided funds for school trips, additional equipment and the Christmas party! Sports day too occurs in the summer, out on the field surrounded by the pine trees. New pine trees were planted in 1983 as replacements for those 1863 trees which had fallen, and these have reached quite a size by 2006.

On the Beatrice Avenue side of the school two mobile classrooms provide the home for 'Chimneys', the educational play centre. This has been operating since 1996, accommodating up to 35 children. The children can begin at Chimneys from the age of two years ten months, leaving when they start primary school, which may or may not be at Whippingham. The centre is self-funded and owned by Mrs Mandy Thorne, who has been there since its beginning. The aim is to make learning fun and make the transfer from pre-school to school easier for the child, by providing high-quality care and education. On Fridays only the older children attend, when they have the opportunity to go into the school assembly. Government funding is now available for all children after their third birthday to have five two-and-a-half-hour sessions of nursery education each school week. 'Chimneys' takes its name from the ornate chimney-pots that once graced every chimney on the school. Sadly few remain in situ today.

At the primary school in 2005 there were 140 children, with number set to rise in 2006. Not all are from Whippingham – a number are from East Cowes and Wootton. There are a few who walk to school, but many arrive by car – 140 years ago all the children would have walked, some from as far as Wootton, as the Queen had land on the far side of Palmer's Brook. Rain or shine, whatever the weather, Vicky Snow's mother walked down the hill to King's Quay, over a footbridge that used to be there, and up through both Woodhouse Farm and Barton Farm to get to school, perhaps an hour's walk. In the 1980s the children living at East Cowes were put on the bus by the

school and then made their own way home.

Mrs Viv Maher was still the headmistress in 2005. Each class now has a teaching assistant, and other specialists assist throughout the school. Recent past pupils will remember Mrs Christopher and Mrs Windsor, both of whom are now head teachers at other Island primary schools.

Whippingham School continues to go from strength to strength. In 1996, after 148 years, the old blackboards and chalk were replaced by white boards and felt-tip markers. Just nine years later the school passed into the electronic age, when white boards that also act as large computer screens were installed, called interactive boards. We wonder what will have happened to the school in 100 years' time!

*The school staff in 2004. Left to right, back row: Carrie Viney (student), Sally Stockley (teaching assistant), Wendy Skinner (TA), Carol Rackett (TA), Ruth Adams (special-needs assistant); middle row: Tracey McNeil (parent), Anna Jones (TA), Cheryl Brazer (TA), Di Blake (helper), Paula Matthews (ICT TA), Angie Cooch (TA); front row: Angie Selle (secretary), Wendy Denham (Year 4 teacher), Jeanette Millward (deputy head, Year 2 teacher), Viv Maher (head teacher), Nicci Billington (Year 1 teacher), Ruth Hitchman (Year 3 teacher), Vicky Jones (reception-class teacher).*

# Chapter 12

# The River Medina, Oysters, Tide-Mill & Marina, Roses & Railways

## Oysters

The River Medina stretches for three miles between Cowes and Newport, and is tidal. Extensive mudflats are revealed at low tide, when it is impossible to take a boat of any description other than a canoe up to Newport. At very low tides it is even possible to walk across the river at Folly, as Sea Scouts found out (and they didn't mind getting muddy!).

In 2006 the division between Cowes and Newport Harbour Authorities is The Folly pontoon. Boats can travel freely up and down the river when they have sufficient water, and have always been allowed to do so. Whenever a boat moors up, however, the appropriate harbour authority takes its fee.

In the past, taxes were also liable on goods brought into the towns, and in the late 1600s Newport folk complained to Parliament that they were losing dues as East Cowes was being favoured by shipping. Parliament did nothing, so Newport bought their own quay at East Cowes and charged ships to use it!

Newport also decided that they wanted the rights of usage of the river. Instead of anybody being allowed to fish the river for their own food, they sold a lease in 1711 to William Cave, so only he could fish there. This annoyed a lot of the local inhabitants, some of whom were oyster fishermen. John Redstone and Edward Faulkner were among these. They were using Claybrooks Luck [stream] for their oysters by permission of Mr Leigh at Heathfield Farm and Mr Barnard at Claybrooks Farm. This stream equates to the Island Harbour Marina today.

William Cave was under the impression that his new lease from the Borough of Newport gave him the rights to Claybrooks Luck so he took a pot shot at the oyster fisherman and confiscated his oysters. The case went to court, and Redstone and Faulkner's case makes amusing reading:

*In the Parish of Whippingham there is a Rivelett of water that Runneth into this... River... it runneth between the said farmlands called Claybrooks and Heathfield and since time out of mind the owners of those farmlands having always fished there and catcht Fish there without lett or molestation they have lately granted by lease all their Royalty and Right of Fishery of the said Lucke to the said John Redston and Edward Faulkner who have lately throwed into the said Lucke a great many thousands of Oysters that cost them a great*

*deal of money and because those oysters growe fatt and large in the said Lucke... Cave the defendant pretends the Lucke doth belong to him.*

*On the 1st of September 1711 Edward King did Dragg and Catch for the plaintiffs Two Thousand of Oysters in the said Lucke and while he was in the said Lucke the Defendant fired a gun which might have endangered his life some of the shot falling a very little distance from him and as the said King was Rowing in a boat with the said Oysters to Carry them to the plaintiffs at Newport the Defendant Cave... took away his said two thousand of Oysters...*

What happened to the oysters in Great Luck, as the creek became known, and Redstone and Faulkner's case, we have yet to establish, but the Harbour Authorities to this day have the right to lease out the main river for oyster fisheries.

It was reported in the *Isle of Wight Herald* on 30 November 1867 that:

*For many years the oysters of the Medina have been noted and declared the best in England. Scarcely a day but that large quantities of oysters are forwarded to London and other parts of England.*

We know there was an Oyster Company in the 1860s, oysters were being farmed in 1711, and probably for many hundreds of years before that. In fact, it may have been during the time of the Romans that oysters were first farmed on the Medina.

Sadly the last Oyster Company on the Medina closed down in 2005, partly because there has been little protection of their oyster areas. At the time of writing oyster fishing is still carried out in season by a few people on the Medina. The river is classed as B-grade water, so the oysters have to be sold to dealers who either put the oysters in grade A water for six weeks or treat them with ultra-violet light to kill off any impurities before selling them.

## East Medina Mill

In 1790 William Porter had a causeway built across the mouth of Claybrooks, or Great Luck and its smaller luck to the south. He was a Newport baker, and he then constructed a tide-mill where the streams ran into the Medina. This was not a small affair, but a major undertaking, for which he obtained loans from a bank. It was the time of the

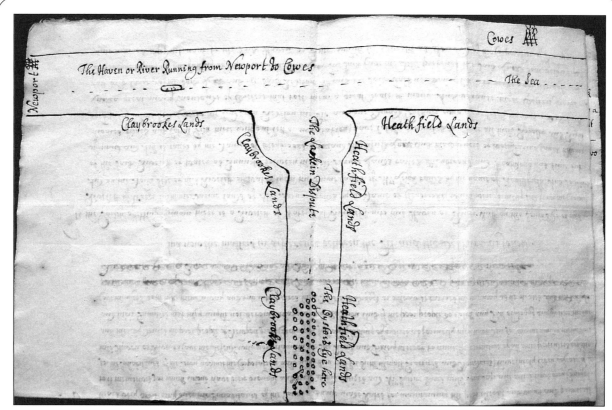

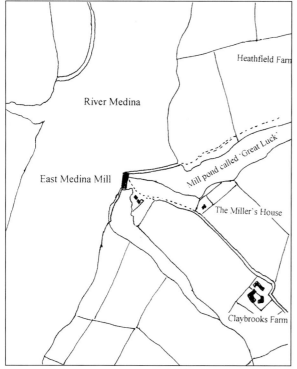

Above: *A map drawn in 1711, showing the disputed oyster-beds in the luck between Heathfield land and Claybrooks land.* (REPRODUCED COURTESY THE COUNTY RECORDS OFFICE, NEWPORT)

Below: *East Medina Mill in 1936.* (R. ADAMS)

Above: *A map of East Medina Mill drawn from the 1841 tithe map.*

Right: *Derelict parts of the mill-wheel after the demolition of the building.*

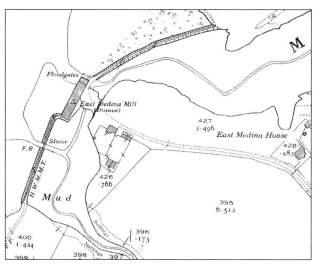

*The disused mill, shown on a 1939 map. (Reproduced from the 1939 Ordnance Survey Map by kind permission of the Ordnance Survey)*

Napoleonic wars and many troops were quartered locally at Parkhurst. These soldiers needed flour and bread, as did the men on ships moored in the Solent waiting to sail to war or the new convict colonies in Australia. Grain travels better than flour, so it was necessary to import grain to cash in on feeding this hungry market. At least five other tide-mills were built on the Island at around this time.

Mr Porter built a mill on the east side of the Medina, and another on the opposite bank a little further south. East Medina Mill was 300 feet long (almost 100 metres), 30 feet wide and three storeys tall, with an attic floor above that. The mill itself was ten bays long and the adjacent storehouse eight bays. Unfortunately, Mr Porter was not sufficiently well financed and the banks who had previously supported him withdrew their funding. Within a year Mr Porter had died and the buildings were left empty.

Certain foreign mercenary troops, known as 'Hessians', from the German state of Hesse, were enlisted into the British Army. They were quartered at East Medina Mill storehouse at about this time, but sadly over 70 people died there in a typhoid epidemic. The story is that the bodies were carried along the footpath beside the river and buried at Whippingham churchyard. Later Queen Victoria's daughter Alice married into the royal family of Hesse, and on hearing the story a plaque was erected at the church to the Hessian soldiers. In the Napoleonic war in early 1800 French soldiers were barracked at East Medina Mill storehouse as prisoners of war.

By 1799 the mill was owned by William Roach, with James Roach running it. The building, kiln and machinery were valued for insurance purposes for £2,000, which was a considerable sum in those days. The Roach family continued to run the mill for the next 140 years, until it closed in 1939.

By 1850 many of the troops had left the Island and milling began to decline. Mr Roach put in new

milling machinery at East Medina Mill, made by Armfields, to improve his productivity over that of some of his competitors, and thus stayed in business.

The principle of the tide-mill was simple – the tide was allowed to flow freely into the two millponds and when high water was reached and the ponds were full the sluices were shut. The water-wheel was a low breast-shot wheel which operated as the tide flowed out of the millponds. It could only turn on the ebb tide because of the shape of the buckets. This wheel, which was 15 feet 6 inches in diameter (almost five metres), and over six feet wide had 30 buckets to catch the water and turn the wheel. The main wheel turned the pit wheel, which was also mounted on the main shaft. The main upright shaft drove all the mill machinery, including the millstones, and was turned by the wallower engaging with the pit wheel. The lock into the marina today stands on the site of the old water-wheel. In the old days the water-wheel was covered by a wooden lean-to building.

To see a tide-mill working today we have only to go over to Eling on the west side of Southampton Water. This is the only remaining tide-mill operational in Britain, restored and milling stone-ground flour just as would have been done at East Medina Mill.

For the next 80 years work continued at the mill, until in January 1930 there was a severe storm which caused a considerable amount of damage. The storehouse roof was lifted off by the hurricane-force winds and hurled through the air. The portion of roof was about 90 feet by 30 feet (30m by 10m) and it landed about 40 yards away (35m), crushing the mill cottages and other buildings. Luckily nobody was hurt, but the two semi-detached cottages suffered badly, the roof being almost totally demolished, with holes and cracks appearing in the walls. Mr and Mrs Phillips, who were inside one of the cottages at the time, had a lucky escape, and their neighbours were away.

After 1930 Viv Thomas remembers going to the mill to collect meal for the hens. The noise of the creaking machinery in the mill, cog against cog, wheel against wheel, has remained in his memory. The mill struggled on until war came in 1939, when the machinery stopped for the last time. The Borough of Newport obtained the mill and used it as a store for waste material that had been collected for the war effort. At some time after this the mill caught fire and half of it was burnt. It remained derelict until 1950 when it was demolished. During this time a firm called Southern Aircraft (Gatwick) leased the land in order to set up a factory for building aircraft, a project that did not materialise.

The miller's house, however, did survive. Built of local red brick, one wonders whether the kiln mentioned in the inventory for the insurance in 1799 was in fact a brick kiln and the bricks were made on site to build both the house and the very large mill. No evidence has been found to support this, apart from that word 'kiln'.

*The marina in 1972, with fixed pontoons.*

*The departure of the* Medway Queen, *passing* Folly *stern first on her way back to Kent for restoration in 1984.*

The miller's house has a definite Georgian look to it and is Grade II listed. Driving by car past the building in 2006, it is little noticed behind the trees and hedges on the right as one enters the marina, a small reminder of East Medina Mill.

## The Marina

In the middle of the 1960s a consortium of local people leased the site to build a marina. In 1965 the marina opened, known the following year as 'The Medway Queen Marina', after the name of the paddle-steamer berthed there, changing its name by 1971 to 'Wight Marina'. The name changed again some years later to 'Island Harbour'. Initially, six fixed concrete jetties were provided for boats. These were not all that successful as occasionally there was a problem with the lock gates which lost water, leaving boats hung up on their moorings! Floating pontoons have replaced the jetties. The lock gates run on old Second World War tank wheels and enable boats to enter or leave for up to three and a half hours either side of high water. Good shower and toilet facilities were provided, and it was intended to provide a swimming-pool, general store, chandlery, squash and tennis-courts. Of these extras, only the chandlery materialised.

*The Medway Queen* paddle-steamer was bought in 1965 and formed a clubhouse for the marina. She had spent her working life, from 1924 to 1963, as an excursion steamer in the Thames and Medway areas. During the war she was used in the Dunkirk evacuation, rescuing about 7,000 troops in seven trips. By 1972 the *Medway* needed numerous buckets to catch the drips of rainwater seeping through the uncaulked deck into the lounge when it was raining, and in about 1979 she was removed from the smaller millpond to the river in an effort by the Paddle Steamer Preservation Society (PSPS) to return her to the Medway for restoration. Unfortunately she immediately sank in the mud and it was not until she was lined with cement that she could be floated sufficiently to be put onto a pontoon in 1984 and towed back to the Medway, where she has been restored.

In 1970 A.H. and C.B. Ridett bought the last paddle-steamer to be used on the Ryde to Portsmouth route, called the *Ryde*. She was built in 1937 for Southern Railway by William Denny & Sons of Dumbarton. At 225 feet long, with a gross tonnage of 566 tonnes, she had a passenger capacity of 1,011. She saw service in the Royal Navy during the Second World War, being used for minesweeping duties in the Firth of Forth. After the war she came back to the Solent and operated for British Rail on the Ryde to Portsmouth route until 1969. She was renamed *Ryde Queen* and was put on a mud berth ahead of the already popular *Medway Queen* and was opened as a discotheque.

By 1972 the *Ryde* was leased by Trusthouse Forte plc and turned into a floating hotel, or 'boatel'. Luxuriously fitted cabins were provided for 33 people, along with a classy restaurant seating 100 people. A bar on the saloon deck had panoramic views of the river and marina. Below the restaurant there was a dance floor and further bar. The engines were exposed, with their gleaming brass rods and shining mechanism.

Regrettably the boatel did not prove as popular as had been hoped, despite the good food, accommodation and position. Trusthouse Forte pulled out, and the discotheque moved into the *Ryde*. In 1977 a fire caused damage to the vessel. At this point the company running the disco on behalf of the owners could not afford to carry on. The fire damage was repaired, but economics forced closure soon afterwards. Since then a number of changes in ownership of the marina and the *Ryde* have generated difficulties for the vessel and made any preservation efforts extremely expensive. A rescue effort was mounted by the PSPS, but negotiations with the owners broke down and work stopped. At the time of writing the *Ryde* is in a very poor state of repair and any chance of restoration looks very doubtful.

On the marina side of things, a new watch-tower and lock-operating office was built in the shape of an enormous mushroom and a 'bistro' arrived. Richardsons moved in, providing not only the chan-

**WIGHT MARINA**

EAST MEDINA MILL.
Nr COWES.
NEWPORT. ISLE OF WIGHT.
Telephone: NEWPORT 4751.

Above: *An aerial view of the marina site on a brochure early in the 1970s. The* Medway Queen *can be seen behind the* Ryde Queen.

Above: *The* Medway Queen *as a nightclub, early 1970s.*

Below: *The* Medway Queen *stranded on the mud in 1981.*

Below right: *A view of the restaurant on the* Ryde Queen *'boatel' in 1972.*

Below: *Accommodation onboard the* Ryde Queen *'boatel' in 1972.*

*The marina office and lock-control tower with the deteriorating* Ryde Queen *behind, 2005.*

*An old ammunition barge rotting away, 2005.*

dlery for those working on their own boats, but a comprehensive yacht-repair facility and cranes to lift out boats of up to 18 tons. If you need a particular part for your boat, then this family concern will be able to provide it for you. Many people store their boats ashore to work on during the winter beside the rusting hulk of the *Ryde*, which provides them with a stark reminder of the ravages of weather on a vessel that is not maintained.

On the mudflats near the marina are the remains of various craft, most only visible at low water, rotting slowly away. The wreck located to the north of the marina is that of an old ammunition barge. Probably built during the First World War, it was typical of the type used to supply Naval ships. It was acquired from Portsmouth Dockyard in 1939 and berthed at Fred Dinnis's yard in Cowes. Even then it was in a poor state and shipping water. It was towed away and beached upriver where it has remained ever since. It was never graced with a name, only a number.

The second wreck lies alongside the marina wall in front of the control tower to the south of the lock entrance. Barely visible in the mud are the remains of

an ex-government barge. In the early 1970s it was used as a teashop and acquired the name *Regal Queen*. It was eventually neglected and is partly broken up.

The third wreck outside the marina opposite the *Ryde* is that of a three-masted Baltic trader, the *Star Pictor*. She was built in about 1912. Wayne Pritchett, the Newport harbourmaster, remembers seeing her in Southampton in 1971 with a completely new mizzen mast. She moved to the mud berth outside the marina in the mid-1970s and was given the name *Svarto*, which the owner claimed was her first name. In the early 1980s she caught fire and her life came to an end.

During the 1990s yachtsmen's cottages have been built alongside Great Luck (the old name of the marina inlet). Further building continues. These have their own moorings, so more pontoon berths have been constructed. All those either living there or visiting the marina in their boats have the benefit of the beautiful countryside with a rich diversity of birds, of which more than 50 species can readily be seen. A kingfisher would whistle a warning and then fly over the marina at about half past four every afternoon 30 years ago. His descendants are still seen today.

*Some fixed pontoons remain, but the marina and lock were undergoing reconstruction in 1981. The first lock-control tower can be seen, with the miller's house in the distance.*

*The wreck of the* Star Pictor, *2005.*

# Roads

In the 1700s the local landholders had to pay for the upkeep of the roads that passed through or next to their land. There were Highways Commissioners who kept accounts of the money expended, and organised the necessary work. The account books are held at the County Records Office. Some of the names of the people who were employed for work on the highway are repeated several times, such as Jn. Moors, Jas. Davis, Wm. Guy, Wm. Burnett, Jas. Keats and Mary Young. Mary picked a lot of stones, probably from the fields. She was paid 4d. a load.

The accounts give us some idea of the methods used for road construction. Larger stones went down first, followed by gravel. There was a gravel pit at the top of Victoria Grove, another in the field north of Whippingham Church and one by Alverstone old farmhouse. William Guy was a labourer who dug much of the gravel. An entry from July 1793 reads 'Wm. Guy for digging 86 loads of gravel at 4d. a load – paid £1.8s.6d.' A load meant one full cart. James Davis was being paid 1s. a day for work on the highways, some of which involved spreading the gravel. John Walker of Padmore was paid for carting five loads of gravel at 2s.6d. a load. John Ralph of Truckles was paid 3s. a load for carting four loads of stones. Sand and stones were also carted from the seashore.

Ditches were dug either side of the road, and in places a 'bunny' or drain was made across inclined roads to help prevent rain washing away the surface. James Masters was paid 2s.6d. for making a bunny across the road in 1792.

Hedges, fences and gates were also attended to. Thos. Dashwood was paid 6s. for 'carpenters work'. In 1794 '3 lugs of Frith' were used to make the hedge in Clavells Lane, costing 7s.6d., and 100 thorn plants costing just 8d. This work was needed after the road had been widened at Clavells. Clavells Lane probably became Mount Road.

The assessment for payment to the highways in 1801 listed J. Rolf at Barton and Woodhouse, Barrington at Osborne, J. Walker at Kingston and Great and Little Padmore, Nick Smith at Alverstone, A. Abraham at Padmore, R. Whitmaich at South Heathfield, G. Read at North Heathfield and J. Ralph at Truckles.

In 1813 there was an act of parliament which enabled the Highways Commissioners to collect contributions for upkeep from those who used the roads. Tolls could be introduced to fund the reconstruction of the surface, and a gate put across the road. A toll keeper was paid to open the gate and he was provided with accommodation. The main road into East Cowes became a toll road, with the toll gate situated just to the south of the Prince of Wales Inn, where the garage is in 2006. George Guy was the toll keeper. His cottage was enhanced by the building of a privy in 1814! Three years later James Guy became the toll keeper.

The main road of 2006 was the main road then. In fact, there is an interesting minute in 1822 in the Highways Commissioners Book: 'Is the road at Whippingham between Padmore and Kingston Farms repairable? Is it a public road?' This refers to Beatrice Avenue, which does not appear on early maps.

By the time Queen Victoria arrived at Whippingham the roads were adequate for her. The royal couple bought up much of the surrounding land and then set about improving the roads within the estate. A total of 20 miles of private drives were created, such as Mount Road from Coburg, to pass Primrose Cottage to Alverstone Lodge. Ditches were dug at the sides of the drives, and the surface kept smoothly gravelled.

Albert also set about re-routing the public highway, Alverstone Road. Coming from the Forge, one travelled about 100 yards before bending left to reach Mount Road near Coburg Cottage. This road was closed off, and only a footpath remains. In 1858 a new road was created to continue Alverstone Road to join directly with Brock's Copse Road at the triangle. The old field boundaries can still be seen, creating odd-shaped fields, waymarked by some large old dying oaks to the north. This gave more privacy to the estate and the impressive gate pillars were constructed at the two entrances to the Queen's Barton and Woodhouse estate, either side of Alverstone Lodge. The Brock's Copse Road also received attention from Osborne estate workers, being levelled, the valley raised, and the road widened through the copse.

Before 1900 there was no road to The Folly. Access had been by boat or by foot across the fields. When a road was created to The Folly Inn and the aircraft sheds of Sam Saunders in 1914, it ran beside a Padmore field boundary. There were large oak trees in this hedge. During the Second World War The Folly Works employed many people, buses bringing them in from various parts of the Island. The road was still gravel at this time. A passing-place was needed in the single-track road, and so one of the large old oak trees became a traffic island. It stood the test of time and increased traffic for another 60 years, but finally in 2004 it became so dangerous that it had to be felled. A new sapling was planted in its place, although it succumbed to the dry summer of 2005. However, in 2006 shoots are appearing from the original Folly oak, and two more saplings have been planted.

Folly Road is still a private road, not adopted by the council. Speed ramps were put in place in the mid-1970s to slow cars. The first casualty on these was Anne Burdett. Not realising the first ramp had been installed by the oak while she was shopping in East Cowes, she flew off her bicycle as she whizzed downhill and received severe bruising!

The main Whippingham Road was once a gentle gravel track, before the days of the internal combustion

*A pavement was installed from Folly Lane to the school in 1948.*

engine. There were no footpaths beside the road, and it was not until the Women's Institute instigated a traffic count in 1948 that something was done about a pavement. The WI found that about 300 vehicles, excluding bicycles, passed the school between 5.30 and 6p.m. on a week day. They asked for, and received, a footpath between Folly Lane and the school, where the bus stops are. The footpath was continued into East Cowes in about 1981.

A traffic count was carried out on the main road near the school in 2005. It revealed that almost 1,200 vehicles (excluding bicycles) passed in the peak time – quite a few more than in 1948.

Sadly, there have been accidents at Whippingham. Nin Woods was killed when she came off her bicycle riding down Alverstone Lane above Alverstone new farm shortly before the Second World War. She was just 17 years old. The bend of Whippingham Road was reduced at the Heights after a fatal accident, and pedestrian islands installed there after a further accident. Street lighting was installed by the entrance to Barton Manor after an accident involving a pedestrian. For many years local people have been asking for a 30mph speed restriction by the school, but so far only a 40mph limit has been achieved. The latest news in 2006 is that there may be a 20mph limit in the near future! Courageous 'lollipop' ladies, or gentlemen, have helped children across the main road to school for over 30 years. Hopefully there will be no more accidents on this extremely busy stretch of road.

## Whippingham Railway Station

The Ryde and Newport Railway Company constructed a station on their line at the nearest point to Osborne House, two and a half miles away. The village of Whippingham was over a mile away. The idea that the building was for the exclusive use of the royal family can be eliminated, as it is believed that the Queen herself only used the station once. However, many members of the Queen's court and government travelled by train to Portsmouth, ferry to Ryde and then took the train to Whippingham. A carriage could easily be sent to collect them from Osborne. A private drive was made through the Queen's land and the distinctive entrance lodge with the royal cyphers still stands at the time of writing on the Ryde side of the crematorium roundabout.

The station was opened on 20 December 1875. The building was a mirror image of Ashey Station, and both appeared much too large for the communities they served. The station had a roomy two-storey building consisting of a stationmaster's house, booking-office and signal-box, waiting-room, ladies waiting-room and toilet, men's toilet and a luggage room. There was single platform 235 feet long and a short siding (172 feet) towards Newport.

When initially opened there were seven trains each way on weekdays and four on Sundays. Trains would only stop on request at Whippingham, and the station was announced as 'Whippingham for Osborne!'

In 1887 the Ryde and Newport Railway amalgamated with other lines to form the Isle of Wight Central Railway. A local gentleman by the name of Henry Pinnock took over as chairman of the railway, having been a director of the Ryde and Newport Railway. He built Belmont Farm on top of the hill above Whippingham Station. The bridge over Belmont Lane at Binfield Corner was called Pinnock's Bridge. At the start of Mill Lane, down to the marina, are two cottages proudly sporting 'H.P.' in their brickwork, for Henry Pinnock.

Mrs Emily Merwood, the wife of James, a railwayman, was given the position of stationmistress in the late 1890s. The couple had been living at the station house for about ten years, and George Merwood, perhaps a relative, had been stationmaster, possibly looking after other stations as well. Emily Merwood adopted a white starched pinafore for her uniform, worn over a functional black dress, with a straw boater on her head. Various postcards of her were produced, including one where she is holding a staff. She was immensely proud of being in sole charge of the station. A ladies' journal of the time reported that it would have been a brave man who would presume to offer Mrs Merwood assistance, so strong, capable and alert was she. Her civility was praised as being an example to all. She had a large black dog called 'Snuff'. She was a busy woman between trains, keeping the station clean, the flower-beds and hedges neat, selling tickets, working the signals, answering the newly-installed telephone and, in winter, keeping a good fire burning in the waiting-room. Mrs Merwood retired in 1912 at the age of 69, but continued to live at the station house with her husband and look after the new stationmaster, James Cooper. Emily died in 1929.

In 1912 a crossing loop was installed operated by an 11-lever signal frame. A new 242-foot down platform was built, complete with a second-hand shelter, possibly an old signal-box from Wootton!

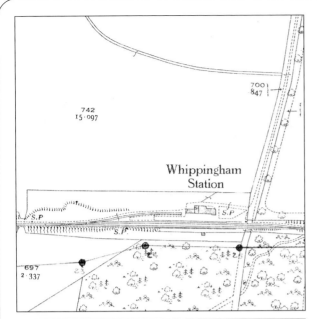

Top: *The 1939 map showing the station.* (REPRODUCED BY KIND PERMISSION OF THE ORDNANCE SURVEY)

Above: *A train coming in from Ryde in the 1930s.* (ANDREW BRITTON COLLECTION)

*Mrs Merwood was stationmaster at Whippingham from 1900 to 1912.*

*The train to Ryde at Whippingham Station, 1933. Note the milk churn on the other platform.* (ANDREW BRITTON COLLECTION)

*Whippingham Station in the 1920s.*

*Station personnel in the 1920s.* **Left to right:** *Signalman Lewis, Ben Steadman and Jim Hooper.*

*George Edwards waiting to hand over the single-line token to the driver of the next train to arrive, 1920s.*

*Phyllis Jolliffe and her mother on the platform, just returned from Newport, c.1921.*

In 1917 George Henry Edwards became the station-master. Among her recollections of life at Whippingham Station his daughter, Mrs Marjorie Smith, recalls how the Royal Naval College provided customers in the years 1903–21. She remembered the young Louis Mountbatten, who always used the railway just as an ordinary passenger. Other recollections included the many heated conversations between Whippingham Station and Newport 'A' signal-box, where the signalman would often give preference to boats on the Medina River by opening the drawbridge rather than pass trains from Whippingham. Another of her memories was helping her father to light the oil-lamps along the platform at dusk and watching a fox trotting along the platform. These memories are recorded in volume four of *Once Upon a Line* by Andrew Britton. Mr Edwards enjoyed taking photographs and snapped young Phyllis Jolliffe and her

mother one day as they returned from Newport.

In the late 1930s, pigeon racing was popular. Roy Brinton remembers the baskets of pigeons being unloaded onto Whippingham Station platform from the guard's van of the train. At a certain time, the stationmaster would give the signal, and Roy and his friends would rapidly open all the cage doors and release the pigeons to fly back to their home lofts.

The Isle of Wight Central Railway was absorbed into the Southern Railway in 1923, and finally became part of British Railways on nationalisation in 1948. The station was only to remain open for another five years, as it closed 21 September 1953. Trains continued to run past the deserted platform on their way to Newport and Cowes. The loop was removed in 1956. Finally, the Ryde to Newport line fell under the Beeching axe, and the last train passed Whippingham on 21 February 1966.

*A shot taken on 19 February 1966 of the 10.18 train from Ryde passing Whippingham Station two days before the closure of the line. (DAVID PETERS)*

117

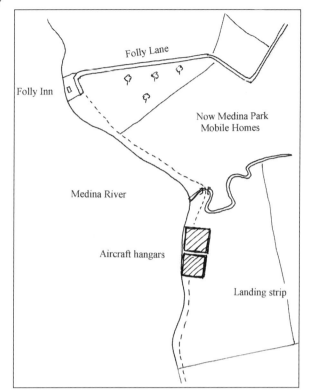

Above: *The Ravaud Aero-Hydroplane with the aircraft hangar being built behind it in 1910.*

Left: *The site of first aircraft works and airstrip, 1910–16.*

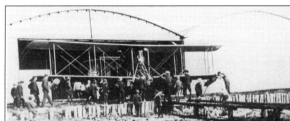

Left: *The Heathfield sheds and the Sopwith Bat Boat being launched in 1913.*

*The prizewinning Sopwith Bat Boat at East Cowes in 1913.*

# Chapter 13

# Sam Saunders

In 1890 Sam Saunders was running a firm constructing beautiful steam launches for the wealthy people who wished to go boating on the Thames. He moved his centre of operations to West Cowes in 1906, then bought a redundant boat work-shed next to the esplanade in East Cowes, where he set about building fast petrol-driven launches for use on the Solent. One shed rapidly expanded to many sheds, and in 1935 the large Columbine Factory was built on the site.

The year 1906 was a time of rapid technological advances – man had just taken to the air and the internal-combustion engine was here to stay. Sam Saunders and his team of designers were developing new methods of travel.

## The Heathfield Aircraft Sheds and Airstrip

In 1909 Sam Saunders announced that he had formed a new department to design and build 'everything required for aero-navigation'. He constructed two large (6,000 square foot) lightweight aircraft hangars on the east bank of the Medina just south of The Folly Inn and the present-day mobile-home site. In 2006, walking south along the river bank from the caravan site, a little stream is crossed by a wooden bridge, and the path leads into the field which once housed the aircraft hangars next to the river. This field, then part of Heathfield Farm, was large and flat enough for a rudimentary airfield to be made.

The first craft that Sam was involved in, however, was a surface-skimming hydrofoil designed by a Frenchman, Ravaud. Called the Ravaud Aero-Hydroplane, it was built at the Heathfield sheds in 1910, and must have caused a stir motoring up and down the Medina in the tests during early 1911.

Sam had patented a very strong type of plywood sewn together with copper wire. This was called Consuta. It was used in the construction of not only his motor launches, but also of the bodies of these early hydrofoils and planes that he built. Consuta was still being used in the 1930s.

In 1913 the Sopwith Bat Boat was assembled and tested from the Heathfield sheds. This was an amphibious plane, designed by Tommy Sopwith, and it proved to be very successful. It did have hiccups – for instance they left it outside the shed one night and in unexpected strong winds the plane ended up upside down on the foreshore mud! However, it could be mended, and was entered for the Mortimer

Singer flying competition in 1913. This involved the aeroplanes making seven successive landings on land and on sea. Of all the planes entered, only the Sopwith Bat Boat completed the course, and hence won the £500 first prize.

The Bristol-Coanda No.120 was another plane rebuilt at the sheds. The original floats proved to be too heavy, so Consuta plywood ones were substituted. This flew on 15 April 1913, but the engine overheated and the plane crashed and disintegrated. The pilot, Harry Busteed, was rescued.

The Heathfield sheds were damaged by a gale in 1914, but rebuilt later that year. A total of 200 AVRO 504s were constructed by Saunders during the First World War. These were land planes that used the Heathfield airstrip. In 1916 the sheds were dismantled. All that remains on this site at the time of writing are the much-eroded wooden planks that once held back the bank of the river beneath the sheds. The earth behind the planks has been washed away, so they stand forlornly in a sea of mud, sole testimony to the Heathfield aeroplane works.

## Folly Works

In 1915 Sam Saunders bought the Padmore estate for £6,000. The estate included the Queen Anne fronted house, the lodge, cottage and stable block and land stretching down to the River Medina. Sam promptly sold 23 acres adjacent to the river to his company for £2,300. To the north of the site is a small stream that comes from a spring on the Padmore land, and to the south of the site is The Folly Inn. The site became known as The Folly Works. A road was built down to The Folly Works from the main road.

Between 1916 and 1918 new wooden sheds were built at The Folly Works adjacent to the river.

*The assembly of Short 184 folding-wing planes at The Folly Works during the First World War.*

*An aerial view of The Folly Works in the 1940s. The air-raid shelters can be seen at the back of the site.*

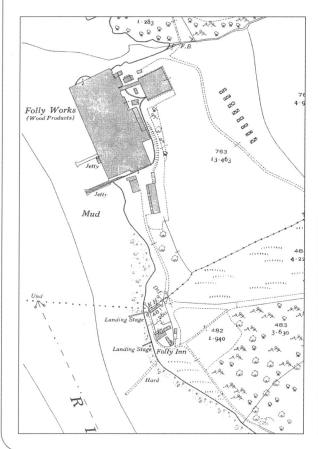

Left: *The Folly Works as shown on the 1939 map.* (REPRODUCED FROM THE 1939 ORDNANCE SURVEY MAP BY KIND PERMISSION OF THE ORDNANCE SURVEY)

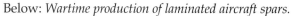

Below: *Wartime production of laminated aircraft spars.*

*Finishing folding canvas-sided assault boats during the Second World War.*

*Putting the finishing touches to a two-man canoe used in commando operations during the Second World War.*

Saunders tendered for and won a contract to assemble Short 184 seaplanes. A total of 30 of these were built for an admiralty contract at a price of £81,000. Sliding doors fronted the river, with ramps for launching the planes from any position along the factory. The remains of the reinforced river banks that were beneath this factory still exist in a somewhat crumbled state in 2006.

Plane manufacture continued in The Folly sheds during the 1920s and '30s. Cutty Sark amphibians were built by the company, the wings being built at Folly Works in 1930. A total of 12 planes were built to this design, both for civil and military use.

Bridging pontoons were under construction for the Army from 1934. During the Second World War aircraft spars and pre-formed parts for aircraft were produced in great numbers. Prefabrication saved considerable time on the part of the aircraft constructors. Not only aircraft were made of plywood. Folly Works built a number of 16-foot-long folding assault boats. Two-man canoes were also produced for commando operations. Part of the firm, called Saro Structures, also produced plywood for air-sea rescue craft, motor launches and motor torpedo boats (MTBs). MTB sides were pressed in their full length of 75 feet.

After the Second World War more products were developed, from hockey sticks and golf clubs to plywood mouldings for train-carriage finishes. Saro Structures went on to prefabricate aluminium roofs and domes, and radio masts, but this finished in 1960.

## The Plywood Factory

The Folly Works site became a major plywood factory, as well as a manufacturing base, when new sheds were constructed in 1919. The Consuta plywood made was for general use, as well as for aircraft manufacture. A large 100psi press was installed – a similar pressure to that used at the present GKN factory. The plywood factory was completed in 1921 at a cost of £43,905. The first superintendent of the new factory was Frederick Goatley. Many of the workers were women, and this continued to be the case for many years.

The later design of sewn plywood manufactured at Folly was of three layers of wood, glued together with the direction of the grain in each layer at an angle to the others and reinforced with rows of stitching with a flax thread. The holes for the stitching were pierced, not drilled. Any thickness from 1/16 inch to 5/8 inch could be made, and up to 50 feet long by eight feet wide. As glues improved the need for stitching the wood diminished, and glue was applied either by large mechanical rollers or by sheets of 'film' glue being laid between each sheet of veneer.

During the Second World War Folly Works was producing 40 per cent of the country's plywood, much

*The 75-foot plywood side of a motor torpedo boat being pressed for the war effort.*

Above: *The workforce at the plywood factory in the 1920s consisted of many young women.*

"G" (SARO) COY. XXth HAMPS. BN. H.G.

NAME...Hcpl...Palmer..H.S    RIFLE NO. F.S..524
                                            5 MAGS

The rifle you have taken on charge this day will be in your safekeeping until such time as it has been returned and a receipt obtained on this card.

Remember to remove the bolt when you leave the weapon at home. Keep the bolt and the rifle in separate places.

The rifle must be kept clean and free of rust.    Have it examined frequently by the Armourer Sgt.

Saro Barracks,                          Sig. of Issuer
E. Cowes, I.O.W.

Rifle returned in                       condition
        Signature of individual receiving the rifle back to store.

Above: *Saro had its own Home Guard.  Mr Palmer was given permission to have a gun.  But was it ever returned!?*

Right: *Firefighting practice at The Folly Works, 1940s.*

*Workers leaving the factory in the 1940s.*

*The stacks of wood veneers all had to be checked for flaws.*

*Unloading veneer from a barge in the 1940s.*

Right: *Loading finished plywood onto a barge for export to the mainland, 1940s.*

*After the disastrous fire in 1960. The Saro signboard can be seen on the ground.*

*Some of the workers stand around helplessly as the factory smoulders in 1960.*

of it for aircraft construction. On the night of 4 May 1942 much of the reserve stock of plywood, which had been moved to 'safety' at Kingston, in the old college engineering sheds, went up in flames when East Cowes was blitzed. Production at Folly Works soon replaced this. The government valued the work of the plywood factory so much that it installed a special power plant to ensure continuity of production should the main Island power station be damaged.

Many of the workers required by the factory came by bus from further afield than Whippingham village. It was at this time that the road was widened by the big old oak tree, to allow the buses to pass one another. Until about 1900 there had been no road from Whippingham to The Folly. The shipyards and aircraft-manufacturing industry at East Cowes and Whippingham had first call on the Island buses. At one time 17 buses a day were bringing workers to the town from Ryde alone. Saro provided its own bus drivers to cope with the early and late shifts, all to keep the factories running 24 hours a day.

Dorothy Wilson remembers that working at the plywood factory was a very cold job during the winter months. She was employed to check sheets of veneer for flaws during the Second World War years. There were three shifts and she was on the 6a.m. to 2p.m. shift when the town received its worst bombing. Then there were the 2–10p.m. shift and the night shift. They were on the night shift for three months at a time.

There were many girls working at The Folly Works, but there was little opportunity to mix with anyone other than personnel in your own workshop. There were men in Dorothy's workshop as well as girls. The girls used to go to The Folly Inn for a cup of tea. One day they came upon a dishcloth left by accident in their teapot, and only found it after they had poured out their tea! On a more sombre note, Dorothy recalls watching the doodlebugs going along Fairlee, wondering where they would land.

The Folly Works had its share of high-explosive bombs, incendiaries and machine-gun attacks. However, very little time was lost as a result of these attacks and numerous warnings. Despite a few casualties the spirit of the Saro team remained as high as ever. During one low-level attack by the Luftwaffe, the Saro Home Guard were credited as having damaged a Dornier with the factory multiple AA guns. The Works Fire Brigade trained to a high standard, with ample firefighting equipment and water storage in view of the highly inflammable stock of timber in the stores.

Saro Laminated Wood Products continued to develop its plywood products through the 1950s. The modern plant coated high-grade plywood with a hard gloss plastic which they designated 'Sa R-Ree Z'. The plywood was used for partitioning in offices, flats and factories.

*A lot of plastic roofing was produced in the 1960s.*

There were two jetties which allowed barges to bring the veneers from the mainland ports, and for the completed plywood to be shipped out to the factories. Railway tracks facilitated the loading.

Plywood manufacture continued on this site until 1960, when there was a very severe fire which destroyed most of the works. Sue Rann at Old Post Office Cottage opposite the Forge feared the sparks would set light to her thatched roof, and Dorothy Wilson at King's Cottages east of Barton Manor could see a red glow in the sky. The decision was taken not to rebuild the plywood factory, but instead to concentrate on the production of thermo-plastics. In 1993 Mrs Hazel Yates was in charge of the works, but the factory finally closed its gates soon after this date.

In 2006 the site is in a sorry state and still disused. Several of the old sheds have been damaged by fires, weeds are encroaching over the roadways, and the fences are rusting away. The site is reverting to nature.

## Sam Saunders

Sam Saunders had moved into Padmore House in 1920. In 1928, at the age of 78, he sold his shares in the company and Alliott Verdon Roe became the chairman. Sam was elected life president of the company, which changed its name to Saunders Roe that year.

Sam Saunders's involvement in the village of Whippingham extended to the residents' social needs. There was no Community Centre, so in 1933 Sam had the present centre built and donated it to the village.

Sam died in December 1933 at Padmore, and his boat-shaped coffin, made of Consuta plywood, was drawn by some of his workers to Whippingham Church for burial. Today the ornate tombstone stands in honour of a remarkable man, one who gave work to many in the village of Whippingham and town of East Cowes.

# Chapter 14

# The Royal Naval College Hospital, Holiday Camp, Saunders Roe to GKN

In 1903 the Royal Naval College Osborne was opened. The college buildings were based around the stable block of Osborne House. The boys were admitted from the age of 13 years and spent two years here training to be officers before going on to Britannia College, Dartmouth. These officer cadets were given a good grounding in engineering at the Kingston workshops by the river with the intention of broadening their basic training, in the hope of encouraging more boys to become engineering officers in the 'modern' navy and breaking down the existing social distinctions.

Among the cadets at the Naval College were several royals. King Edward VIII and his brother Albert, King George VI were at Osborne College, as was their cousin who later became Lord Louis Mountbatten, Admiral of the Fleet and later Lord Lieutenant of the Isle of Wight. They were among 4,000 naval cadets to be marched in single file along the Cadet's Walk that crossed the Kingston Farm fields between the college and the workshops.

While entry at 13 years old may have been a success in some ways, it meant that many boys entered Osborne College straight from home tuition or small preparatory schools. Most had not had the opportunity to mingle with large numbers of their age group before this time, and consequently were ripe to catch many infectious diseases. Only one boy had to return to the college carrying, say, measles, for the whole of his class to catch it, with the likelihood of it spreading to other classes very rapidly.

Much was said of Osborne College being built on an unhealthy site. Classrooms created out of the Queen's stables did lead to some concern, and it was said that a condition known as 'pink eye' was derived from this. It was investigated thoroughly, and no link with the location could be found. Conjunctivitis was believed, erroneously, not to be contagious. There were frequent catarrhal infections as well. Each morning, on getting up, all the cadets were required to use the cold plunge pool at the end of each dormitory.

Questions were asked in the House of Commons about the high incidence of disease. In 1907 the authorities refused a request to rebuild the accommodation blocks in brick, but did agree to build a small isolation hospital, which was constructed on land below Kingston Farm, approached from Cadet's Walk.

As a direct result of a 'flu epidemic that spread through the college in 1910, resulting in 260 cases, it was decided that more hospital accommodation was required. So that year the 'Infectious Hospital' was constructed for the college on a field opposite the gates to Barton Manor. Crown Estates owned the land, which was transferred to the Admiralty. Initially two wards were built, but by 1915 there were four light airy wards each capable of taking 20 boys. A substantial house was added for staff accommodation. A sewerage system was constructed to serve the hospital, and the remains of this still exist in the fields between Beatrice Avenue and the river.

Cases of influenza, measles, German measles, mumps, and chickenpox were among those treated. The numbers of these could be alarmingly high. In 1911, for instance, there were 383 cases of infectious disease recorded, out of a total number of 440 cadets. In 1915 when a question was again asked in the House of Commons, there were 136 cadets on the sick list that week. Of these 106 had influenza, 12 had measles, 10 had conjunctivitis, 5 had pneumonia, 2 had mumps and one had tonsillitis, among some 330 cadets present at college. The worst epidemic was in 1917 when a cadet introduced a particularly virulent strain of measles to his companions. A considerable number of cadets succumbed to measles, accompanied by bronchopneumonia, which sadly caused six deaths.

According to the memoirs of Osborne cadets, many had experiences of the hospital. The boys were unanimous in their praise. The nursing staff were very efficient and looked after the boys well. Michael Partridge, in his book *The Royal Naval College Osborne – A History, 1903–21* includes some of these memories:

*The nursing was very good, they took great care to see that we were properly looked after whilst we had 'flu and in the post-'flu conditions, too, [they] made quite certain we were rehabilitated. They were very good nursing staff, I think. The surgeons were good too.*

*The staff accommodation building at the hospital in 1956.*

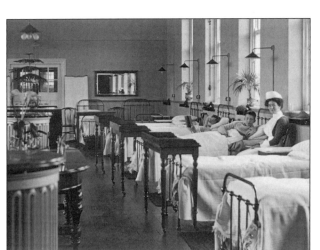

*A ward at the Royal Naval College Hospital, c.1910, although this may be in the smaller on-site hospital, not at the infectious diseases hospital.*

*At the end of 1918... there was a terrible outbreak of 'flu... practically everyone went down with 'flu. Aspirin had just been invented and one of our really clever naval surgeons who was there insisted we were given aspirin and that did undoubtedly save a lot of lives...*

In 1921 it was decided to close the Naval College. The experiment to encourage the standing of engineering officers had been tried, and most of the boys had enjoyed starting their education in the Royal Navy at Osborne. Dartmouth now had sufficient capacity to house all the cadets required for the postwar navy, and the boys left 'unhealthy' Osborne. The college dormitories were dismantled in 1934.

The Infectious Hospital was valued at around £30,000 in 1921. The Admiralty was still working on 1914 prices so were not quite sure. The management of the site reverted to Crown Estates. The hospital was about to embark upon a new lease of life.

## East Cowes Holiday Camp

From 1927 to 1939 the Royal Naval College Infectious Hospital buildings were leased for use as a holiday camp. The proprietor was Mr Allnatt, who had a registered office in London. His first intent had been to lease the Osborne Naval College buildings themselves for use as a holiday camp. He offered to buy the whole college site in 1930, as long as he could have access to the sea at Osborne Bay. The intention at this time was to run a college for foreign university students, especially Austrian and German. The idea came to nothing.

Numerous school groups, church groups and youth organisations brought parties of youngsters here for an annual holiday. Many of the children were from London, so it must have been a wonderful experience for them to wake up in the countryside and walk through fields. The four hospital wards were used as dormitory accommodation, with the main house for the dining-rooms and classrooms. Groups of as many as 170 children with nine teaching staff could be accommodated. Three of the Naval College dormitory blocks at Osborne were also rented in 1929, and this is probably where they put up a group of 350 youngsters from Staffordshire.

Miss Allnatt, the daughter of the proprietor, was the camp nurse. She was described in one testimonial as 'so fascinating that any scratch was excuse enough to visit her!' The manager was Mr G.L. Oldham. He took every care to make the holiday a delightful experience for everyone who stayed there. In the words of the captain in charge of the 1st Walthamstow Girls Brigade:

*He is a wonderful man, who is always sought after, always helping someone. His good nature is infectious and his helpers have caught it, the popularity of his staff is marvellous and every one of them is a friend.*

The cook was very highly praised in every letter – 'The food, both in the cooking and the quantity, have been of the very best.' 'The food – words fail to express our appreciation!' 'Perfectly cooked and served up.'

Because the camp was in permanent buildings and the catering was supplied, life was perfect for these youth groups. They could make their own entertainment in the grounds. Football posts were erected in the field, which was large enough for several different games to take place at once. There was a small swimming-pool. Groups could go for walks in the countryside (there is mention of the nurse being good at dealing with blisters!) and Osborne House was handy to visit. Parties of children could walk down to the seafront to swim. Residents of the town have told of memories of the Hitler Youth Movement being marched down to the beach from the camp, singing as they went. Mr Oldham would arrange coaches for outings to places more distant if required.

Mr Othen and his son Frank were running the eight-acre market garden to the south of the site. The swill from the holiday camp went to feed the 200 pigs they kept there, along with 300 fowls. These were fattened up for Christmas. Mrs Othen also worked in the market gardens, and they had a round in East Cowes delivering fresh vegetables by horse and cart on Wednesdays and Saturdays. Some of the vegetables went to the holiday camp.

Young Frank would go to Whippingham Station on a Friday with the horse and cart, taking the bags and cases of the visiting youngsters, who would walk to the station. He would then collect the luggage of the next visitors. Frank remembered the girls from Cadbury's chocolate factory staying at the camp.

Several schools and youth groups came back year after year. The children so enjoyed the experience

*An aerial view of the Osborne Works site, early 1960s.*

*The third test facility built at the site, the test tank built in 1956.*

that the staff knew it was worthwhile. Many of these children would have no other holiday, and would have spent a year saving up to be able to come.

One interesting coincidence is that one of the parties, described as a 'Welfare Party', was from the firm Guest, Keen and Nettlefolds Ltd, of Birmingham – the firm which now operates from this Osborne Works site is the same – GKN!

After the 1939 summer season the holiday industry ceased to exist on the Isle of Wight, as it became a prohibited area during the war. The Infectious Hospital was about to take on a third role.

## Osborne Works – SARO to GKN

In 1941 the old Infectious Hospital site was taken over by Saunders Roe, or Saro, as it was affectionately known. They were given the use of the site for wartime production by the Ministry of Aircraft Production (MAP). Additional buildings were added for use by the firm, as well as a raised aircraft-spotting post, to warn of air attacks, at the north-west corner of the site.

Some first toeholds on the site had been achieved in 1939 when permission had been granted for the Saro Rugby Club to use the pitch west of the site, and SLWP (Saro Laminated Wood Products) Sports Club were allowed a football pitch on the site. The works site opposite Barton Manor gates was called the Osborne Works. This caused some confusion as Saro also had its head office and design department at the Osborne House stables. After the war Saro leased these sites from the Crown.

### Test Facilities

Hydrodynamic development of the hulls for flying boats and high-speed craft led to a requirement for test facilities. Those created at Whippingham were probably the most comprehensive in the country outside of government establishments.

The first indoor test tank for seaplanes and boats

was constructed at the site in 1947. It was 618 feet long, eight feet wide and had a strong mobile carriage running on rails over the water surface. The carriage could not only support the model plane or boat, but also up to four observers. The models, up to six feet long, could be moved through the water at a speed from 0.05 feet per second up to 43 feet per second (30mph).

The second tank, the 'Ditching Tank' which opened in 1950, was an open-air facility. It had a large gravity-operated catapult at one end, so that models could be launched at variable speeds, angles or rates of descent into a large basin of water, and the results recorded.

The third, an indoor test tank, was built in 1956. It was 250 feet long by 12 feet wide and had a monorail inside capable of moving an unmanned carriage at speeds of up to 50 feet per second (34mph). All the sensor information was immediately relayed back to a central control console at the side of the tank. The operator not only controlled the model, but also had all the data presented to him immediately on dials and pen recorders.

Another building housed a wind tunnel where aerodynamic testing of models was carried out, the air flow eventually provided by a jet engine in the early 1950s.

In addition to these facilities the company also developed free-flight radio-controlled models so that other characteristics of the craft could be studied. This technique was also applied to model boats and hydrofoils.

Research and development facilities were set up in additional sheds. Equipment was installed for testing structures for vibration, fatigue and static loading (this on a rig known as the 'Elephant'), together with the metallurgical testing of materials. A large autoclave was installed in the main test house for operations requiring a vacuum; this building was also the home to the highly-skilled model makers. Testing was also done on hydraulic and electrical systems. In fact all the behind-the-scenes tests that need to be carried out before an aircraft part takes to the air was done at Whippingham.

In addition to the work for Saro the research team at the Osborne Works carried out work on a commercial basis for other companies. An example of this was the fatigue-cycle testing of Comet fuel tanks for De Havilland after the early Comet disasters.

A full-size mock-up was built of the enormous Princess Flying Boat fuselage in the late 1940s. This was housed in the largest shed at Osborne Works. When the managing director visited the mock-up his only comment was that the unusual spiral staircase between the two passenger lounges should be altered, because it had 13 steps. The designers had to work out how to fit a fourteenth step in!

A large cylindrical tank, quite a landmark and rather like a small gasometer, was built next to the eastern dormitory. This was used to pressure test, under water, a full-size mock-up of the Princess fuselage and, later, the Comet fuel tanks. A smaller tank was built to test the SR53 and the SR177 cockpits.

Following the company's research on hydrofoils in the test tank, a full-size mock-up was also built of the high-speed hydrofoil for Canada. Later this was built by Saro at Beaumaris.

In October 1948 the electronics division of the company was formed, starting at the Osborne Works. Research led to the development of several new areas; e.g. special generators, test instruments, printed circuits and strain gauges. An aircraft simulator was built for the SR.53 fighter plane, and automatic sequence ground control for the Black Knight and Black Arrow rockets.

The company went on to produce many early complex analogue computers in the 1950s. These computers needed a large room each – developments in computers have come a long way since those early days! The electronic division moved to the Kings

*An inside view of the test tank which was 250 feet long. The test tank built in 1947 was 618 feet long.*

*A special-purpose digital computer designed and built by the electronics division in 1956.*

Building (the old Kings cinema) in East Cowes in the early 1980s. At one time 80 people were employed on the electronics side at Osborne Works.

Also on the site in the late 1950s was a storage facility for the highly volatile rocket fuel HTP (High Test Peroxide), requiring very special precautions!

## The Saunders Roe Apprentices School

Apprentices were an important part of the firm and their training received careful consideration. Facilities were soon made available at the Osborne Works for this. The apprentices during wartime were generally local Isle of Wight lads, who would live at home, catching the workmen's buses to attend lessons at the Osborne Works and work in the East Cowes factories. There were some mainland apprentices during the war, but they lived in digs in the town. There were small workshops and a classroom in the old hospital wards where the lads were trained. The apprenticeship lasted five years.

V.T. Stevenson was superintendent of training from 1940. In 1945 he improved the Indentured Apprenticeship Scheme such that it became recognised in the industry as second to none. He pioneered up to two days a week for apprentices to attend technical colleges, developed 'sandwich schemes' and a full range of night schooling. He also made it possible for promising apprentices to take university degrees. V.T. Stevenson played a great part in establishing the I.W. Technical College, which opened in 1951. He retired in 1978.

In 1945 the Saunders Roe Group Technical College and Apprentice Residential Centre was established. Initially this used two of the old hospital wards as dormitories, and the surgeon's house as a dining-room with accommodation for V.T. Stevenson's family. The other wards were used as classrooms and workshops. The disinfection/incineration block was used for hobbies.

'Pop' Stevenson, V.T.'s father, was one of the instructors at the Saro Training School. He and the other instructors, such as Frank Daltry, ran the workshop where the apprentices learned to achieve precision with the use of hand tools. There were also a number of small machine tools which allowed instruction in the basics of metal machining. 'Pop' was always ready to help the lads with their hobbies and past-times, and as he lived on the site he was always kept busy at weekends and evenings.

Mrs Rosa Stevenson, V.T.'s wife, supported her husband by running the hostel for apprentices. Her role would best be described as 'Matron', but this title does little justice to the many things she did for the boys.

The number of apprentices increased sharply in the early 1950s, when a third hospital ward was converted into another dormitory. The capacity of each dormitory was about 28 lads, utilising the side

Above: *The 1954 intake of apprentices.*

Right: *'Pooge' Saunders teaching technical drawing in around 1956.*

*The 1956 intake of apprentices.*

*Apprentices relaxing in 1953.* Left to right: *Peter McGee, David Kitchen, ? Russell, ? Pritchard, Graham Britton.*

Above: *'Pop' Stevenson instructs Graham Pike, c.1956.*

Below: *Dormitory for the apprentices, c.1956.*

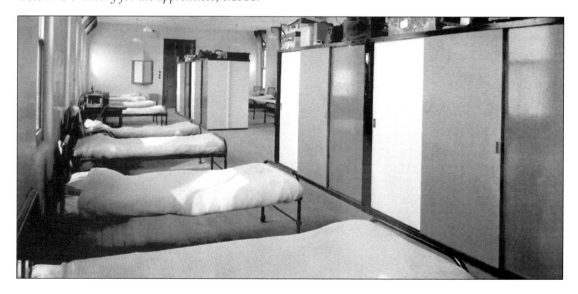

*One of the old hospital wards was used as the training workshop, c.1956.*

*A 1956 'Head of the River' gig-racing crew.*

rooms for older apprentices and the single rooms for Prefects. These were senior apprentices who were supposed to keep order! Therefore, about 84 apprentices could be 'living in' and extra accommodation was developed for other seniors at Millfield in East Cowes. A gymnasium and common room were added at the hostel for the boys in 1954.

Generally the hostel was a very happy place. In the mid-1950s the lads paid 30s. for their keep out of their initial weekly wage of 45s., but they had to pay extra for their lunches and laundry, or do their own! Many of them received a small grant, to break even, from the Ministry of Labour and National Service. There was always a mass exodus to West Cowes on a Friday lunchtime to collect this and Ada at the Labour Office would have all the named envelopes laid out ready for the lads to collect.

Ron Scruby was appointed chaplain to Saro Company in 1953. He organised many activities for the apprentices, including football, rowing and holiday trips to Loch Rannoch in Scotland. Two new gigs were constructed, *Ebb* and *Flo*. With these the lads were able to take part very successfully in local gig races. These included the 'Head of the River' for apprentices in the port of Cowes, the 'S.E. Saunders', the 'Sir Arthur Gouge' and The Folly Challenge cups.

Roy Jones coached the apprentices' rugby team from 1956. He joined the training-school staff as training officer in the early 1960s and was appointed training manager in 1978 after V.T. Stevenson's retirement.

There was the opportunity for amateur dramatics with the drama club, and many other social events in the evenings in between night school, or at weekends. In 1956 the apprentices were even given 'credit' for breaking up a meeting of the Communist Party in West Cowes. It was at the time of the suppression of the Hungarian uprising. Most of the apprentices attended, armed with a few tomatoes and bangers. Unfortunately there was a power cut, so the speaker (John Gollen, head of the British Communist Party) never reached the podium and the 6d. entry fees were

returned to the students who put the money into the Hungarian Relief fund.

At one stage the apprentices had access to Barton Manor and its beach but this was curtailed due to some inappropriate behaviour, by a few! However, this did not stop a few moonlit excursions to Barton Manor's lakes for fun and games, especially when they were frozen.

The differing social and educational backgrounds of the hostel intakes played a major part in character forming, and could be argued to have been as effective, in this sense, as university.

Due to the general malaise of the British aircraft industry after 1957, there was a gradual reduction in numbers of apprentices taken on by the company. The hostel closed its doors to residents in 1974.

The training school continued to serve the company, but the old hospital wards and surgeon's house (the centre block) were demolished in the late 1990s. During the time the site was an Apprentices' Training Establishment, over 1,100 lads served their apprenticeships at Saunders Roe. These lads, trained in Whippingham, were to go on to become the renowned designers of planes, rockets and hovercraft, and experts in many forms of aircraft and other engineering disciplines.

*An aerial view of the site, early 1960s. The battery site in the distance is being built on.*

Above: *Three of 'the evacuees', the five girls who came down from the Saro London office in September 1939 to live and work at the Community Centre, pictured with two local colleagues. Left to right: Kathleen (Kit) Kerr (Londoner), ?, Una Bennett (Londoner), Margery Hodgson (Londoner), Dolly Thompson (local).*

Above left: *Una with the car belonging to the boss at the Community Centre in 1940.*

Left: *Three likely lads in 1940 – Guppy, Pressy and Ossie. Pressy was Norman Pressy and Ossie was Ossie Chapman.*

Below left: *The group who worked at the Saro office in 1940. Left to right, back row: Cicily ?, Mr Cole, Sybil Brazeley, Una Bennett, Doreen Oxford; front row, seated: Thelma Bartlett, Dolly Thomson, Norma Moss, Joan Rice.*

Below: *The caption on the back of this photograph reads 'Guppy, Ossie, Pressy and someone left over from one of our parties.' 1940 high jinks!*

# Chapter 15

# The Community Centre

In 1930 Sam Saunders decided to present Whippingham Church with a Church Hall. The vicar then was Revd Mostyn Pritchard and he decided not to accept the building unless it was accompanied by a £5,000 endowment. Sam could not accept this condition and instead gave the spacious hall to the community, although the firm of Saunders Roe still held the lease.

It was completed in 1931, probably constructed of bricks from Sam Saunders's own brickyard at Gunville. His bricks at that time cost £4 for 1,000. It was designed by the Newport architect Cheverton.

Queen Mary agreed to open the building during one of her fairly frequent visits to Cowes and they arranged to meet at Trinity Wharf at 11.00a.m. Sam waited until midday and, as there was still no sign of the Queen, he returned to his house at Padmore. The local blacksmith, Frank Rann, promised to send his son, 12-year-old Bob, to fetch Sam from Padmore if the Queen appeared. About an hour later the Queen arrived by car and Bob raced off. Unfortunately, Queen Mary lost no time, immediately declaring the building open and departed before Sam arrived. Bob Rann recalled that Sam Saunders was very annoyed, to put it politely!

The hall was used for various village events. There are tales of exciting dances held on Saturday nights for the villagers. One regular activity at the hall from the earliest days was a Working Men's Club. This provided relaxation and amusement for the men of the village for some years. However, Grace Davison understood from her mother that the club became a little bit rowdy when drink was sold at meetings so the Working Men's Club came to an end before 1939.

The Barton and Whippingham Women's Institute started their meetings at the Community Centre in 1934. Their meetings continued there until 1939, when the centre was no longer available for village entertainment. This was because the offices of Saunders Roe were evacuated to the Island from London and took up residence there. Staff both lived and worked at the centre.

Five girls came down from London on 13 September 1939, ten days after war was declared. They were accommodated in the Esplanade Hotel at Ryde for a few days until the Community Centre was fitted up for them. The side nearest the main road was altered for the girls, with partitions making three little single bedrooms and a twin room. Una Bennett, usually called 'Ben' shared the latter. Margery

Hodgson, Joan Rice and Kathleen Kerr were three of the other Londoners. Una was just 17 years old.

The kitchen and cloakroom facilities were available to them, with a dining- and sitting-room. Mrs Edwards from Alverstone Road came in every day to cook for the girls. The remainder of the building was one large room, used as the Saunders Roe office. They were joined by several other Island girls in the office, some of them from East Cowes. A surface air-raid shelter was built, although Una does not remember it being used while she was there.

Bob Rann came across from the Post Office Cottage every day to deal with all the black-out boards that had been made for the many windows at the hall. It was while doing this that he met Una, and two years later they were married. After serving in the navy for the duration of the war, Bob came back to work in the Forge with his father. Bob and Una lived in the village, for many years at the Truckles east cottage near the church.

Una remembers her time living and working at the Community Centre with some affection. The girls called themselves 'the evacuees', which was what they really were. They had guests to parties at the centre, and made friends with numerous young men from the neighbourhood!

Una's father was an Islander, born in Newport in the same street as Bob's father! Una had lived in London most of her life, with only short visits to the Island to see relations. Of the other London girls, three returned to London after the war, but Margery Hodgson married and stayed on the Island, though not in Whippingham.

In April 1950 the building was purchased from Saunders Roe for £3,925 by the council for the Administrative County of the Isle of Wight. It was then used as an annexe to Whippingham School. The eastern side of the hall was divided to make two

*The caption on the back reads 'The Community Hall recently opened', so this is an early 1930s photograph, and includes a glimpse of a bus.*

classrooms and suitable toilet facilities were added. The reception and class one used the building, and the school lunches were served there. The older children used the 'top' school, which in 1983 was renovated and enlarged and all the children were moved to that site.

In 1984 there was much discussion in the village as to what was to happen to the 'Community Centre'. Some people in the village felt that it should be returned to the community, while others felt it was unnecessary to keep the building. The County Council had plans to sell it for conversion to two bungalows. A public meeting was held, and after much discussion the meeting voted narrowly in favour of keeping the building as a Community Centre.

Whippingham Community Association was formed and took on a lease from the County Council. Under the terms of this lease the association is responsible for all maintenance and improvements to the building. The association pays rent of £1,600 a year. The council did contribute 50 per cent of the cost of double glazing when the windows needed replacing, but the Community Association have paid for water heaters, central heating and electric heaters, together with interior decoration. All the domestic requirements, such as water, electricity and rates are the responsibility of the Whippingham Community Association. Thanks to them the village has a building for numerous functions, which enrich the lives of the community.

One of the earliest activities to be organised by the Community Association was a gardening club. Flower and garden produce shows have been held regularly, and also sales of bedding plants. Members club together to send off bulk orders for seeds and other garden requirements, making a saving on the cost. Speakers and outings to gardens or horticultural establishments complete a varied programme of activities. The garden shows have been very popular, but a series of poor summers have led to a lower number of entries, although the cake section is still well supported!

The Friday afternoon tea dance has been a great success since 1987. The sprung wood floor is one of the best for dancing on the Island. On average, 30 people regularly attend. The dances are open to all – Whippingham residents, those from East Cowes and beyond, and all enjoy their afternoon of exercise! They had the excellent services of the late Edgar Hoffman on the music system for many years.

At present the association is entirely reliant upon lettings for its income. Whist drives, quiz nights, many parties and even a wedding reception have been held in the centre. Brownies have had holidays at the centre, and dog-training classes were a regular feature. Weekly there is a youth group working on the performing arts, and pantomime rehearsals take place in the run up to Christmas. Public meetings are held for local residents, such as that regarding the trailer park for the ferry companies on the old Brickfield site, when the hall was full to bursting.

An enthusiastic core of villagers has been involved with the Community Association since 1983. Ray and Audrey Thorne, Tony and Grace Davison, Edgar and Mollie Hoffman, Mr and Mrs Fred Blackman and Anne Burdett were involved from the start, and others have joined in as time has passed.

The Whippingham Partnership met at the Community Centre, receiving funding from the I.W. Council until 2006. They organised projects for the village, such as flower planters, riverside clean ups, and dog-waste bins. They contributed towards the costs of researching this book, and members of the Environment Group are creating a Heritage Trail around the village.

Talks were held in 2005 to enable the Community Association to purchase the lease of the building from the council. We await the outcome of their discussions, and hopefully the Community Centre will continue to be used by the community as Sam Saunders intended.

*Some of the group who attend tea dances at the Community Centre in 2005. Left to right: Andrew Read, Roz Saunders, Ron Chamberlain, Mary Wilkins, Maisie Baxter, Audrey Nash, Peggy Blackman, Ray Thorne, Vera Early, Audrey Thorne, Doug Early, Gwen Kersey, Ron Sibley, Esba Bull, Charles Bull, Catherine Howland, Frank Howland, Molly Gustar, Marion Crowe.*

*Dancers on the floor at the weekly tea dance in 2005.*

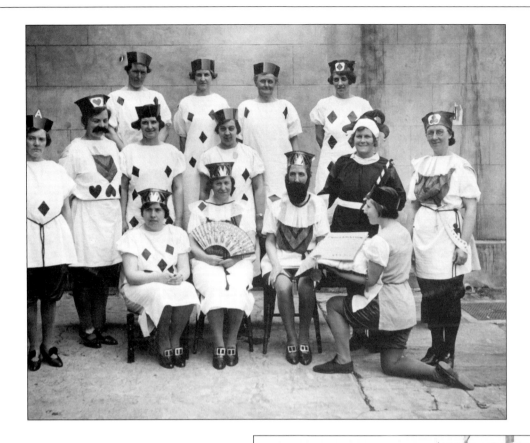

Above: *Whippingham WI practice for a pageant in the 1930s. Left to right, back row: Win Gregson, Mrs Johns, Win Gregson's housekeeper, Mrs Titmus;* middle row: *Florence Allam, Mrs Godsland, Nancy Glasspell, Mrs Wooldridge, Mrs Snow, Mrs Moody;* front row: *Ena Johnson, Ruth Ross, Miss Blanchard, Peg ?.*

Above: *Mrs Grace Davison plants a tree for the Osborne WI at school in 1974. Helping her were Katherine Saint (the eldest girl) and Darren Blanchard (the youngest boy).*

*Sylvia Brownscombe and Joyce Fernley of Whippingham WI with the contents of their 'Meg and Mog' book bag.*

## The Women's Institutes

There has been a Whippingham Women's Institute group since 1934. They first met at the Community Centre, although from the early days they saved for a hall of their own, selling dressed rabbit skins, jam and old newspapers. The earliest minute books are unfortunately missing, but the wartime accounts of the work of the WI can be found in Chapter 17.

Numbers have fluctuated from 20 in 1947 to a peak of 39 in the 1980s, returning to 20 in 2005. Meetings have moved from venue to venue, with the church rooms at the Rectory being used for 30 years. With the return of the Community Centre to general use in 1985 the WI moved back there. Apart from a year or so, the meetings have always been in the afternoons.

The format of the meetings has remained the same. A welcome is followed by the singing of 'Jerusalem', then a business meeting followed by a speaker, finishing with tea. There are always one or two competitions, for which points are collected throughout the year culminating in the presentation of the silver rose bowl at the AGM. Speakers are enjoyed, on a variety of subjects, as are those who show a new craft or activity that all can join in with.

The WI has been active in encouraging improvements in the village, such as requesting a pavement along the main road, supporting a request that rural villages should have electricity installed, organising a bus shelter as a coronation memorial in 1953, and planting bulbs won in the Best Kept Village Competition. Funds were raised for a village minibus and until 1974 there was always a prize given to Whippingham School of 10s.6d. In 1990 Mrs Wooldridge was unfortunately knocked down by a car and the WI encouraged the Highways to install a 40mph speed limit through the village on the main road.

In 1960 Whippingham WI gave £100 from their hall fund for the new kitchen at the church rooms, and some years later gave money to help with the Island WI headquarters in Newport.

Many local, national and international good causes have been helped over the years. For instance, silver paper and milk-bottle tops were collected for the Guide Dogs for the Blind fund, hot-water-bottle covers knitted for the patients at Fairlee Hospital in 1958 and jerseys knitted for sending to Kosovo in 2000. 'Book Bags' were made for local schools, which consist of numerous wonderful props for telling a specific story to young children.

Whippingham WI has been complemented since 1965 by Osborne WI. This group initially met at the school, then moved to the Community Centre, and now meets at the Church Hall in the evening. This enables those ladies to attend who are perhaps out at work during the day or have children to care for. Mrs Jan Broughton of Barton Manor Farm was elected as their first president.

Work in the community has always been at the hub of Osborne WI's philosophy. From 1966 members worked a rota system to arrange flowers at Frank James Hospital and this led to additional work serving evening suppers and clearing away. This helped to relieve pressure upon staff, which was greatly appreciated by both patients and staff. In 1970 members became very involved with the campaign to gain OAP concessions on Southern Vectis buses, writing letters to everyone involved.

The highlight of 1970 was winning the WI competition at the Isle of Wight Agricultural Show. Subsequent entries have frequently received high marks. Members have been especially interested in craft work. Mrs Veronica Hewlett specialised in 'scraper board work', and the Duchess of Kent admired and bought two pieces of her work at the show.

Through the Associated Country Women of the World (ACWW), a 'pen pal' link was made with ladies in Kempsey in New South Wales, Australia in 1972. This has continued ever since.

A choir and a drama group were established early in the 1970s and members have performed in competitions as well as locally and at residential homes. Many interesting and successful skits, plays and monologues have been written by Mrs Grace Davison and Mrs Doris Osborne. They were one of the most popular acts at the 'Old Time Music Halls' held at East Cowes Town Hall for several years as part of the annual Victorian Festival.

Other community action has involved tree planting, especially in the grounds of Osborne after the 1987 hurricane, trees at school, and planting bulbs in the village and various other events in East Cowes. In 1992 foetal stethoscopes were presented to Miss Val Attrill, midwifery manager at St Mary's Maternity Unit. Flower festivals have been arranged for Whippingham Church.

In 2005 Osborne WI celebrated its ruby anniversary with a party, a poem written specially for the occasion by Mrs Osborne, and a beautiful cake made by Mrs Tuckwell. Members received an additional birthday present when they successfully applied for a grant to enable 14 of the members to go on courses at Denman College, run by the WI.

The ladies of both the Women's Institutes in the village are still as enthusiastic as ever, and find true comradeship in their membership.

# Chapter 16
# *The Folly Inn & Regatta*

The first known instance of The Folly Inn being shown on a map was on the 1783 Admiralty chart of the River Medina. Here it appears as a small 'Noah's Ark' representation with the name 'The Folly'. It was on land belonging to the Padmore estate, but when Padmore was leased by Benjamin Cook to William Cheek of Niton in 1774, The Folly was excluded.

There may have been an earlier vessel on the mud at this point, called *The Maudelyn*, which, way back in 1532, the court leet ordered to be removed as it was a danger to shipping.

According to the author of *Sketches and Descriptions*, written in 1792, the name of 'The Folly' on the east shore of the river is derived from a barge, formerly moored near the side of the river, which used to be 'the scene of high entertainment amongst the bons vivants of an earlier age.' In 1792 the barge had been hauled up the gravel hard and built upon. Some stories say that the old barge broke adrift from her moorings and was washed up high and dry onto the beach. The Medina makes a bend here and this part of the river is called 'Windy Corner' by the locals.

*The Folly* was a vessel 60 feet in length and had been in the Burnett family for many years. Captain Thomas Burnett had been the owner-master of several locally built trading craft, including *The Three Brothers* and *The Bee*. He had the rights to several oyster-beds in the river and owned seven oyster vessels. Captain Burnett was married twice and had five daughters by his first wife, but none by his second. He was at The Folly in 1840 and employed someone else to run this remote inn. He died in 1842 and was buried at Whippingham Church.

After the death of Thomas Burnett, William Smythes appears to have taken over the lease. Later, between 1845 and 1856, James Smythes was paying rates for The Folly.

The story that the present inn is built over the remains of the vessel *The Folly* is quite true. When working on the reconstruction of part of the pub in the early 1960s, the ribs of the vessel were found, and a small section exposed behind a glass panel in the floor for all to see. A deck hatch was found during alterations in a ground-floor ceiling.

The 1853 Admiralty chart gives us a clue as to why the inn prospered there. It is called The Folly Halfway House on this chart, reminding us that it is halfway up the river towards Newport. From East Medina Mill the river almost dries out at low water springs. Barges caught by the low water would wait in Folly Reach before proceeding up to Newport on the next tide. The bargemen would be happy to partake of refreshment at The Folly.

By the 1860s the Jolliffe sisters owned the Padmore estate. They tried to negotiate a new lease so that the Oyster Company would take over The Folly, with the proviso that 'no beer or spirits, or oysters or anything whatever to be sold at the premises.' There was to be no access except by boat or from the public path to the south, which was to be fenced to enclose the footpath. There was to be no trespass across Padmore land. Obviously this agreement was not completed as The Folly continued to function as a public house through the century.

It is interesting to note that at this time there was no proper public access from the village to The Folly. There were only footpaths along the river or over the fields. However, villagers certainly used the public hard at The Folly in 1860, as the ferryman Hollis called there twice a week to pick up passengers from Whippingham on his trips to Newport market. The hard spit of gravel made getting onboard quite easy at high tide, but more difficult at low tide!

In the 1920s and '30s East Cowes people would row up the river to The Folly on a Sunday for a 'boiled-egg tea'. There was a good pear tree in the garden which is still there between the inn and the slip in 2006.

A good landlord makes or breaks an inn. One of the many good ones at The Folly was Bob Savage. He was the tenant from around 1905 for many years. He had been in the Royal Navy and was a heavyweight boxing champion in the Navy competitions. His relationship with the youngsters who frequented the river was good, although Uffa Fox talks of being caned by Bob for misdemeanours. Afterwards Bob would put

*The ribs of* The Folly *were exposed during renovation in 1964 and displayed behind glass.*

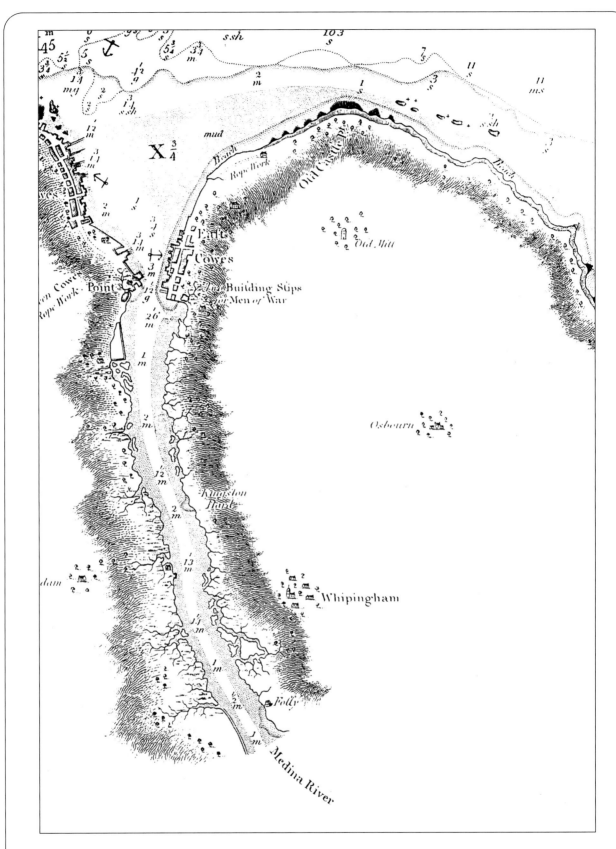

*The Admiralty chart of 1783 marks The Folly.* (BY KIND PERMISSION OF THE UK HYDROGRAPHIC OFFICE. WWW.UKHO.GOV.UK)

*A cement barge sails along the River Medina in the 1940s.*

*A small jetty was constructed over the mud, c.1910.*

the punishment aside and be friends with the boys again. He taught them how to box. Uffa tells of his first lesson when Bob spun Uffa round and round then invited the boy to hit him. Uffa swung a fist and promptly toppled over, and Bob pointed out that you should never let your opponent make you dizzy!

Before the First World War groups of schoolchildren from Whippingham were taken down to The Folly at an appropriate tide to be taught to swim by Bob Savage. Those who Bob knew could swim already were allowed to swim to the other side of the river, where the Werrar brickyard had its drying sheds.

Bob Savage was still tenant in 1933 when the Padmore estate was sold by Sam Saunders's trustees. He was offered the inn for £160, but he thought it was a bit expensive. Instead the brewers W.B. Mew Langton bought The Folly for £185. Until his death Bob continued renting the inn from Mew Langton. There was only a six-day licence to start with, but when the Ship and Launch Inn at Hurstake closed down in 1936 The Folly licence was increased to every day of the week.

A road had been made to The Folly Works which also served the inn. An extension to the north of The Folly Inn was added in 1948/9. This gave a much enlarged bar area. The wall and concrete seating area on the riverside of the inn was built just before this.

In 1960 there were just three permanent moorings laid down in the river. One was used by Mr Mew, one by *René Phillipe*. She was a motor cruiser used as a floating base for a sailing school.

In November 1960 Janette and Murray Dixon took on The Folly Inn. There had been a disastrous fire at the Saro Folly Works next door, cutting the workforce from over 1,000 to 120. The inn had depended heavily upon the workers for its income. The girls had popped into the inn for tea at breaktimes and lunchtime. End-of-shift beers had been good trade for the inn.

Mew Langton decided that the inn should be developed to appeal to yachtsmen, and Murray, nephew of Uffa Fox, seemed an ideal candidate as publican. On the first day they moved in, Janette had

a party of 11 booked in from Saro for their lunch. She had only an Aga and a little Calor gas stove, and went into East Cowes to buy a joint of beef. Somehow she coped – possibly being the granddaughter of Fred Reed, one-time publican of the Ship and Launch Inn in East Cowes, might have helped.

There had been a storm at the beginning of that November which had flooded Mew Langton's brewery at Newport and washed away many barrels of beer. The Dixons were still fishing these out of the river by The Folly at the end of November!

Gradually the yachting facilities were improved and the pub started to increase its yachting clientele. The concrete scrubbing-off hard beside the jetty was made and concrete was laid down at the end of the gravel spit to the south. There were some old outbuildings in The Folly garden to the south and mesh doors were put on these so that people could padlock them and store their outboard engines for their dinghies.

As the trade from the water increased rapidly, yachts anchoring in the fairways caused difficulties for the commercial traffic passing up and down the river. Murray Dixon suggested to the Cowes Harbour Commissioners that a string of visitors' buoys would ease the congestion, but they felt it would not be a viable proposition. So Murray organised moorings himself and visiting yachtsmen put their contributions in a beer mug on the counter! This encouraged both Cowes, under the new harbourmaster, Henry Wrigley, and later, Newport, to increase the mooring facilities.

The field at The Folly Inn, owned by the brewery, was a proper campsite at this time, licensed by the council. During Cowes Week families would sail over for the week and the families would camp there. Sailing clubs from the mainland would organise dinghy weekends to The Folly and use the site.

The boat *René Phillipe* came from the mainland, with Barry and Pat Stoneman, and moored near The Folly. They set up a sailing school which operated from the boat, the pupils staying onboard. Pam and Alan Cundall bought *René Phillipe* in 1963 and continued the sailing school successfully, with its fleet of dinghies. They could take up to eight pupils at a time. Additionally friends would take out pupils on larger craft so they could gain more experience.

In 1964 Alan Cundall became the first Folly harbourmaster, and for 34 years he could be seen cheerfully making the rounds of the visiting yachts, collecting mooring fees from visitors, checking boats after storms and generally looking after the river craft and their users.

Not all his duties were pleasant. On one occasion he had to go out to a local resident sailing on the river to inform him that his father had suddenly died and tow the unfortunate sailor back to The Folly. It was an unhappy occasion for Alan as well because he was a friend of the family concerned.

If not on the river, Alan could be found in The Folly harbourmaster's office (initially a wooden shed), or partaking of refreshment at The Folly Inn. He retired in 1998.

Pauline and David Faudrey managed The Folly Inn for a couple of years before moving to the Fishbourne Inn and after them, in 1975, John McQueen Mason and his wife Lucy (a niece of Uffa Fox) took over The Folly. It was then owned by Whitbreads, who had bought out all the Mew Langton public houses and brewery which had been previously bought by Strongs. The inn had been extended a little to the south, and while John was there this extension increased in size. There was plush carpet on the floors and polished wood, so yachtsmen left their wellies lined up outside the door.

John and Lucy had been in partnership for a few years with Murray and Janette Dixon when they still ran The Folly Inn, but Whitbreads wanted to make it a managed house and the foursome left to go to the Clarendon. When the breathalyser was introduced it killed a lot of the trade, so John and Lucy returned to The Folly and the Dixons started up Murray's Restaurant in Cowes.

There was an old gentleman by the name of Charles Patrick who for several years before this lived in his car at The Folly. He had a refrigerator on the passenger seat and slept on the back seat. Later he moved into a small launch that had washed on shore, and still spent much time in The Folly. In the nine years John knew him he never had mail, apart from football coupons, nor any visitors. John gave him tobacco and cigarette papers on special occasions, and looked after him when he was ill. He died in about 1984, and two years later a chap came into the inn looking for the landlord. The man turned out to be Charles Patrick's son, and he wanted to thank the landlord for all he had done for his father.

Another item that stayed in John McQueen Mason's mind was the occasion when he had to call out the police launch. Trawling for fish was prohibited in the River Medina, but one night John spotted a trawler at work. He alerted the police, who instead of contacting the police launch sent a van with two men, which was not very useful in chasing a trawler! The police launch at that time was the *Ashburton* and they patrolled all the Solent and Chichester Harbour as well. While moored in Folly Reach one black stormy night, the author found the presence of the police launch very reassuring, even if their megaphoned message was 'Are you ok? Force 10 imminent!' – just as the boat moored astern broke adrift.

In the freeze up of 1976 a barn owl was noticed on The Folly roof one evening. This was not that unusual, as the owls were regularly seen hunting over the neighbouring fields and the rough ground around the Saro works. What was unusual was for John to find the bird sitting on his wardrobe at 9p.m. John went down and asked Lucy for some thin strips of beef to feed it, which the bird took delicately and with gratitude. The barn owl thought it was on to a good thing, and John had visions of serving behind the bar with the owl on his shoulder, pirate fashion! However, Lucy had other ideas and, when the bird was found sitting on the rail at the foot of their bed after closing time, she refused to go to bed, so John had no option but to put the bird outside in the cold!

As the yachting custom and fame of The Folly grew, more moorings were laid down by Cowes and Newport Harbour authorities. The Folly jetty is the dividing line between the two authorities. In 2005 there were many swinging moorings, and some pontoon moorings attached to lines of piles. In the

*Visiting The Folly for a boiled-egg tea, c.1910.*

*Bob Savage pulls a pint at The Folly Inn, 1930s.*

*The Folly with new windows and pebbledash on the walls, and a handrail on the jetty, c.1920.*

early 1980s a solid-brick building was constructed as a harbour office near the slip. The harbour office also incorporates the office of the Medina Mariners Association. Next to the office are vertical stands for members' rubber dinghies, and to the south of The Folly is an area reserved for members' pram dinghies.

The Medina Mariners Association (MMA) was formed in 1972 with Murray Dixon as a driving force and Norman Parr as the first president. Careful links were forged with the brewery Whitbreads. The aim was to preserve the River Medina in an unspoilt state. Islanders were becoming increasingly aware of the developments that were ruining the rivers on the mainland and wanted to see the Medina remain with a green riverside. Based at The Folly Inn, MMA run a variety of activities for members, as well as keeping to their brief to conserve the River Medina.

Their views have been expressed on various developments along the river, and in some cases the planning authorities have listened to MMA and other conservation groups. In 2001 the inspector at the inquiry into the unitary development plan was taken by boat along the Medina by MMA, to see what the effect the development on four more fields south of East Cowes would have. Unfortunately the inspector did not view the plans in the same light as the conservationists, and more of the river bank is now destined to be developed.

MMA's activities range from the provision of two dinghy parks, clearing rubbish from the banks of the Medina, cruiser races and outings, dinghy races, and winter talks on various nautical and conservation themes. Their patrol boat, *Emma,* was joined by another, *The Arthur Lowe,* gifted in memory of a late member of MMA and 'Dad's Army'. He used to moor his steam yacht *Amazon* at Medham while performing at the Sandown Theatre during the summer season. A rota of members runs patrols up and down the river to keep an eye on things.

Money has been raised by the club to send local people on *The Lord Nelson,* which is specially equipped for the disabled sailor. Other people with disabilities are helped to get afloat on shorter cruises from The Folly on members' craft. One activity that MMA has been running for the last few decades is The Folly Regatta.

The first Folly Regatta was held on the afternoon of 20 September 1913. Previously a regatta had been held at Newport, extending down the river, but as none was planned that year, Bob Savage, the genial host at The Folly Inn, took on the organisation. The weather was perfect and there was a very large attendance both ashore and afloat, suggesting that the regatta should become an annual event. The nearby aviation grounds and sheds of Messrs Saunders and Co., from which Mr Hawker had started on his recent record-breaking round-Britain flight in the Sopwith water plane, had helped to popularise the locality. The firm helped with some fund-raising towards the cost of staging the regatta, together with various local dignitaries, such as Messrs Mew, T. Sopwith, T. Roach and W. Harvey, a popular local farmer at Kingston. Crouchers Ltd of Newport kindly loaned their motor barge *Tally-Ho* as a committee boat.

The regatta committee consisted of Messrs W. Ansell, T. Tewkesbury, J.R. House, A. Payne, G. Smith, D. MacDonald, R. Savage, and E.C. Johnson. Mr Ansell was the starter for the races and Payne and Tewkesbury (of East Cowes Sailing Club) were the judges. Owing to the large attendance afloat it was often difficult to keep the course clear!

Races included a sailing handicap for members of East Cowes Sailing Club – won by W. Austin; a four-oared galley race – won by Mr B. White's crew from Newport Rowing Club; a four-oared gig race – where the team from S.E. Saunders beat the team from J.S. White's; a punt race, a single-oared sculling race, a shovel race (two men in a boat with shovels instead of oars!) won by B. Oatley and R. Oatley; a ladies paired oared race – won by Miss Moore and Miss Watts; a dinghy race for boys; a race for bona fide bargemen – won by F. Riding and A. Cole; a boys' swimming race and a ladies single-handed race – where Miss B. Savage came second after Miss Daisy Sheaf.

On shore there were even more amusements. There was a large refreshment marquee, run by Bob Savage, and the band of Princess Beatrice's I.W. Rifles played pleasing selections during the afternoon and through the evening for dancing. There was walking the greasy pole, a treacle-bun eating competition for

*The 1947/8 extension to the north.*

*The harbourmaster's launch passing the old Folly Works in 1997.*

Left: *Gigs at The Folly during the 1950s. All the main ship and aircraft building firms in East Cowes had their gigs, and the apprentice crews competed in the 'Head of the River' race.*

Left: *The* René Phillipe *tied up to the landing stage, c.1965.*

Below left: *Alan Cundall, harbourmaster, collecting the mooring fees in 1997.*

Below: *Alan Cundall, shortly before retiring as harbourmaster in 1997.*

*The harbourmaster's offices, new and old, in 1997.*

*The Folly in about 1965.*

school boys and a ladies' tug of war – married ladies versus single and the latter won!

Despite the success of The Folly Regatta in 1913, the First World War probably curtailed events during the following years and the event ceased to take place. It was revived at a meeting at The Folly, still run by Bob Savage, in the mid-1930s. Uffa Fox was elected president of the committee and 22 of his friends were each given tasks to do on the premise 'You suggest it, you do it,' more commonly quoted as 'You says it, you does it!'

The posters were headed 'Fun and Frolic at The Folly' and advertised dancing on the spacious lawn. The lawn was the rough sloping grass field that had been scythed for the occasion. A brass band was seated on two farm wagons so that all could see them as well as hear the music.

There were rowing races, sailing races, every kind of shore sport and fun for children and grown ups. One popular event was the beer-barrel race. A tub of beer was tied up on to a pile in the river – the rowing boats raced to the beer and the first one to get the barrel won it. The innocent thought that all they had to do was to row to the pole, but the barrel was lashed so tightly that all the boats were jostling about under the pole before it was cut down. Quickly the river was full of sinking boats, swimming men, oars and paddles, and eventually all the men reached the shore swimming, pushing the barrel before them, and all shared in the contents! It was slack water, so the boats could wait – the beer wouldn't!

There were several events including residents of Newport and East Cowes. The Newport borough surveyor took the opportunity with a lot of Newportonians to 'Beat the Borough Bounds' that afternoon, ending at The Folly with a very impressive procession. They were given a trip across the Medina at Folly by the Cowes harbour launch so that they could continue the beating the following day.

The Championship of the Medina was a swimming race which started from the Cowes Floating Bridge, the men and boys diving off from the top deck. This was started by the chairman of Cowes Council, and swimming up with the flood tide the racers were

timed in when they arrived at The Folly by the mayor of Newport, who also presented the trophy.

The Folly Regatta was revived soon after the Second World War and much enjoyed by everyone in the late 1940s, '50s and '60s, run by a committee that enjoyed convivial meetings at The Folly.

Medina Mariners Association took over organisation in the 1970s. Car parking became a problem, until land was made available at the disused Saro works. Part of the field had become The Folly car park, but some running races were still held for the children. There used to be room for a large marquee serving teas and drinks. This was usually sited where the MMA have their main dinghy park now. The Unity Stompers Jazz group always performed during the late '70s and the '80s. The Folly had seen the beginning of this popular band, who asked if they could practice at the inn, a move welcomed by Murray and Janette.

A popular race for the youngsters was a cork race, where one crewman rowed and the other collected floating corks that had been tipped onto the water. The winner was the boat which picked up the most corks. Again lots of barging and pushing, and entertainment for those ashore as boats capsized! The Sea Scouts seemed to be quite good at this, probably practising during their weekly meetings, sailing at The Folly during the summer!

As more moorings were laid down in the river by the harbour authorities space for the regatta

*The Folly Regatta in 1948.*

143

*The Folly Regatta in front of the inn, 1948. Mew Langton's beer tent can be glimpsed behind the trees. As yet there is no sea wall in front of The Folly.*

*Visiting boats at The Folly Regatta, 1948. The Naval cutter on the right is the* Bromesko, *under restoration in Wootton Creek in 2006.*

diminished. Races had always started with the Gurnard Sailing Club racing round and up the Medina to The Folly. The space for sailing races in the river was much reduced.

In 2005 problems arose concerning insurance. With public liability making the event so costly, the MMA have decided that they can no longer afford to run The Folly Regatta. It is sad to think that a tradition will be broken by twenty-first-century red tape, a tradition that has given pleasure to so many. However, we hear that there may again be a regatta from Newport to Cowes, so perhaps the wheel is turning full circle!

After John and Lucy McQueen Mason left The Folly the interior was given a 'makeover'. Old timber was used to line the walls, ceiling and floor. The effect was very rustic and it took the locals rather a long time to get used to it. However, it is very efficient as it has never needed repainting! In 1996 Andy and Cheryl Greenwood took on the pub for Whitbreads and established themselves as firm favourites, and the pub became even more popular

with visiting yachtsmen. Club outings of 50 or 60 boats visit The Folly at the weekends during the summer season, jostling for a berth six abreast on the visitors' moorings. Green King own the inn at the time of writing, which can seat 200 indoors and almost as many outside. Visitors arrive by boat, car, amphibious vehicle, or helicopter, and have included royalty who appreciated fish and chips! A canoeist on a high tide actually came in the door – and watch out for dancing on the tables when things get lively at weekends!

After a year away from the Island in 2002, Andy and Cheryl are back where they belong, at The Folly. The ambience has grown on the locals, who continue to enjoy eating and drinking there. Whether sitting by the log fire on a winter evening, or by the window 'checking the boat' on a rainy day in spring, or basking in the summer sunshine by the sparkling river, the atmosphere is most enjoyable. Men sail here from far and wide. We have an advantage as we live here, within walking distance of The Folly!

*Crowds flocked to The Folly Regatta – here in the 1950s. Mr Leonard Mew's boathouse is on the extreme left. Clare Lallows put up the flagpole.*

# Chapter 17
# The Second World War

Whippingham, like many other villages, experienced great change during the war years. A major anti-aircraft gun emplacement appeared on the top of the plateau, with smaller guns elsewhere, large numbers of troops came and went at various times, and hundreds of workers came every day to The Folly plywood works. The office of Saunders Roe moved into the Community Centre and air-raid precautions were put in place throughout the village.

The air-raid warden for much of Whippingham was Mr Brinton, from Astolat on the East Cowes Road near Brickfield Corner. By day he was a turbine engineer at J.S. White's at West Cowes. His son, Roy Brinton, had the task at the start of wartime preparations of delivering a form to every house. The homeowner filled this in to detail all the people who lived there and whereabouts they slept in the house, in case there was damage to the property at night. Roy had to go back and collect all the forms on his bicycle.

Sadly this information was needed in 1942. On the night of 4/5 May there was a concerted blitz on East and West Cowes. The routes into the towns were also hit in an effort to delay fire-engine reinforcements. Point Cottages were where the roundabout is by the crematorium. Two large families lived there and their houses received a direct hit from an armour-piercing bomb. The crater made was two storeys deep, so one can imagine the destruction. Mr Brinton, being the smallest of the local wardens, was given the unenviable job of crawling beneath the splintered roofs and floors to extricate the remains of the children and their parents. It took him a long time to get over this grisly task.

That night, in the dark, the men were aware of something like a body hanging from the telegraph wires. They had to wait until daylight, when it was revealed as a macintosh – it stayed there for months. In all, nine people were killed at Point. Three of the children killed had attended Whippingham School, and a poignant entry was made in the log book by Miss Moody.

The worry and confusion created in the minds of those who lived through the raids is shown in a letter written from Four Cottages on 5 May. 'It was a night and no mistake, hope you will understand as I don't know how to write.' The children suffered from lack of sleep during the air raids and would frequently arrive at school tired out. Protection during school time was catered for by an air-raid shelter in the playground. It was a frightening time for the children when the big guns were firing only 300 yards away.

The chief air-raid warden for the area lived at Summer Cottage, Binfield Corner. He was called Mr Jolly and had a car and a telephone. When the wardens were needed in a particular area they would all pile into his car. One such occasion was the first hit by a doodlebug in the area, just south of Mill Lane. The wardens happened to be having a meeting at the time at Astolat, so into the car and off they went. Roy Brinton followed on his bicycle. The only casualty that time was a cow.

Bombs landed in various locations during the war. In August 1940 there was a raid on Folly Works. Plywood was being made there for airforce planes and boats. Veneers, pontoons and boats were destroyed in the raid. An incendiary raid in March 1941 also caused damage at Folly Works. They had their own fire-fighting crew and fire watchers at night.

There was an unexploded bomb on the railway line near Whippingham Station and a delayed-action bomb went off in the village in November 1940. In April 1941 a total of 50 incendiaries fell between the church and Kingston Farm.

Mrs Jolliffe and her daughter Phyllis both joined the VADs, the Voluntary Aid Detachment, part of the Red Cross. Nursing skills were taught at courses held at the barracks in East Cowes. Mrs Pim of Osborne House was the commandant. The 12th Field Ambulance HQ was at Barton Manor. This was run by Royal Army Medical Corps personnel.

*The VADs after inspection at Albany Barracks, East Cowes, c.1935, wearing their medals won for examinations completed.* Left to right, back row: *Mrs Florence Jolliffe, Mrs Constable, ?; the rest include: Mrs Hart who went into nursing (standing on the right); Mrs Pim the commandant (seated fourth from the left); Mrs Edgerton (fifth from the left).*

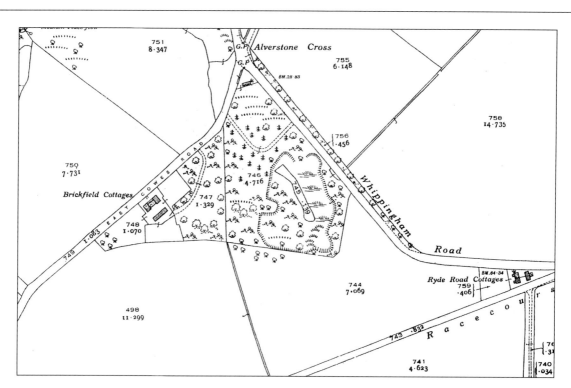

*Ryde Road Cottages, known as Point Cottages, 1939. The crematorium roundabout covers the site in 2006. (Reproduced from the 1939 Ordnance Survey map by kind permission of the Ordnance Survey)*

Whippingham
East Cowes I.O.W.
May 5/42

My dear Kitty
I could not come to you today as the glass is blown out of the windows & I have to board them up the glass is all over the rooms I had to go to Newport this morning to get some small tacks to board it up I thought the house was coming down so I dont know now when I shall be able to come, as I have not been to see Fred yet. I saw him in Newport this morning & told him I would come as soon as I can, those houses up at the point where Frank Hendy lives are down flat to the ground, they got out 6 little Children dead but so far they have not got the Hendy's out or had not when I was in Newport all the windows are blown out at Palmers Brook so I dont know what they will do, I will try and come over one day this week I come back the same

day & then I can see Jess as well Son said he would get a note to you by their Van today or rather Jess so I asked him to let you know, I am worried so I dont know what to do they say Osborne House is down but dont know if is true West Cowes is knocked about terribly so they say, it was a night and no mistake hope you will understand as I dont know how to write hope you & all are well with love I am as ever Father

P.S Will came up this morning to see if I was alright, about 2 a.m. very good of him poor boy, he does not get much rest,

*This moving letter to his daughter at Chale was sent by Mr Allam after the night of 4 May 1942. He was living at Four Cottages.*

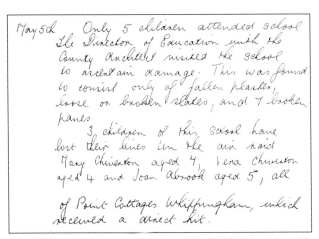

*The 1942 school log book entry after the 4/5 May air raid.*
*(BY KIND PERMISSION OF THE PRESENT HEAD TEACHER)*

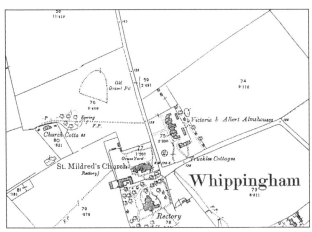

*Map of 1898 showing Church Cottages. (REPRODUCED FROM THE 1898 ORDNANCE SURVEY MAP BY KIND PERMISSION OF THE ORDNANCE SURVEY)*

Included here were Female Auxiliary Nursing Yeomanry (FANYs).

By the present Forge bus stops there was a security checkpoint across the road. This consisted of a number of old oil drums filled with concrete, in which poles had been set. Wire was strung between the poles. The road was closed off to half its width, and vehicles had to negotiate a chicane and show their passes to the guard on duty.

Apart from the anti-aircraft battery at the Heights, troops were stationed in the Whippingham area on several occasions. Canadian troops trained in Whippingham for the ill-fated Dieppe raid in August 1942. They had to practice house-to-house fighting and used the cottages in the field immediately to the north of Whippingham Church for this purpose. They were empty at the time and the troops had been given permission to use them. However, they were rather too enthusiastic in their task and much damage was caused to the buildings. The cottages are shown on old maps, but nothing is left of them now. Very few of those troops survived Dieppe.

More Canadian troops were stationed in Whippingham ready for D-Day in June 1944. Many were camped on the shore by Woodhouse Farm. Their tanks were drawn up under the trees by the shore – hazel paling fencing was laid down on the ground so that the tracked vehicles did not destroy the surface. One of their lorries knocked the corner of a barn down at Woodside Farm. Unfortunately a calf was killed in the accident. The farmer was nowhere to be seen, so the carcass was rapidly removed in the lorry, barbecued and eaten. When the farmer arrived that evening searching for his calf there was nothing to be seen!

All along Brock's Copse Road, amongst the trees, there was an ammunition dump on both sides. A vast quantity was stored there. Different types of shells had different colour-coded end labels. This arsenal was guarded by one elderly gentleman who occasionally rode up and down the hill on his bicycle.

His main task was to keep inquisitive young boys like John Warne and his friends away from the shells! All this ammunition was destined for France with the troops, and it disappeared on D-Day.

The build-up of craft in the Solent was remembered by all who saw it. 'There were so many ships out there it looked as if you could walk to Portsmouth.' Then on the morning of 6 June they were suddenly all gone. 'It was so quiet, the Solent was deserted.' Villagers had become so used to seeing the fleet when they looked out to sea that an eerie feeling descended on the area, and everyone listened to their radios for news.

Each member of the force embarking from the Isle of Wight wore a blue-and-white armband, showing an angel protecting the Needles rocks. One is pinned into the school log book. While there were still alarms and doodlebug raids, the time of nightly air raids was soon over.

Reading the Women's Institute minute books for the wartime period gives us a glimpse of what life was like in Whippingham during the Second World War.

## The Women's Institute, 1939–45

At the beginning of the war the ladies of Whippingham WI were meeting at the Osborne Sea Cadets Hall. This building was part of Queen Victoria's stable block but had been converted in 1903 into the Royal Naval College. The college dining-room, created in the carriage house, was used by the local Sea Cadets as a meeting hall, with other organisations also using the facilities. The Whippingham WI had lost their meeting room at the Community Centre when Saunders Roe moved its office staff into the building for the duration of the war. When the Osborne Hall was destroyed by bombing the WI moved to Padmore House, at the invitation of Mrs Barclay, but when her son was killed she moved away. The Rectory was then used, until Mrs Ivor Tillett invited the WI to use the billiard room at Barton Manor.

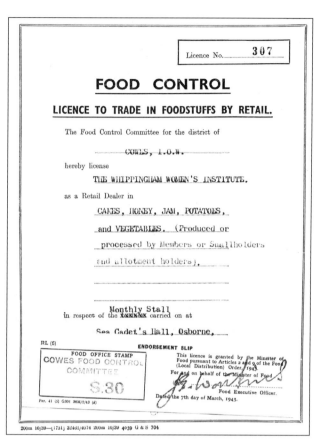

*Permission from Food Control for the WI to have a produce stall at their meetings in 1943.*

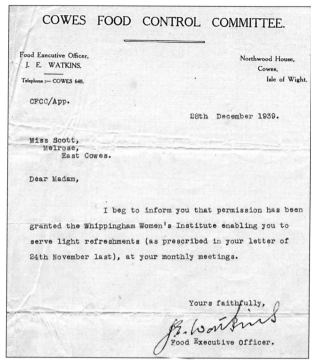

*Permission from Cowes Food Control for the WI to serve light refreshments in 1939.*

It was agreed at the outset of rationing that each member would bring a spoonful of tea and her own sugar to meetings. Throughout the war Mr Moody gave milk for the refreshments. Special permission was given for the WI to serve refreshments, and they also had permission from the Cowes Food Control Committee to hold their produce stall at each meeting.

Three years running the WI held a 'Dig for Victory' exhibition at Whippingham School. They showed trays of vegetables, fruits, jams, bottled fruits, eggs, mushrooms, blackberries and so on. They showed many 'thrift' handicrafts, and also bundles of wood collected from the river bank. There were competitions for the children, such as the biggest marrow, rabbits and knitted dishcloths, with saving-stamp prizes. The free exhibitions were visited by friends and villagers with the hope of finding inspiration to achieve similar results from their gardens and the hedgerows. At the close of the exhibition in 1942 a message sent to the commanding officer at the near by camp (the Battery) brought an officer closely followed by two soldiers with a large wheelbarrow. Mrs Rann filled it with 'gift' vegetables and apples, topped with a large bunch of flowers, and the barrow was joyfully wheeled away!

In 1944 a village produce market was held, with a demonstration on bottling tomatoes. A total of 57 people paid a penny each to enter the market and make their purchases.

In 1942 rosehips and horse chestnuts were collected in a national campaign, but only rosehips were needed in 1943. That year, in December, the WI were asked by the WVS for help with collecting vegetables for Navy ships in the harbour, and they would be called for every Tuesday at the Post Office. By January 1944 there was a comment in the minute book that 'green vegetables are very short, but even one cabbage would be gratefully accepted for the Navy!'

Mr Thomas gave 100 seed potatoes a year for WI members to grow in their own gardens. In the autumn the resulting spuds were brought to meetings and the sacks were given to either a nursing home in Newport or to Frank James Hospital in East Cowes. A comment from the matron at Frank James was that such a gift was so much more valuable than money.

Presents to the retiring WI president or secretary were extremely functional during the war, such as half a dozen eggs, some seeds, or a bar of soap. Not until the mid-1950s did fancy gifts reappear – talcum powder or a box of chocolates.

Even in 1942 the WI were entertained at one meeting by Mr Bright of the CPRE who gave a talk on postwar planning. The minutes read 'We hope in all we do to be given wisdom to make this country a better place for all and not to spoil England with ugly buildings in the countryside.'

Many of the monthly competitions for WI members had a thrift theme during the war. These included something made from unpicked wool, herbs from the garden, 1lb of blackberry jelly, a homemade calendar, and a patchwork cushion. Times were still difficult after the war, and it was not until 1954 that 'a fruit cake' appeared in the competitions.

Links were established with WI groups in Canada and Australia. Food parcels arrived to be shared among members. Tomato seeds arrived from Canada in February 1943, along with various tins and packets of food. In December 1945 two fruit cakes were in the latest parcel received from Australia. Members cut one at that meeting and saved the other for the next meeting! In March 1946 it was recorded that 'A parcel from Australia was opened during the social half hour; we each had a sweet.' Later parcels provided members with the opportunity to draw for a tin each, a record being kept of those absent so that they should have first draw from the next parcel received.

Parcels were still being received in 1951. But soon after the war Whippingham WI were sending presents to Holland. In 1945 each member brought a tin and clothes were knitted and sent. A link was established and four Dutch ladies stayed in Whippingham in 1947 for a holiday.

Throughout the war sacks of clothes were sent to Canning Town Settlement in London. Gifts were sent to wardened accommodation that had been set up. Bunches of primroses were picked by members, carefully packed by Mrs Rann and sent by post to Canning Town. The home was visited in 1947 by a member. She brought back wool that had been donated to the home so that Whippingham members could knit it up into baby clothes to send back to London.

Whippingham WI members were only doing the same as other people in the community, although they perhaps received more helpful hints through their organisation. But Whippingham in 1940 was a country village, and villagers had always grown their own vegetables and fruit. Queen Victoria had ensured that each cottage had sufficient land, and had pigsties built for her cottagers. Some new houses had been built along Alverstone Road and East Cowes Road at Binfield Corner. Astolat, built in 1937, had three quarters of an acre, and Mr Brinton found that he could be self-sufficient in fruit and vegetables during the war.

The WI gave ladies encouragement and they shared their ideas so that all in Whippingham could 'Dig for Victory!'

## Whippingham Battery

Until 1939 this was just a field, part of the Barton Manor Farm. As part of the preparations for war, the field was requisitioned and a battery built there for heavy anti-aircraft guns.

The surveyor for the work was an officer by the name of Norton Green. The huts for the men were erected first and appear on the 1939 Ordnance Survey map. Green then oversaw the construction for the installation of four 3.7 inch guns. These were in place by August 1939. They were manned by the Royal Artillery and had a complement of 120 officers and other ranks of the 57th Regiment Heavy Anti-Aircraft 213 Battery.

Whippingham also had two low-calibre anti-aircraft guns. The first of these was to give some protection to the main battery. It was sited at the lower end of the footpath leading west across the field west of the Battery. Another was positioned by the River Medina 100 yards north of The Folly Works. For a short time one was installed opposite the Brickfield Cottages. Mobile searchlight batteries were deployed at various places, including East Medina Mill.

By June 1942 a newly developed GL Mark II radar station had been added to the defences at the Battery site. This was manned by girls of the Auxiliary Territorial Service (ATS). When the girls and women joined up they had to take a series of aptitude tests to decide which job would be best for them. Many of the girls had volunteered from London as they felt that they would be protecting their families if they could help stop the aircraft bombing London. The ATS became the Women's Royal Army Corps (WRAC).

One of the radar operators at Whippingham was Mrs Mary Skinner, and we are indebted to her for talking to us of her memories of that time. She was in a team who had worked together in Essex and Liverpool before being sent to the Island. They arrived at Whippingham in the summer of 1944 from a short posting in Lymington, where on one occasion they had been sent to pick strawberries, as there was no local labour available!

The camp by this time was known as 526 Battery. It was linked with another camp at Nettlestone. The commanding officer was based at Whippingham. It still had four 3.7 inch guns at this stage.

The radar installation consisted of a transmitter which was in a small cabin with two girls working it and a power unit. The transmitter sent out a signal which bounced off the target plane and back to the receiver, 200 yards away. The receiver had a cathode ray tube in a small cabin which housed three girls and their NCO. The first girl tracked the aircraft, the second fixed the bearing and the third girl (Mrs

*The Battery camp (unnamed) in 1939. (REPRODUCED FROM THE 1939 ORDNANCE SURVEY MAP BY KIND PERMISSION OF THE ORDNANCE SURVEY)*

*The team of radar operators who were sent to Whippingham in 1944. The photograph was taken at Liverpool earlier that year. Left to right: Carolyn Bailey, Mary Skinner (née Davis), Doris Bullock, Dorothy Till, Florence Burnham, Noreen Hawkins.*

Skinner) fixed the elevation. There was a diesel-powered generator to provide power, which had to be swung to start it. That was a tough job with which the men would sometimes help, especially in winter.

Signals were then sent to the predictors. There was a telephone which was wound so many times in order to call the person at the other end. These predictor girls worked out in the open in all weathers, always wearing their steel helmets. They worked at ground level. From them there were underground cables to the gun emplacements. The cables conveyed the information for setting the guns before firing. If it all went correctly the gun fired and the shell exploded just as the plane entered that airspace.

There were three teams of girls to operate three shifts on the radar, and carry out their own maintenance. Cleaning and greasing the dipole aerial was described as a horrible job.

By 1943 there were probably around 100 girls based on the site, accommodated in wooden huts. There were 12 girls to a hut. In each hut there was one stove and a bucket of coke. By each bed was a 'soldier's box', which contained all their possessions. Each bed had a mattress made up of three separate sections, commonly known as 'biscuits'. These were separated out to form a mattress for the bed, but during the day they had to be piled up one on the other, the pillow and sheets folded up on them and the two or three grey blankets wrapped around them in a neat roll. The occupant's name labels on the blankets had to be left showing clearly with precision, ready for inspection every morning. Those girls who had been on the 2a.m.–6a.m. shift could get a short sleep afterwards, but their beds too had to be rolled up by inspection time, between ten and eleven o'clock every morning.

The girls' ablutions block had showers, but only the early birds caught the hot water! A bath was

allowed once a week. The girls did not have to do their own washing as it was all sent out to a local laundry. The daily work uniform was a khaki 'battle dress' top and trousers, boots, leather anklets, and sleeveless tan leather jackets. The khaki service dress, a skirt and jacket, had khaki lisle stockings which were 'horrible' and the uniform colour was not attractive! A khaki hat or forage cap was worn.

In the cookhouse the eating was done in shifts. The food was very basic with none of today's herbs and spices, but adequate. Some ATS girls were assigned to cooking tasks. They wore white head-scarves. Everybody had their own cutlery, enamel mug and plate and did their own washing up at the end of the meal. There was usually porridge for breakfast, of varying quality. The tea was kept in big churns, already sugared so it was not popular with those who didn't take sugar.

The ATS girls had to do guard duty on the gate to the camp sometimes, which Mrs Skinner didn't like. On other days they would be on fatigues. The men always did the night guard duty. Guard duty entailed standing by the long white pole across the entrance to the site, and opening it vertically to authorised personnel. Mrs Skinner was always afraid that she would not recognise someone whom she should salute, or that she would let in a lorry load of unwelcome visitors! It could also be a very boring job.

The wages of an ATS girl were 14s. a week to start with. When the girls had passed their trade test this went up to 18s. This was paid weekly, in cash, the girls saluting to receive it. At the same time coupons were given to allow the girls to purchase soap or chocolate. The NAAFI canteen on site sold buns and cups of tea or coffee, together with things like soap, shampoo and toothpaste. Soap and chocolate could only be purchased with coupons. Cigarettes, scarce in the shops, were also available at the NAAFI.

Mrs Iris Palmer worked at the Whippingham NAAFI canteen from 1942, as a member of the Women's Voluntary Service (WVS). At that time she lived in East Cowes and had a special permit to allow her to travel to and from the camp. Her work was described as being of 'National Importance' and to those who relied upon the NAAFI canteen it probably was! Later Iris lived in Alverstone Road, just a field away from the old Battery site.

The ATS girls had a 24-hour pass once a week, from 1p.m. to 1p.m. the next day. As Mrs Skinner's sister lived in Portsmouth and was expecting a baby, a visit to her was a break from the camp. Not many people went to the mainland except on leave. Mrs Skinner did not explore much of Whippingham during her stay here, apart from a few visits to church. The girls didn't need to go off the site as everything came to them. Talks and entertainment were provided. There were dances to which local girls were invited in the early days. Mrs Grace Davison remembers going to the dances with her sister.

Every three months the ATS girls were given a week's leave. As service personnel they did not have ration books. Instead they received a special form which they would give to whoever they were staying with so that additional food could be purchased. By December of 1944 Mrs Skinner left the ATS and Whippingham for the birth of her first child. Her husband was with a bomber squadron in Lincolnshire.

By June 1944 the V1 bombs were coming over from Germany. Commonly known as doodlebugs these were rarely picked up by radar and were very difficult targets for any gun. By late 1944, the guns at Whippingham were four 5.25 inch guns. Only Nettlestone on the Island had similar guns. These were turreted guns on extensive concrete bases. The noise they made when they fired was even greater than the 3.7s, and the vibrations and noise could be heard in Marks Corner, several miles away across the river in Parkhurst Forest. The guns at Whippingham are reported to hold the record for the highest shot-down plane over Britain during the Second World War, possibly five miles up in the sky.

Some men working in the battery were not classed as medically fit. They were either older men or waiting for transfer to other Army units. There were fewer men than women working on the site. There was physical training, cross-country runs and route marches to keep the men, and girls, fit. However, the guns were immaculate, and with much cleaning and polishing they kept the guns of Whippingham firing at any enemy plane that came within range, defending not only the Island but also Southampton and Portsmouth.

By January 1946 the guns of Whippingham had been dismantled and removed. Viv Thomas pastured his cows around the emplacements and huts. In 1960 when Whippingham School held its pageant the Army huts could still be seen in the background. Some of these huts had been occupied by local agricultural workers for a few years after the war. It was all the concrete for the gun mountings that made it impossible to return the site to agriculture after the war and led to the development of housing in place of the Whippingham Battery in the late 1960s.

*Left: This 1960 school pageant photograph shows some of the camp huts in the background, soon to be demolished to make way for Campfield Road and the rest of Whippingham Heights.*

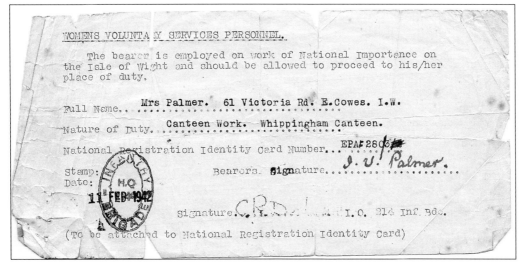

*Iris Palmer's WVS 'essential war work' pass to work in the canteen at the camp.*

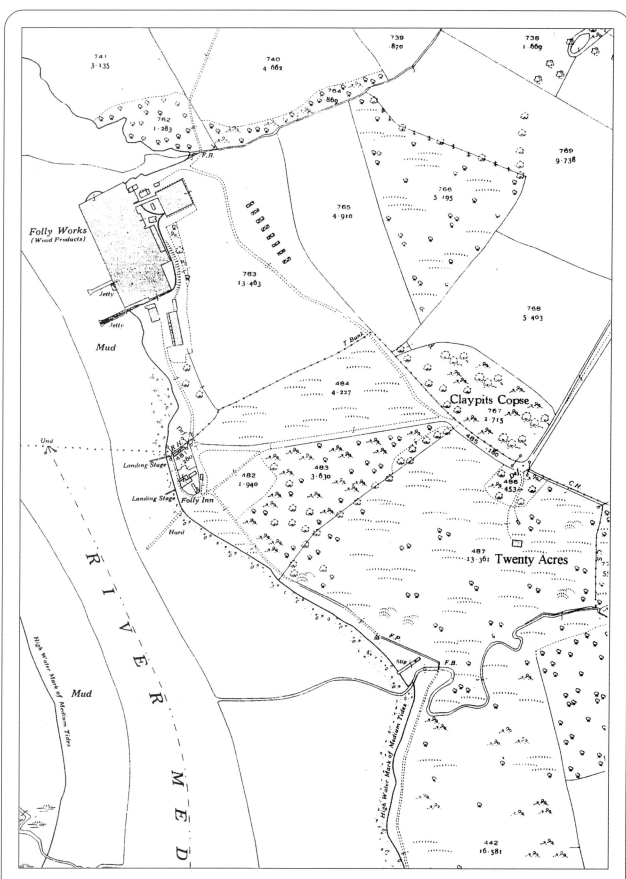

*The 1939 map shows Twenty Acres house built and a slip on the foreshore, both constructed by Uffa Fox.*
*(Reproduced from the 1939 Ordnance Survey map by kind permission of the Ordnance Survey)*

# Chapter 18
# Twenty Acres, Uffa Fox & Medina Park

In 2006 Medina Park is a residential mobile-home site, with 150 homes. Until 1935 the land was part of the Padmore estate, the one part of Whippingham that had not been bought into the Queen's estate. There had been some industrial use of the land, as clay had been dug for the brickworks at Werrar on the opposite side of the River Medina. Clay had been dug from the foreshore and from a field. The name is remembered in 'Clay Pit Copse', and small ponds can be seen as the possible remains of clay diggings in the copse. There is no evidence of a brick kiln on this east shore of the river. Werrar brickyard was still operating in 1935.

In 1935, after the death of Sam Saunders, Padmore was put up for sale. In the sale catalogue it was suggested that the area would be suitable for developing a holiday camp. However, 20 acres of land by the river was bought by the yacht designer Uffa Fox, who then set about building a house, which he called Twenty Acres, looking south up the river. He also brought his floating-bridge workshop (and former home) and moored it by the river path through his land, just south of The Folly. On it he was designing and building world-medal-winning dinghies, with customers such as the olympic yachtsman Sir Peter Scott, well known as a naturalist and artist. Sir Peter wrote in his autobiography:

[The dinghies] *were built with the precision and artistry of a violin; Uffa had set new standards of workmanship in boat building, and to own one of his fourteen footers in the 1930s was to own the most perfect little boat in the world.*

At Twenty Acres, Uffa created a self-sufficient house, with his own water-catchment tanks to collect rainwater from the roof and a well-insulated building with lots of novel ideas. The fireplace in the kitchen had a pit that the ash dropped into, ready to be raked out from outside once a month.

All the fireplaces had an external coal bunker with a chute to oak-panelled lockers beside the fires, rather than carrying coal in through the house. Vents beneath the fires controlled them excellently. As befits a yacht designer, much of the furniture was built in, made of oak and teak, with the rooms panelled and floored in hardwood as well.

The semi-circular drive to the house was constructed over a pond. The pond was filled with cut blackthorn bushes, with lorry loads of large flints deposited on top. Gravel finished off the drive once delivery lorries had compacted the stones. No electricity was laid on to the house as Uffa wanted the house to remain isolated. Oil-lamps and candles provided light.

In less than five years, Uffa sold Twenty Acres to Harry Dowsett. Uffa Fox went on to design, among other things, a lifeboat that could be dropped from a plane to enable a ditched aircrew to make their way back to English shores. Hundreds of airmen owed their lives to his design, and to Uffa's simple instructions printed on silk on how to sail the boat! An engraving of the lifeboat being parachuted to the sea is shown on Uffa Fox's tombstone in the churchyard at Whippingham.

Back at Twenty Acres, during hostilities there was a large hut built on the site to accommodate the soldiers manning the searchlight battery or small anti-aircraft gun north of Saro Works. The searchlight itself was located at one time on the site of Island Harbour, but they were mobile installations and moved around as required.

By 1951 the owner of Twenty Acres was Arthur Guy who was raising pigs on the field. He took up the suggested holiday camp idea. The first site was Claypits Site, then the 'Shop Site', at first with chalets. The left-over Army hut provided some accommodation and more chalet huts were built, painted dark khaki green. Later the first caravans were introduced. Until 2004 one of the concrete toilet blocks remained on the shop site, converted into a bungalow. The caravans were placed between the oak trees and around two circular recreational lawns. A shop was provided and a telephone.

*The green by the site shop, mid-1970s.*

*An advert for the holiday caravan site, late 1950s.*

In the 1960s the site gained residential status. By 1973 all but one of the caravans at the Claypits Site on the north side of Folly Lane had its own toilet plumbed into a main sewer. At that time each caravan was open to the wind beneath it and still had wheels and a tow bar. Gradually the undersides of the vans were boxed in, and new additions arrived on lorries without wheels of their own. More areas of the field were developed and the number of caravans increased steadily. Each subsequent area of vans seemed more palatial than the previous one. For instance, in the early 1970s when the southernmost road was put in facing up the river, it was called 'millionaires row' by the other caravan dwellers!

It was at about this time that the new double caravans started to be introduced, which seemed palatial in comparison with the 30 foot by 8 foot singles, or even smaller original vans. Consequently more land was required. The riverside field, where wild orchids used to grow in profusion, was the first to have mainly double vans, and by 1985 the 'new pig field' uphill from the caravan site was acquired and gradually completed and landscaped as the older single vans were sold off and double vans introduced in their place. The latest development has brick-built garages alongside each mobile home.

Described now as 'Retirement Homes', families of all ages lived there in the early days. It is a beautiful place to live, close to the river, boats and the countryside with its abundant birds and animals. Squirrels are frequent visitors and the calls of wading birds and geese drift up from the river. The thick clay soil is excellent for roses but needs hard work to create a garden. But the small gardens are carefully tended and appreciated by all.

With 150 homes, Medina Park is a large community within the village of Whippingham, dependent on Folly Lane for road access.

*An aerial view looking at the caravan site and The Folly, c.1975. Note the old Whippingham Dock showing up well on the extreme right.*

# Epilogue

During the course of compiling *The Book of Whippingham* various important aspects have emerged.

Firstly, Whippingham had the huge impact of having the Queen and her consort living nearby and owning most of the village. Nearly every man and boy worked for the Queen in some way or another. The Queen oversaw their schooling, their health care and their happiness. New housing was provided for the royal estate workforce, and tenants were given every consideration.

This state of affairs continued for some even after the death of the Queen. The Tillett family held the Barton estate together until 1953, and the other farms still remained as Crown lands until 1956. Restoration of much of the Barton Manor Farm buildings, thanks to the Goddard family, saved Albert's model farm. The estate roads, some of those 20 miles of private drive built for the Queen, still remain private. Consequently there has been a certain 'hibernation' of the whole estate, and much of the Victorian building is still intact. Unfortunately, some slight alterations are beginning to creep in, such as the removal of some of the redundant chimney-stacks when in need of major repair. It may be desirable to arrange some kind of conservation area for much of the Queen's old estate of Whippingham, which would acknowledge how well the estate has been preserved. The church and Almshouses are protected by a

*The Almshouses in 1981.*

Conservation Area of their own already, as well as being listed buildings, but their environs may be affected by the encroachment of East Cowes further south in the near future.

The second impact on the area has been the industrial development connected with The Folly Works, and in the last 50 years by the enlargement of the Osborne Works opposite the Barton Gate. Sam Saunders was in the forefront of seaplane development and plywood manufacture. Large aircraft hangars were built beside the Medina and flimsy craft took to the water and thence to the skies.

During the war the necessity for strong but lightweight plywood for the construction of planes meant that hundreds of people were employed at Folly Works. Saunders Roe took over the Osborne Works, and there the electronics division expanded. The village certainly did its bit for the war effort. Since 2000, much more of the GKN Aerospace works has relocated to the Osborne Works. We await new plans for The Folly Works. One drawback to any development might be the narrow Folly Lane, which is still privately owned.

A third aspect has been the change in agricultural practices. From being a labour-intensive industry, mechanisation has greatly reduced the number of workers involved in farming. The type of agriculture has also changed. There are no longer any dairy herds in the village. One by one the farmers have given up dairy farming as it has become uneconomic. When we look at our countryside here in Whippingham, remember that we are looking at farms. To continue looking at farm land in the future, that land must produce an income, whether it is crops or pasture or some fresh activity.

A fourth aspect has been the tourism and leisure facilities that are provided by the river. Many people come to the Medina, appreciating it as one of the more unspoilt rivers of the Solent, but with the famous watering-hole of The Folly conveniently situated halfway up to Newport. There is a limit to the numbers of yachts that can be accommodated and still retain that charm. An increased number of moorings, while providing additional income for the harbour authorities, may in fact not be a good thing for the river.

Trying to protect the river bank and the Sites of Special Scientific Interest for the future is also a concern. Experts say the wildlife has been studied carefully, but still development goes ahead. Once upon a time (in 1970) there was a decision that a 'country and waterside park' should be established which would protect the whole of the Medina Estuary from development. This plan has been ignored in every development plan produced for the Island since then, and now there is a suggestion that regeneration for the Island should be concentrated on the Medina envelope. Hopefully people will realise the beauty of the valley before it is too late, and prevent further development along the Medina.

The church remains a magnet for those interested in the royal family, and visitors come to see it from all over the world. Whippingham is proud to show the extent to which the rest of the village was linked to the royal estate. The small exhibition in the Church Hall gives just a glimpse into the past.

Whippingham residents plan to have a Parish Council, and a Management Committee has been set in place in 2006. Once elected, the Parish Council and residents will have a statutory voice in future developments that might affect the village.

This book does not pretend to be a complete history of the village. There is so much more research that could be undertaken, given the time. The more one researches the more one finds that there is to learn. Here we have only touched the surface in an effort to record some of what is known, drawing together material from various sources and memories from those older residents of the village. I will have made mistakes, for which I apologise. There is a will to continue collecting information about our history, either through the Community Association or at East Cowes Heritage Centre. If you have more to add, please let us know.

I hope that this book has broadened your view of Whippingham and enabled you to understand how the village has developed. Whether you live here, work here or use the area for recreation, I hope you enjoy all that the village has to offer.

*Frosty morning at St Mildred's, November 2005.*

*Folly Reach looking north down the Medina, 1997.*

# Subscribers

William and Shirley Allcock, Whippingham, Isle of Wight

Anthony D. Allen, Whippingham, Isle of Wight

Terence Arnold, East Cowes, Isle of Wight

Edward Baker, Truckles Cottage

Jennifer Baker, Whippingham School 1954–1960

Ann D. Barrett, Ryde, Isle of Wight

Sarah Bhatt, South Woodford, London

Nicci Billington, Wootton Bridge, Isle of Wight

Paul Bingham, Newport, Isle of Wight

Mrs Margaret Blow

Roger J. Bowley, Island Harbour, Isle of Wight

Marcia L. Boxall, Dashwood House, Whippingham

The Boxall Family, Whippingham, Isle of Wight

Peter Brading, Ashley Down, Bristol

Roy Brinton, Isle of Wight

Ken and Sally Brown, Whippingham, Isle of Wight

D. Burdett, Chairman, Isle of Wight Society

Carisbrooke Castle Museum, Newport, Isle of Wight

Mr and Mrs G.A. Caws

Karen M. Caws (of Whippingham).  La Mancha, Spain

Mr Roger Caws, North Fairlee Road/ex Binfield Farm

Paul Chapman, East Cowes, Isle of Wight

Charles Charleston

Christian R. Chessell

Alan Cramp, Shalfleet, Isle of Wight

Heather April Cripps, Nutbourne, West Sussex

Alan Cundall, East Cowes, Isle of Wight

Colin Cundall, Northwood, Isle of Wight

Rev Dr James C.C. Darling

The Darling Family

Mrs Grace L. Davison, Whippingham, Isle of Wight

Laura Davison, Aberdeen, Scotland

Peter and Maureen Dixon

L. and J. Dyett, Bedfont, Middlesex

Mr Adrian Terence Edge (Terry), Binfield Corner, since 1960

Ethel Winifred Elsley (née Ryall)

John Farthing, Newport, Isle of Wight

Maureen I. Fautley, Osborne, East Cowes, Isle of Wight

Rita Ferguson, East Cowes, Isle of Wight

Harry and Linda Flack, Whippingham, Isle of Wight

Kevin Foss, Whippingham, Isle of Wight

Alan and Jennifer Gray, Wootton

Mary and Stan Greenen, Newport, Isle of Wight

Arthur Gregory, Whippingham, Isle of Wight

Geraldine Maud Gregory, Whippingham, Isle of Wight

Richard Griffin, Wootton, Isle of Wight

Ian Groves, Stone Steps, Calbourne

Michael T. Hann, Otley, West Yorkshire

A. and A. Hansen, Damerham, Hampshire

John Hayward, Carisbrooke, Isle of Wight

Mrs Muriel Hayward, East Cowes, Isle of Wight

H. Haywood, Whippingham, Isle of Wight

Duncan Heenan, Dolphin House, Niton, Isle of Wight

Peggie Heenan (née Rann)

Mary Hewlett (née Jackman), Woolston, Southampton

Janice Hollingworth, Cosby, Leicester

Isle of Wight Heritage Service

Isle of Wight Library Service

Mrs Phyllis Jerome (née Jolliffe), Whippingham

The Johnson Family, Whippingham, Isle of Wight

Shirley A. Knight, Whippingham, Isle of Wight

Doris M. Lewis, Wootton Bridge, Isle of Wight

Steve and Hilary Lloyd, Newport, Isle of Wight

The Loader Family, farm workers on Osborne Estate

The Lovejoy Family, April Cottage, Whippingham

Royle Luckett

Mrs Viv Maher, Headteacher, Whippingham School

Sylvia and George Marlow, Whippingham, Isle of Wight

Daphne A. Mattey, Wootton Bridge, Isle of Wight

Iain A. McGillivray, Whippingham

Jean P. Merry, Whippingham, Isle of Wight
Roy Middlebrook, Newport, Isle of Wight
Arthur Moody, Whippingham
Jean Morris, Chilwell, Nottinghamshire
Jean and John Nash, Brighstone, Isle of Wight
Patrick A. Nott, Ryde
Sheila A. Oakley, East Cowes, Isle of Wight
Michael P. Parker, Whippingham, Isle of Wight
Malcolm C. Pay, Whippingham, Isle of Wight
Ruth Pearce (née Brook), Etwall, Derbyshire
David and Mary Peters, Whippingham
Dave J. Quigley, Osborne, Isle of Wight
Barry Quinn, East Cowes, Isle of Wight
Clare L. Randall, East Cowes, Isle of Wight
Mrs D.E. Rann, Whippingham, Isle of Wight
Trevor Rann, The Forge
Una M. Rann, East Cowes, Isle of Wight
Tom and Julia Richards, East Cowes
Fred Richards, Alverstone Road,
    Whippingham, Isle of Wight
Sue Richmond, Whippingham, Isle of Wight
Michelle Richmond, Everton, Bedfordshire
John and Jo Rowell, Glebe Cottage,
    Whippingham
The Russell Family, Whippingham
Mr and Mrs R. Saint, Whippingham, Isle of
    Wight
Beryl and Brian Sargeant, Folly Lane
Tony and Chrissie Saunders, Whippingham
George Sherman, Victoria, Australia
Andrew Sim, Gatcombe
Glenn M. Smith, East Cowes, Isle of Wight
Ronald Smith, Newport, Isle of Wight
John Snow, Cowes, Isle of Wight
Brian A. South, Whippingham, Isle of Wight
Kenneth Richard Stanton, Whippingham, Isle
    of Wight

Brian and Genevieve Taylor
Charles S. Taylor, Cowes, Isle of Wight
Gerald Terrett, East Cowes
Kevin Thomas, Whippingham, Isle of Wight
R.V.J. Thomas, Alverstone Farm
Sophie D. Thompson, Whippingham, Isle of
    Wight
Raymond and Audrey Thorne, Whippingham,
    Isle of Wight
Di and Pat Tiller, Greenlands Road, East Cowes
David and Maureen Titchener, Folly Lane,
    Whippingham
Trevor J. Towill, Ryde
Angela M. True, Whippingham, Isle of Wight
Mr and Mrs D. and J. True, Woodside Farm,
    Wootton, Isle of Wight
Dr Raymond V. Turley, Southampton
Jennifer and James Viney, Newport, Isle of
    Wight
John F.W. Walling, Newton Abbot, Devon
Shirley and Don Webb, Cowes
Jill Weeks
Terence Westmore, East Cowes, Isle of Wight
Danial W.J. Westwood, Whippingham
Thomas E.R. Westwood, Whippingham
Whippingham Primary School, Whippingham
Mrs Dorothy L. Wilson, East Cowes, Isle of
    Wight
Paul and Joyce Wise, Whippingham, Isle of
    Wight
Clive S. Woodford, East Cowes, Isle of Wight
James Wooldridge, Whippingham, Isle of
    Wight
Mr Tim Wooldridge, Gorleston-on-Sea,
    Norfolk
Lee Wright, Whippingham
Mark Wright, Winchester, Hampshire

# Community Histories: Further Reading

*The Book of Addiscombe* • Canning and Clyde Road Residents Association and Friends
*The Book of Addiscombe, Vol. II* • Canning and Clyde Road Residents Association and Friends
*The Book of Ashburton* • Stuart Hands and Pete Webb
*The Book of Axminster with Kilmington* • Les Berry and Gerald Gosling
* *The Book of Axmouth & the Undercliff* • Ted Gosling and Mike Clement
*The Book of Bakewell* • Trevor Brighton
*The Book of Bampton* • Caroline Seward
*The Book of Barnstaple* • Avril Stone
*The Book of Barnstaple, Vol. II* • Avril Stone
*The Book of The Bedwyns* • Bedwyn History Society
* *The Book of Bere Regis* • Rodney Legg and John Pitfield
*The Book of Bergh Apton* • Geoffrey I. Kelly
*The Book of Bickington* • Stuart Hands
*The Book of Bideford* • Peter Christie and Alison Grant
*Blandford Forum: A Millennium Portrait* • Blandford Forum Town Council
* *The Book of Blofield* • Barbara Pilch
*The Book of Boscastle* • Rod and Anne Knight
*The Book of Bourton-on-the-Hill, Batsford and Sezincote* • Allen Firth
*The Book of Bramford* • Bramford Local History Group
*The Book of Breage & Germoe* • Stephen Polglase
*The Book of Bridestowe* • D. Richard Cann
* *The Book of Bridgwater* • Roger Evans
*The Book of Bridport* • Rodney Legg
*The Book of Brixham* • Frank Pearce
*The Book of Buckfastleigh* • Sandra Coleman
*The Book of Buckland Monachorum & Yelverton* • Pauline Hamilton-Leggett
*The Book of Budleigh Salterton* • D. Richard Cann
*The Book of Carharrack* • Carharrack Old Cornwall Society
*The Book of Carshalton* • Stella Wilks and Gordon Rookledge
*The Parish Book of Cerne Abbas* • Vivian and Patricia Vale
*The Book of Chagford* • Iain Rice
*The Book of Chapel-en-le-Frith* • Mike Smith
*The Book of Chittlehamholt with Warkleigh & Satterleigh* • Richard Lethbridge
*The Book of Chittlehampton* • Various
*The Book of Codford* • Romy Wyeth
*The Book of Colney Heath* • Bryan Lilley
*The Book of Constantine* • Moore and Trethowan
*The Book of Cornwood and Lutton* • Compiled by the People of the Parish
*The Book of Crediton* • John Heal
*The Book of Creech St Michael* • June Small
*The Book of Crowcombe, Bicknoller and Sampford Brett* • Maurice and Joyce Chidgey
*The Book of Crudwell* • Tony Pain
*The Book of Cullompton* • Compiled by the People of the Parish
*The Book of Dawlish* • Frank Pearce
*The Book of Dulverton, Brushford, Bury & Exebridge* • Dulverton and District Civic Society
*The Book of Dunster* • Hilary Binding
*The Book of Easton* • Easton Village History Project
*The Book of Edale* • Gordon Miller
*The Ellacombe Book* • Sydney R. Langmead
* *The Book of Elmsett* • Elmsett Local History Group
*The Book of Exmouth* • W.H. Pascoe
* *The Book of Fareham* • Lesley Burton and Brian Musselwhite
*The Book of Grampound with Creed* • Bane and Oliver
*The Book of Gosport* • Lesley Burton and Brian Musselwhite
*The Book of Haughley* • Howard Stephens
*The Book of Hayle* • Harry Pascoe
*The Book of Hayling Island & Langstone* • Peter Rogers
*The Book of Helston* • Jenkin with Carter
*The Book of Hemyock* • Clist and Dracott
*The Book of Herne Hill* • Patricia Jenkyns
*The Book of Hethersett* • Hethersett Society Research Group
*The Book of High Bickington* • Avril Stone
*The Book of Honiton* • Gerald Gosling
*The Book of Ilsington* • Dick Wills
* *The Book of Kessingland* • Maureen and Eric Long
*The Book of Kingskerswell* • Carsewella Local History Group
*The Book of Lamerton* • Ann Cole and Friends
*Lanner, A Cornish Mining Parish* • Sharron Schwartz and Roger Parker
*The Book of Leigh & Bransford* • Malcolm Scott
*The Second Book of Leigh & Bransford* • Malcolm Scott
*The Book of Litcham with Lexham & Mileham* • Litcham Historical and Amenity Society
*The Book of Loddiswell* • Loddiswell Parish History Group
*The New Book of Lostwithiel* • Barbara Fraser
*The Book of Lulworth* • Rodney Legg
*The Book of Lustleigh* • Joe Crowdy
*The Book of Lydford* • Compiled by Barbara Weeks
*The Book of Lyme Regis* • Rodney Legg
*The Book of Manaton* • Compiled by the People of the Parish
*The Book of Markyate* • Markyate Local History Society
*The Book of Mawnan* • Mawnan Local History Group
*The Book of Meavy* • Pauline Hemery
*The Book of Mere* • Dr David Longbourne
*The Book of Minehead with Alcombe* • Binding and Stevens

159

For details of any of the above titles or if you are interested in writing your own history, please contact: Commissioning Editor, Community Histories, Halsgrove House, Lower Moor Way, Tiverton, Devon EX16 6SS, England; email: katyc@halsgrove.com

*\* 2006 publications*